SOON COMES SUNRISE
Philippines, WW2 and an American Boy's Struggle to Survive, Escape, and Eventual Return as a Missionary to Help Those Who Saved His Life

Second Edition

By
Chuck Alianza

Contents

Copyright 2018, Chuck Alianza

All Rights Reserved

No part of this book may be reproduced, stored in a retrieval system, or transmitted by any means, electronic, mechanical, photocopying, recording, or otherwise, without written permission from the author.

Author Contact: Aklan2000@aol.com

Cover Design, Proofing and Publishing Assistance: www.cyruskirkpatrick.com

Dedication:

To my daughter Carla, whose life was cut short by tragedy, exemplified love, dedication and concern for the Ati tribe that was indispensable.

A portion of the proceeds from the sale of every book will go to help support the work in that small tribe that is not insignificant in God's eyes.

If You Like This Book, You May Also Like:

A Cold War Teacher's Tale

The Challenges, Fun and Historic Moments with Our American Schools Overseas
By *Carol O'Donnell Knych*

A Compelling Historical Account of an American's Life Alongside the Iron Curtain

ORDER AT: https://www.amazon.com/dp/1540493776/

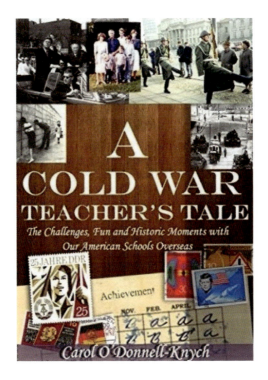

Contents

	Introduction	7
1.	Father	14
2.	America	25
3.	Foundations	38
4.	Birthday	45
5.	Attack	60
6.	Evacuate	68
7.	Hopevale	84
8.	Diamonds	98
9.	Massacre	108
10.	River Crossing	113
11.	Respite	126
12.	Escape	138
13.	Submarine	141
14.	Freedom	153
15.	Second Letter	159
16.	Return	166
17.	Interisland Travel	181
18.	Malay	186
19.	Return to Hopevale	199
20.	House Moving	210
21.	Paralysis	226

22.	Helicopters	234
23.	Flood	239
24.	Indebtedness	246
25.	Snakes	247
26.	Rabid Dog	252
27.	Mountain People	262
28.	Sometimes it Gets to Me	268
29.	Killer Bees	289
30.	Malay Mission Hospital	310
31.	Interrogation	318
32.	Cezar	325
33.	Doctor Nelson	329
34.	Aunt Sadie	339
35.	A.B.W.E.	344
36.	Fish Poisoning	358
	Epilogue	387

Contents 8

Acknowledgements

There is not enough room to mention all who have contributed in one way or another to the publishing of this book. To those who have enthusiastically proclaimed it, I say, "Thanks." And to those who questioned the clarity or purpose, I also say, "Thank you." Without their shake of the head and red pencil scribblings, it would not be what it is.

A special thanks to Carol and Joy for their many hours of critiquing, taking kinks out of awkward sentence structures and shining light on my far from perfect English grammar.

Of course, for the cover design, proofing and publishing assistance of Cyrus Kirkpatrick, I am indebted.

INTRODUCTION

Dried sweat and Camp Pendleton dust stained my Marine Corps uniform. It was 1954 and we had just returned from two days and one sleepless night in the boondocks of Camp Pendleton, California, playing war. "I'm going to teach you how to stay alive," our platoon sergeant had said and there wasn't one of our 22-man platoon that doubted him.

Sergeant Tabola had just returned from a tour of duty in Korea and uppermost on his mind was to keep his men alive. He had seen, felt, and smelled death up close and he couldn't talk about it without the corners of his mouth pulling down tight, and if the bill of his cap wasn't almost touching the bridge of his nose we were all sure we would see tear-dampened fire in his eyes.

Pitch black. Midnight. We were told we had to crawl through a hundred yards of waist-high grass, snakes and all, down a ravine, up the other side and somewhere over there would be an enemy post with a message on it. "Read it and get back," he said. If we were caught it was a severe reprimand. He reminded us that if this were real there would be no reprimand. We would be dead. The "enemy" was the second platoon. They were to stop us, or they would face the reprimand.

One man fell into the ravine and had to be carried back with a broken leg. Many had their hearts into it, but so did the second platoon. Two of us found the post. We took our shirts off, draped them around me to hide the light as I huddled close to the post, struck a match and quickly read the message. Some of us got back undetected. I did. I knew how to stay alive. Somewhere I had learned that.

***

Impatient, we stood in formation in front of our barracks while the company clerk called out names from a two-day pile of mail. Eager voices responded and he tossed the letters in the general direction. The letters passed from hand to hand accompanied by whistles and graphic remarks if hints of perfume or scribbled notes appeared on the envelope.

Then while others rushed in to shower, dress, and head for town to guzzle a few and look for some weekend excitement, I dropped to the wooden steps and studied the envelope. In the upper left corner: E. Alianza, Philippines. My father's name was Emiterio. But he was dead. Years ago. At least our letters all came back marked, "deceased."

Like slow-motion movies, double exposed, rolling on top of each other, dark memories scrolled from a corner of my mind that I thought I had locked up tight. *Smothered. Couldn't breathe. A blanket pulled tight over my head. Then ripped away. A sobbing gulp of air before my eyes focused on the gun barrel an inch from my face and my Father's voice, "When I tell you to stop, you stop!"*

"You don't do that. That's Ruth's kite!"

Blood oozed from fang marks on my left palm. Pain engulfed my body, shaking, sobs of fear. "Looks like a snake bite ... I have to go to work."

"Why only three bullets?" Mother questioned as Father handed her the gun.

"One for each of the children and one for you. It's better than capture."

A traitor was discovered, made to dig his own grave, then shot.

Wet and cold, I climbed shakily off the bamboo raft. Father stood across the thundering, rain-swollen river, then blended back into the jungle. I never saw him again. "Will he be coming later?"

"He never kissed me good-bye. But you must never forget that your father is a good man."

Lots of things I didn't forget. But I had tried. I opened the envelope slowly and unfolded the paper. The penmanship was shaky but concise, well thought out. I read the words. All three pages. Then in a flash, smashed the pages into a tight ball and wrapped my fist around them. I stood and squinted into the fiery afternoon sun and took a deep breath of dusty Camp Pendleton air. It burned all the way down into lungs that seemed intent on squeezing shut, refusing to accept. I shoved fists deep into my pockets. I couldn't throw it away. He was still my father. Somewhere, sometime, someone had taught me how to stay alive. I had to read it again.

Chapter I
FATHER

Father was a man who climbed on board life and rode it, taking the reins and spurring it to the next horizon. It was his and he wanted to see it all.

He was an average man. Until a foreign power ravaged his island nation. Until they demanded he surrender his American wife and children or be hunted down and killed. Until he said no. That was my father.

His name was Emiterio Alianza Alianza. His father had married a distant cousin and so, by the customs of the

Philippines, as the eldest son, he inherited his mother's maiden name as his middle.

The name Alianza means alliance, or covenant, so all his life he would carry with him a repeated reminder of what he stood for. Though he had little formal education, he was intelligent, resourceful and proud. Three generations of Alianzas had taken their first breaths in the loosely knit group of islands called Philippines. In Emiterio Spanish blood still dominated and carried with it not only imposing height, but the pride of the Spanish Conquistadors who first discovered and named the group of islands after their beloved King Phillip.

It was 1925 when the urge to go to America to "seek his fortune" first surfaced in Emiterio. It was not financial fortune that he sought. His father, Amay, the patriarch, had built a sizable sugar plantation on the sprawling plains of the fertile Iloilo river on the Southern shores of Panay, the third largest and centrally located island. As the eldest son, this would soon be his inheritance. But to him, horizons were there to be explored and oceans meant to be crossed

In Amay, the Spanish blood was tempered by a sincere love for the people and the land. And the people loved him in return, although love was not the only force that forged the bond. The plantation provided jobs for hundreds of people who for the most part would otherwise be living off the land. The mill to process the sugar cane, the company transporting the product to the docks, and even the ship line that took it to Manila, all prospered from the plantation.

It was not Philippine custom to suddenly spring an idea or decision on anyone, so Emiterio casually dropped the thought of going to America into the fertile conversations of the family and allowed the seed to grow. It didn't take long for all to realize that for Emiterio, the decision had already been made.

Amay pondered these thoughts long before making any comment or judgment. It was hard for him to think of his eldest leaving now that the time for shifting of responsibility was drawing closer. But he knew all about the feeling that tugged at the heart of his eldest, of gazing at the horizon and wondering what was beyond. Emiterio's younger sister, Patricia, was more vocal in her feelings. She did not possess her father's compassion for the people, or indulgence for a brother who would put in question the family name and his own loyalty to the family by leaving.

Her motivations, however, were mixed. The thought of shouldering the responsibility of the plantation should her elder brother leave was balanced by the pride and status it would certainly carry. Changed would be her dreams of a flowing social life, carried by the family name. She would have to work. She knew that Federico, her father's life long friend and foreman could well handle the plantation, but he was not an Alianza and the plantation was built on the name.

Emiterio Alianza often stood gazing out across the vast fields of sugarcane shimmering in the summer heat. In the midst, as if a mirage through the heat waves stood the mill. It was silent now, but next week the harvest would begin, and the air would be filled with the clatter of the mill, of plodding water-buffaloes straining against creaking carts, of sun glistening on hundreds of lean brown shoulders, of the sing of machetes on ripe sugar-cane stalks, and dust. It was in the quiet of a day like that that the undercurrents, only lightly hidden, surfaced to be judged upon.

Emiterio's eyes were distant, focused past the fields and the dark mill, as if cutting through the brown hills to the sea and beyond. He did not acknowledge as Patricia drifted beside him and leaned on the bamboo rail of the verandah. Hers were the same dark eyes as his that commanded attention, analyzed and understood. She also shared the lift of the chin that was unmistakably Alianza. The shape of her eyes was carried down from the grandmother side though. Patience is the attribute most always associated with the Chinese blood that ran through her grandmother's veins, but that part of it Patricia did not inherit. Spanish blood pumped her emotions.

She let her gaze follow his and waited the proper time before speaking. "Soon the harvest begins, *Manong*, and there will be much work for us all." She punctuated her statement with the proper respect term for older brother, but there was a breath of derision in her voice.

Chapter I

Emiterio stepped forward leaning heavily on the rail, his eyes beginning to betray a decision already made.

"Feding can well handle the plantation, little sister. He has been doing that since before you were born."

Her voice softened, "But he is not family, *Manong*." There was no mistaking the emphasis. To the Filipino family it was no small matter to turn so much authority over to a foreman. Even to one such as Federico.

Federico had been with the Alianza family for years and perhaps knew the plantation better than all, except of course Amay himself. He had stood beside the elder Alianza from the beginning. Their sweat had mingled in those early days and their blood had drawn the boundaries of what was now a vast complex of holdings throughout the valley. It employed hundreds and held the loyalties of even more. But Federico was not an Alianza.

Emiterio turned to face his younger sister. Her chin lifted as their eyes met and held. Spanish heritage ran deep with the Alianzas and she made sure no one forgot it. But he was the elder and she quickly broke off with a wave of her fan.

Amay, the revered father and elder Alianza, sat across the verandah from his children. His eyes were on the cloudless sky, but his ears missed nothing. The topic of his first-born son leaving had been in the air for some time now, and he listened quietly, revealing little of his feelings until all had their say. Then he would decide. His health had been waning over the past several months and he knew the time was near for him to turn over his iron control to his children. Emiterio, the eldest, was the obvious choice. He held the respect of all the employees as well as the community in spite of his youth, and was by far the favorite. The sudden yearning to go to America was something that Amay had not expected, although he had admitted to his son privately that had the opportunity been there when he was a youth, he might have chosen the same.

"Come, it is time for *merienda*." he waved to the table and with the same motion dismissed the young girl who just brought the tray loaded with cups of steaming coffee and rice cakes.

They sat quietly watching their coffee cool for a few moments. Patricia ventured out, "Another good harvest soon, Father. All because of your hard work."

"We have all worked," he said quietly.

"It will always be a work to be proud of. It has brought much prosperity to the whole valley," she continued.

Amay raised his eyes to the fields, and Emiterio raised an eyebrow to his sister. "The Alianza name is one to be proud of," she went on. "Our name is known throughout the province—"

"And perhaps soon even in America." interrupted Emiterio.

"And it will continue to be an honorable name," Patricia came back, her voice low, pointed. "As long as there is loyalty." She raised her fluttering fan nervously.

Chapter I

Amay reached for his coffee then suddenly grabbed at the large bandanna that he always kept close as he doubled over in one of the coughing spells that had been so troubling him of late. Patricia jumped up to rub his back and coo over him until it passed. His shoulders, once square and tight, were now bowed, and Emiterio looked away.

Tuberculosis was a ravaging killer in his country and Emiterio had watched many strong men wither as leaves in drought before dying emaciated and beaten, both in body and spirit. But now father, the patriarch, the builder and sustainer, the man of covenant, fighting, but with no more weapons

People could see it in his eyes. Deep set, they were once a symbol of authority and an ever-changing mixture of courage and caution, but now to a casual observer they were sunken and drawn. Behind those eyes was what mattered though; wisdom to build an empire and a quiet but powerful charisma that had, with few exceptions, drawn the entire valley in support of the mill. Amay was not one to forget their support, nor would they let him down.

***

After dinner Emiterio strolled back out to the verandah and lowered himself into one of the bamboo chairs. He stretched his legs out and waited. The verandah had become the place where decisions were weighed and made. The backdrop of rustling cane and the imposing mill had a way of drawing everything into perspective. The plantation was the pivot around which all Alianza decisions were made. They had brought it into being and it was their life.

The door swung open slowly and Amay stepped out and stopped. His stance was almost worshipful; head tilted back, drawing the world into perspective under the blazing heavens. The cane was now touched with the fire of sunset, and crimson rays played with the silver of his hair. His gaze was all encompassing. His frame straightened as if drawing strength from the sunset and the now black silhouette of the mill. He moved to where Emiterio sat and lowered himself into the adjoining chair.

Neither acknowledged the presence of the other. It would be no more necessary then the right hand acknowledging the left as they lace together in reflection. The silence was a bond between them, communicating where words often failed.

Amay spoke first as was right. "Soon the cane will be harvested. Then again begins planting." His voice resonant, soft, was but a continuance of the deep reds and purple fingers of light that probed the darkening sky. "Without care it will not survive. It is strong only when it is nurtured." His words blended into the rustling of the cane. Then silence commanded, waiting for understanding.

Chapter I

Emiterio's eyes were dark, reflecting the silence of the mill. Amay went on, not interrupting thought, but giving it substance.

"The Banyan tree of the deep forests is not as the sugarcane, my son. It is king. The sky only is above it, and it does not hide its roots. They spread wide for all to see."

He paused, as if his mind's eye was surveying the majesty of the king of the forests. "Its branches also are the home of many," he went on, his voice rich with the pride and strength that made him who he was. "They are resting places for the weary. No one takes care of the Banyan, but it takes care of many with only its presence."

For the first time Emiterio turned toward his father. The elder's silhouette now blended with the mill against the darkening sky.

"Your head is high my son," he went on, his face unchanging, "as the highest limbs of the Banyan reach for the sky."

The substance of understanding flooded over Emiterio and in the darkness of the verandah he saw his father. Hidden was the graying complexion and the shoulders that wearied. All he could see was the wisdom and love that was Amay Alianza. Emiterio looked away toward the horizon and let his father's words wash through him. He knew them to be words written in stone.

"Your wish is to be next to the sky and be nurtured by no one, my son, and that you must do, but do not forget your purpose." He paused, the silence emphasizing his final words. "And do not hide your roots. They are strong, and they are you. Without them you will never be the man that you must be."

Long moments passed. Slowly Emiterio Alianza Alianza pulled forward in his chair, then turning toward his father, he took the elders hand, pressing it to his own forehead, the cultural sign of deepest respect. Amay's eyes glistened in the gathering darkness and he nodded almost imperceptibly.

The next few days were taken up with ambling talks between two friends. Federico and Emiterio were saying good-bye. Walking through the mill, Emiterio's hands brushed across the still machinery as they talked, as if sending encouragement into the dark steel and in return giving to him the needed strength to leave. Federico walked close beside him as they talked, their hands often touching, conveying what words could not. On horseback, they traced the perimeter of the vast holdings, stopping at strategic spots to discuss and exchange thoughts, and at other times they rode silently, not needing words. Then each evening on the verandah a father and son watched the sun set behind the mill and talked of business and family. And of giants pushing toward the sky with branches the homes of many and roots spread wide, a stance of strength. They communicated, and they talked, strengthening a bond that they prayed would stand the test of time and distance. Two men were saying a good-bye that both knew was final and that neither would speak of directly.

Chapter I

Some days after the harvest was in, Emiterio stood on the dock chatting with dockworkers while waiting for time to board. Soon he would step aboard the interisland freighter that would take him to Manila; the same ship that hauled the raw sugar for the Alianza Plantation. He had preferred not to be seen off by family. It was difficult enough to leave them, but with words like disloyalty and disregard for family drifting about, he preferred a quick, clean good-bye.

Family loyalties were strong in the entire culture, not just with the elite. And as he stepped up the gangplank and onto the ship, a dockworker he knew well threw a comment into the air about lack of loyalty in the younger generation. Emiterio dropped his suitcase and before it hit the deck the hapless worker careened toward the rail, a heavy right hand having smashed him off balance. Emiterio paused at the rail only long enough to see that the man surfaced safely through the turbid waters of the harbor. As he thrashed toward the dock, Emiterio Alianza Alianza picked up his suitcase, turned his back on the life he had been born into, and boarded the waiting freighter. His heart, however, never left.

Chapter II
AMERICA

The Alianza name was unknown in America and there was little need for sugar plantation heirs on the California agricultural scene. In fact, there was little need for anyone anywhere in the late 1920s. Terry, as my father's name was shortened to in America, soon found work in *The Brandycake Cafe*, a small cafe in South Pasadena, California. There he practiced the hobby he had developed and loved while on the plantation. He became a cook in a cafe crowded with farm workers. He now served food to the caliber of people he had hired and fired on the plantation.

One evening his walk back to his small apartment slowed as he heard music drift out of an open door. Drawn by the music and the same inquisitiveness that stretched him to see over the horizon, he stepped aside from the dusty South Pasadena street through the open door. It had previously been a neighborhood grocery, or hardware store. Another victim of the great depression that had smothered so many. Inside, chairs were drawn up in casual rows. Most were filled with men who had no other place to turn. Terry chose a chair on the left, near the front, and listened as a woman quietly spoke of the plans God had for everyone. Not new words to Terry, but he welcomed the rest and refreshment. It had been awhile now since he had paused to seek that strength and guidance in his life. It seemed he had been doing okay by himself.

As he listened his eyes were drawn more and more to the speaker's young assistant seated to the side, her violin lay across her lap, her fingers slowly caressed the violin's bow which she held. Her blue-gray eyes seemed to speak of an inner contentedness that set her apart from the often frantic and always busy searching's of most: a path that he had caught himself wandering onto of late. Her light brown hair pulled back into a soft wave that ended in a roll on the back of her head, a head that she held high with a slight tilt. Mouth soft, ended in hints of upward curl at the corners. Her eyes moved slowly, seeming to communicate silently with each person, then moving on to the next. They settled on him and he decided that he must meet her. That he did, and soon there grew an attraction that fulfilled their very different goals.

Olive Eliza Burger came from a conservative midwestern family, quiet, yet strong in their reliance in God through all aspects of their lives. Their family was close, taking pleasures in the simplicities of life and utilizing even hardships as doorways to help and strengthen each other. Olive was the one in the family born perhaps fifty years ahead of her time. She was the one who would have been near the head of a protest march carrying a rather small but straightforward banner that said simply, "WHY?" or "WHY NOT?"

Her fear and respect for the God whom she loved and served would have held her back from carrying a large banner, but she would have been in the march nevertheless. Listed in first place under the question of why, would have been the question; if God so loved the whole world, why are we content to be content while so much of the world lives in darkness? But she was ahead of her time and her protests would have been no more than an unfocused light within. In Terry she saw a strong hand that slowly but surely focused her purpose in life. He was the mysterious and dark Orient. He was a link with, and possibly the answer to the question: why not? He was the fulfillment of her missionary desire to go into all the world. He was—could she dare use the word—escape, from what appeared to her an unending, straight line through life. His was the path less traveled.

She pursued the man she loved, to a point that drew her even past the straight hemmed limits of the conservative lifestyle that she knew. "He's a tiger," the waitress at the Brandycake Café had warned her in confidence. Her dark eyes never wavered, but she didn't expand on her warning, relying on the woman's instinct to decipher. Olive ignored that warning, however. She scarcely heard the words and chose to not even ponder the meaning. Love can leap immense gulfs and not even be aware of their dangers.

Chapter II

They were wed in Santa Rosa, New Mexico, on December 2, 1932. It was only there that Terry knew of a man qualified and willing to marry them. After all, this was 1932 and he was a Filipino, of the Orient, and she was a conservative American Protestant of English-German heritage. On November 15, 1933, a girl was born to them, Florence Ruth. She was the pride of Terry's life.

Scarcely a year later, word reached them of the death of Amay, Terry's father, the clan patriarch. The Depression was at its darkest and it would take time to save enough money to go home. Then another delay. Olive was expecting another child. On December 19, 1935, I, Carlos Burger Alianza was born to them, as was custom inheriting my mother's maiden name as my middle. Another year and a half passed before enough money could be saved for the voyage. Father wondered secretly why the family did not send money for the trip, but knew instinctively that a reason beyond questioning existed. He kept his thoughts to himself.

It was 1937 when Mother, Father, my sister Ruth and I boarded the S.S. President Coolidge, bound for the Philippines, but before the ship could clear the Golden Gate Bridge, an oil tanker concealed by fog lumbered across the bow. Too late to take evasive action, the collision tore a gaping hole in the bow of the Coolidge, spilling a cargo of paint from the fore hold forming a multicolored splash in the fog. The ship limped back to dock and the choice was given to either wait for repairs or proceed to Vancouver by train where another ship, the

President Jackson, was preparing to sail. The choice was made and following a long train ride, we boarded the Jackson on April 3, 1937.

On the long trip over, a young woman who was also on route to the Philippines contacted Mother. She introduced herself as Sadie Buss, and they soon became fast friends, sharing times of prayer and mutual encouragement each day. It was a stormy ocean crossing and Sadie often carried me about the deck as I was just learning to walk and the rolling deck proved too much for my newfound legs.

Upon arrival in Manila bay, Mother and Sadie Buss parted, with the vow that they would continue praying for each other. Father booked passage as soon as possible on an interisland ship. Destination; Iloilo, the port city on the island of Panay, third largest in the archipelago called Philippines. The city and the port were at the mouth of the Iloilo River, which flowed out of the rich valley of the same name. In that valley was a plantation that Emiterio Alianza Alianza called home, and one he prayed his hazel-eyed wife and two children would be welcomed as family.

Chapter II

Father was, of course, welcomed home with open arms. A family party was soon in progress and Mother was introduced to the Filipino customs and traditions. The least of which included never to say anything that may embarrass another. It didn't take Father long to discover that echoes of disloyalty still could be heard in the shadows. He knew that he had lost his inheritance; that his disloyalty to the Alianza name was proven when he failed to return for his father's funeral.

For Olive's sake, these family talks were, for the most part, in English. To her, they were informal, light hearted social times much as she had enjoyed at home where in no seeming order, everyone interjected their own thoughts and perspectives on every subject that touched their lives. They were interspersed with laughter and reflection, philosophy, and news. Terry talked of the hardships caused by the great depression, and of the second child, the boy, the first-born son, whose birth had drained any savings he had to come home on. Others updated Terry on the situations at the plantation as well as the surrounding community. All agreed that Terry had been greatly missed around the plantation, but Patricia had held it together on the passing of Amay. How fortunate that Patricia was able and willing to take on a man's job, they said.

Mother replied with social nods and assents when she was turned to, but soon realized that conversations went on without her if she was not quick to answer. What she later came to understand as "Filipino English", with its seeming disjointed and often convoluted sentences, was quite frustrating to her untrained ear, but her warm smile kept her in good stead. She never realized that the subject of Terry's resuming responsibilities at the plantation was never brought up. To Terry, however, the absence spoke volumes, and after several weeks had passed, he announced that he was taking his family to another town several kilometers distance where he knew of a small farm for sale. It seemed, he told the family, that the hectic life at the plantation was not what Olive desired. The family all agreed that his choice was good and they wished him well.

The property lay just across the river from the town of Calinog. There an old house stood, surrounded by two

Chapter II

acres of flat land beside the road. Father decided to build a new house toward the back and gardens in the front. The new site was cleared of underbrush before Ruth and I were even allowed to explore the area. Directly in back of the new site the ground sloped away. There, like gigantic clumps of grass twenty feet across and fifty feet high, large stands of bamboo grew wild. Individual stalks, some bigger than a man's leg, crowded each other for space, groaning and creaking with the slightest breeze. The slope ended at an embankment where steps had been cut into the bank. In a small grotto at the bottom of the bank, a spring bubbled out of the rocky side of the grotto and fed a quiet pond fringed with reeds and small floating plants.

We moved into the old house while Father and neighbors built the new one. According to custom, the first step in building a new home was to set bamboo poles on the ground in the location and shape of the planned house, then wait a few days to be sure it was okay with the spirits. This also gave time for the owner to consider all aspects of his decision.

Mother said it was the only time she had ever seen Daddy scared. He woke one morning in a cold sweat saying that the spirits were not happy. Leaving the house in a near panic, he went straight to the new sight, adjusted the poles, then waited. Not many days after, construction started and it was all right then. Mother didn't question his actions or his fear, knowing that to him there must have been a good reason.

Almost every day Ruth and I headed for the spring in the small grotto and became acquainted with frogs, small turtles that hid under floating leaves, and nervous little fish that would flip water with their tails each time we waved our arms. Then we would climb the slope and watch the new house take shape for a few moments.

In traditional Filipino style, holes were dug in the earth at each corner and about two arm lengths apart throughout the floor plan. Large bamboo was then dropped into these to form the foundation for the house. After aligning and tamping dirt around the poles, they were cut to about five feet in height. On top of these would rest the floor and the rest of the house would rise from there.

Life was warm and Mother always listened to the adventures we spilled out to her. When the new house was finished, we moved in and I guess the spirits were pleased because nothing bad happened. Gardens grew and flowers filled the air. No one knew that like the inheritance, this too was not to be.

It was about that time a teenage girl came to live with us. Her name was Florencia Palentia, but we called her Nini. In the culture most everyone had nicknames and Nini was much easier to say. Father said she was the daughter of a distant relative who needed a home. Mother welcomed her eagerly. She was a good cook and often relieved mother of much of the household responsibilities as well as taking care of Ruth and me. She made a game out of going down to the spring for water. She taught us how to catch the turtles. Look for the floating leaves that have ripples around them, she said—for there would be a turtle hiding underneath. She showed us how we could take a turtle up to the house away from the pond, turn it on its back and spin it. When it would stop spinning, it would flip itself over and always turn straight back toward the pond. It was one of those little mysteries my young mind filed away to work on from time to time.

Nini collected drinking water from a trickle that came from the side of the grotto. She would hold a cupped hand under the trickle until full, then let it fall into the pitcher she held underneath. Again and again she repeated the process until the pitcher was full. I asked at one point why she cupped her hand to catch the water first. "You get more water" was her reply. I watched the trickle fall from the rock, into her hand, then into the pitcher and my mind filed that away, too.

Soon Mother went to work teaching high school across the river in town. I think it was really fulfilling for her. She talked about her students all the time and soon she had a Sunday School class going at the house. I didn't know much about Father's work except that he went off every morning and it had something to do with buying and trading water buffalo and horses. Mother said he was good at it.

Rainy seasons seldom caused life-style changes. There was no electric service to be suddenly disrupted and phones were only something Mother tried in vain to explain to two children too young to remember. When she told of being able to talk to others over long distances, my mind could only picture standing on the rooftop with a megaphone. She tried her best to explain electricity traveling through wires to light up the house and do other things beyond my comprehension. In my mind, hollow wires carried kerosene from a far off source to the lights.

Transportation was the main change that the rainy season affected. The trucks that rumbled through on the road from the big city, through town, and on towards the mountains were not as frequent, and much to our dismay, we were not allowed to play outside as much. The times when we did however were times of memorable abandon. The rain fell warm and cleansing. Puddles were made for playing and bits of wood and bamboo were transformed into ocean going ships. Mother stayed home often as few children came to school anyway. As the river rose men would stand on the banks and discuss whether the bridge would hold or not. Then one day it didn't. The brown rampage of water overpowered the bridge and all travel into town was stopped.

Father had stood with four neighborhood men on the banks of the flooded river that separated us from town. Most of the bridge had been swept away and there was no real reason to cross anyway, however idle conversation bantered on whether or not a man could swim the torrent. "No man can swim that, even if life depended on it." Heads nodded in agreement. All except one.

Chapter II

"If there is enough reason it can be done," Father answered quietly, his eyes gauging the current. There was no response except, it seemed, for a more intense visual of measuring and calculating.

"It's very strong." The reply finally came. Again heads nodded. For some perhaps the torrent received the nod. For others it may have been the challenge. Father took another moment to gauge, then pulled at the knotted string holding his machete scabbard at his waist and handed his machete to the one that had spoken. Then without a word he turned and made his way along the bank toward the bend in the river a hundred yards upstream. As he approached the bend, he unbuttoned his shirt and dramatically threw it to the ground before turning the bend to be hidden by foliage and the mist of rain.

The four men watched silently until he was out of sight, none daring a comment. A moment later a derisive note came from one of the four. "He'll hide in the bushes then go home and laugh at us with his hot coffee while we stand in the rain watching for nothing." A guffaw, then laughter split the air as they turned toward their homes with thoughts of hot coffee. One turned back for a last look. The smirk on his face disappeared with a jolt.

"Look!" His eyes flashed toward the center of the river where a man, his arms flailing at the boiling maelstrom fought his way toward the far shore. He paused a moment to get his bearing then struck on with renewed vigor as the current swept him closer toward the last piling of the broken bridge. His effort was almost too much as the rampage drove him directly into the wooden piling precariously holding the end of the bridge. The current tore at his body and legs but his arms were locked around the post. After a moment to breathe, he inched his arms up the pole until his body was free of the pull then swung his legs free and wrapped them around the pole above the wrenching current. Moments later he stood atop what remained of the shuddering bridge, chest expanding, pulling in life giving air, legs spread in triumph. Then with no more than a flick of his hand toward town, he turned and strode toward the dark silhouettes of rain soaked buildings, lantern light dispersing shadows from the windows. There would be much talk around hot coffee that night.

My five-year-old mind was not impressed by what I heard. Impressions are made by the abnormal and I had nothing to compare it to. This was my father and it was normal. Abnormal is when fear is present, or changes unexplained.

Chapter III
FOUNDATIONS

Mornings generally started early so evenings ended early. A tuck into bed, a goodnight prayer and a few quiet words of love were routine. One evening Father interrupted with a hushed call from outside at the bottom of the steps. He had gone to the outhouse a few moments earlier and Mother seemed a bit annoyed that her few moments of quiet with us were cut short. Her annoyance was easily hidden though, and displaced by curiosity that he should be back so quickly. His evening stroll usually included a look-see at the chicken coops in the back where our laying hens were kept. The rest of the chickens ran free and roosted in the tree beside the house. Father would then return, climb the stairs and secure the house for the night.

    I slipped out of bed and peered through the bedroom doorway as Mother lowered herself to one knee at the head of the stairs.

    "Hand me my *bolo*!" Father's voice was quiet as he answered her unasked question. Quiet, but with an edge that was not questioned or hesitated on. Mother's eyes didn't leave the shadow below her as she slipped her hand up the inside of the doorpost where she knew his machete hung. Quickly she handed it down to him.

"Is something wrong?"

"No, nothing. I'll not be long." He blended quickly into the shadows.

"Mom, what's wrong?" I called as I slipped hurriedly back into my bed.

"Nothing, dear. Go to sleep now."

The night sounds retreated into a vacuum waiting to be filled. A few moments passed and Daddy returned, climbed the stairs and hung his machete beside the door. Mother followed him into the kitchen. Their muffled voices drifted in as I again slipped out of bed.

"You better not!" My sister's warning whisper from across the room startled me and I eased back, relenting to wait. Sleep didn't come easy for me and when it did come, morning seemed just an instant behind.

I threw the covers back and raced into the kitchen remembering the muffled voices from the night before. As I slid the kitchen window open, Ruth jostled into me wanting to be first to look out. Below us on the ground stretched eleven feet of snake. A squeamish sound escaped Ruth's clenched teeth and her short nose wrinkled sharply before she covered it with one hand and turned away pulling her shoulders up and trying to hide behind them. It was big, much bigger than the black poisonous snake that Daddy had killed in the bedroom windowsill not too many days before.

"That fox that we thought had been getting the chickens," Daddy began later at the kitchen table, "it's not a fox, and I got him." He paused only a moment. "It was a python. That's why my snares would never get it. It slipped right through." He sipped at his coffee before continuing. "We never heard the chickens cry but just the flapping of wings because it had their head in its mouth first."

"The hen last night . . . is it dead?"

"No, but it won't have feathers on its neck for awhile. Just imagine my surprise," he went on, "I opened the door of the out-house and there's the chicken hanging out of its mouth right here!" He raised his hand to eye level a foot in front of his face and let his fingers fall like the death flutter of a chicken's wings. A squeal escaped my sister's throat and Father smiled, reaching over to touch her cheek.

"Scared?" He asked. Ruth pulled her shoulders up and leaned into the hand at her cheek.

I thought of the several chickens that had disappeared from the tree limb that leaned against the house just outside the bedroom window and a chill coursed down my spine. I could still feel the squirm under my bare foot the day I was running down the path to the rice fields and stepped on a small snake. But that wasn't fear, just a chill, a shock.

Fear, perhaps was learned a bit later when I woke early one morning with a burning fire in the palm of one hand and uncontrollable shaking through my whole body. The entire family was wakened by my cries and try as I might I could not cease my cries and sobs. That's where the fear entered because hurting as my hand was, it was not the cause of my crying. I didn't know what made me cry, and neither did Mother or Daddy. Mother wrapped a blanket about me and held me to comfort me.

In the palm of my left hand were two puncture wounds an inch apart and Daddy thought it looked like snakebites but he didn't have time to look for a snake. He had to get to work. Later as my shaking subsided Mother made a thorough search of my bed. There hiding in the folds of my blanket she found a centipede at least six inches long. With my father's machete she quickly chopped it in half. That's when she discovered that centipedes had to be smashed to be killed, otherwise the two halves just run off in different directions before eventually dying. That too, was my first introduction to emotions that could divide and run in different directions. Mother's concern and comfort could not offset father's seeming unconcern and busyness with other things.

As pain brings awareness, so too can joy. The light breeze was promising for kite flying as one morning I followed my sister and father up the hill in back of the house. At the summit, Daddy prepared the kite while Ruth sat intent at his feet. I watched from nearby but was soon distracted by an ant carrying an immense grain of sand away from his hole. It was at least three times his size and although he struggled, he didn't give up or stumble. My interest was so taken up that I missed the first flight of the kite. It was Ruth's cry that brought me up to see the kite circling wildly, then tail up plummet out of sight over the crest.

Chapter III

I jumped up, now thrilled to be part of the fun. I was closest to where it fell and could outrun Ruth anyway. Daddy would be pleased and I knew Ruth would be also. In spite of its nose-dive into the rocks, the kite was unhurt and I picked it up. I held it high over my head and ran back to where they would be eagerly waiting my triumph.

"I got it! I got it!" I shouted as Ruth reached out to claim her kite.

"You don't do that!" Father said. "That's Ruth's kite!" The stab was unexpected, but the thrill of retrieving the kite was enough to carry me through and I knew better than to question Daddy. I turned away as Ruth took the kite from me and I went back to watch the ant and the enormous burden it carried.

Bumps are part of growing up, they say. Makes you stronger, builds character. But it does little good to tell that to the one getting the bump.

Running and playing with abandon are gifts of childhood. That's when memories are born, life patterns cast. A child doesn't have the stumblings of the past to look back on as warning signs. He just does it with all the energy he has.

In the midst of one day's memory making, I scraped a knee. It was only a small scratch. It barely bled, and Mother had cleaned it as best she could with the little alcohol she had left and sent me back out to play. You don't put a five-year-old ball of energy to bed for a scratched knee. But it had not healed but enflamed, the infection growing in size and standing almost a half-inch high. When it began spreading up my leg as well as down, mother hurried me across the bridge to the hospital in town.

"If it does not stop when it gets to his thigh, it will be necessary to amputate."

Mother looked at the doctor a long moment, her gray eyes weary, fearful, yet accepting. A coarse whisper escaped her lips. "Thank you." She then turned toward the concrete steps leading to the second floor of the hospital, walked past the steps and stopped beside the folding cot where I lay. There were no rooms available and I lay in the darkness of a stairwell on a folding cot. Painkillers kept the pain down to a throb even as the infection approached my thigh.

Not three feet away in a second cot a young girl lay, perhaps seven-years-old, just two years older than me. She was quiet now. Only her face revealed the torture that claimed her body. Her arms were crossed over her thin chest, secured with twisted straps. Her legs lay askew from their fight with the bonds. She was under heavy sedation and Mother knew she might not wake again before the tetanus claimed her. If she did wake, the spasms would wrench her body, as before, her face torn into an almost inhuman shape. It was far too late for recovery and Mother's gray eyes, softened now by love, moistened with prayer, fearful and hesitant, but prayers indeed, that the tortured shape before her would pass on while she slept. Her heart ached for the girl. There had not been one visitor to see her in the five days she had been there.

Mother then turned toward me. My left leg lay bare on the sheet, blood red and swollen to nearly twice its normal size. She lowered herself to the edge of the bed, laid her hand gently on my forehead. It felt cold to me. So cold. Erysipelas, the doctor had called it. Most likely picked up through the scratched knee. The doctor had agonized with her each time a medication failed to stop the bacterial infection. And now she had seen in the doctor's eyes that he was out of options.

Later she revealed to me the storm that raged inside her soul. The doctors at home would have the answers, if we were home. If we were home in Pasadena, California, she whipped back at her own voice, this would not have happened. But this was not Pasadena, she argued back. This was home. This was the home she had chosen. Prayer always headed Mother's priority list, but this time there was no alternative. Nothing else.

That day marked the change and the swelling began receding. One week later I was home and being decidedly more careful than any five-year-old could be expected to be.

Chapter IV
BIRTHDAY

December 19, 1941. My sixth birthday. Anticipation was in the air as I sat quietly watching my mother create my birthday cake. We had moved into the countryside out of the town of Calinog the week before, shortly after hearing of the bombing of Pearl Harbor.

The attack was not totally unexpected. Seven months prior it was reported that two thousand American troops had unloaded in Manila harbor, prompting speculation that there was indeed trouble brewing with Japan.

Mother was always the softening in a hard day, the open window in an otherwise dark room. With war clouds threatening on the horizon, she was baking me a cake.

Suddenly excitement caught my ear. *"Cano! Cano!"* The words echoed between several children, before penetrating the split bamboo walls of our small house. I jumped up from where I sat, watching Mother carefully arranging firewood under the oven. My bare feet hit the bamboo floor and in three steps I was across the room. Knees thumped onto the wooden bench under the window before my mother's voice could catch up with me. She was saying something about a cake falling, but my attention was already out with the boys as they

Chapter IV

skipped excitedly, pointing back down the path toward the road. One boy approached the house, arms windmilling, but the sight of Mother through the open door kneeling in front of the oven waving a smoking stick at him stopped him before he could bound up the three wooden steps. The stick bobbed leaving a smoking exclamation point hanging in the air before mother returned it to the fire. She nodded gratifyingly at the oven, turned to the boy and paused for affect until she knew she had his attention, then lifting her chin and eyebrows just enough, waited.

"Americans are coming!" He repeated in his best school English. Mother gave him her 'well done' nod, then standing, walked lightly to the door. Shading her blue-gray eyes from the afternoon sun, mother squinted past the banana plant beside the steps. Her gaze followed the path to where it dipped from sight behind the bamboo stand. She seemed to be going through a mental list of the only other Americans she knew of in this area when she dimly heard him mention that they had a boy with them.

"It must be the Rounds." she said, anticipation playing across her face.

"Doug's coming to my birthday party!" I exclaimed, sliding off the bench to mother's side.

"Surely they wouldn't come way out here just for a birthday party." I puzzled at her words and she looked down, our eyes locking. "But then maybe they did." she added pulling me close. "Sixth birthdays are very important."

Her thoughts had been distant; perhaps back to father's last words before he had slipped out the door to the emergency town meeting before dawn. "Don't go where you can be seen from the road until I return." he had said, "Especially if there are strangers around." I wondered how Mother would know a stranger if she saw one anyway. We had only moved there from town a week before. "I'll find out what the situation really is." His smile and touch appeared to give her a measure of warmth in the predawn chill. Perhaps she wanted to forget what she had learned of the Filipino's innate ability, yes, even inbred social longing to hide all negative feelings.

She turned back to the room seeing what she could tidy up before they arrived. Besides a wooden table, four chairs and a bench, a wood-burning stove filled one end of the kitchen flanked by a clay water jug and a screened cabinet for food. The bamboo floor was self-cleaning. Anything too small to kick out the door would fall between the slats for the chickens below to eye and decide on. There wasn't much to do. They'd just have to accept things as they were. Then looking down at her brown cotton print dress, she smoothed at the wrinkles and turned to the small mirror on the wall. She wiped away a charcoal smudge on her face.

This was not the life-style she had left America for.

Mother assured us again and again over the past week that this war would not spread to the Philippines and, somehow, we would all be stronger for it and after it

Chapter IV

was over, Father would regain his inheritance. She felt a confidence in it.

But now with America's retaliatory declaration of war on Japan, there was little doubt, even though no communication had passed down from Manila since then. A day to remember, December 7, 1941, although here on this side of the international date line it was Monday, December 8, a fact that somehow deepened the feeling of alienation that at quiet moments surfaced from some dark place. Mother took a deep breath and turned to the oven and the birthday cake. "There they are!" I shouted as I stood on the bench, knees braced against the windowsill. I raised an arm to wave, then didn't.

They were undoubtedly Americans. Their stride marked them even before their clothing or height could be distinguished. So different from the Filipino's, everything-is-under-control-and-anyway-it's-too-hot-to-hurry, stroll. He was dressed in khaki with a light brown hat perched squarely on his head. She, in white, nearly as tall as he, easily matched his purposeful gait. My attention, however, was on Doug. He was a year older and taller than I and quite a bit taller than the village boys excitedly bouncing and running beside him. He gestured and laughed along with their abandon. Shyly I stepped forward to meet them and was soon caught up in the carefree world of children that stretches' sparkling to the horizon but never sees beyond tomorrow.

Louise Rounds stood tall, straight, holding herself equal to Mother's five-foot-nine, and showed pronouncedly the effect of one accustomed to walking long hours. Mother embraced her warmly then turned to greet Erle who had stepped aside, his lean frame seemingly propelled by nervous energy. Hat in hand, he wiped perspiration from his face with an already damp kerchief, eyed the house, then tested the steps before stepping inside.

"How long has it been?" Mother's eyes swept between them.

"Wasn't it last year, when you were still in Calinog? And before that on the ship over."

"How did you find us?"

"Oh, it wasn't hard to find you." Louise responded. "You know, you're the only American within fifty miles. We just went to your house in town and one of your neighbors guided us here," she reflected, swiping unconsciously at the perspiration on her forehead. "Why, anyone could find you."

That thought had probably already crossed Mother's mind and she found little comfort in it. After a cup of cooling water, Louise and Mother sat facing each other across the narrow table. Erle paced the small kitchen examining everything in an off-handed way, then dipped another ladle of cool water from the jug. He replaced the lid carefully and seemed to scrutinize the effectiveness of it. It received a passing grade. He ran his hand up one of the posts that stretched to the roof peak, then guided by his nose, leaned low over the hot oven, touching it lightly with fingertips. "Something smells good." He straightened, glancing quickly at Mother while testing his fingertip temperature with a thumb.

"It's Carling's birthday cake," she answered.

"Today?"

She smiled with a nod.

"December 19, I must remember this day." Erle put in.

"Oh, I'm sure you will," Mother answered. Erle lowered his frame to the bench beside his wife. "By the way, where's Terry?" His voice was casual but measured.

"In town at a special meeting." Mother went on to explain Father's concerns about the bombing and the absolute lack of radio communication.

"We're concerned too, Olive. That's really why we're here." He paused, fingers tracing circles on the table. Then laying his hand palm down softly but resolutely, he measured his words. "If there is an attack, you know Iloilo City will be one of the first targets of the Japanese—third largest city in the country and only two hours flight from Manila—risky to live so close." He paused, perhaps seeing the question in Mother's eyes. Louise shifted uneasily and Erle hurried on. "The Americans on the university staff, in fact all Americans are leaving the city. There's a place way back in the hills one of the evangelists visited awhile back. Quite remote, he said, and the people are receptive, they can be trusted." He raised a hand waving away any doubts. "It's only a precaution, you understand. The Japanese will never get that far, that is, if anything ever does happen. You know, this may well be completely unnecessary." He finished up on a light note.

Mother pondered his words, looking toward the door. Probably wishing that Father were there. I was too. Father wasn't a university professor but he was in touch with the people, and Mother felt more confident with that than with speculation. Louise touched Mother's hand. "We know you're in a different situation, with Terry being Filipino and all, but you're still an American, and your children are at risk too, you know." Mother's eyes hardened for an instant and she reached out wrapping an arm around my waist. There was no greater concern in her life than our safety. I knew that.

Erle interrupted her thoughts. "It would be safe for you there."

"We found you here." Louise reinforced. "Anybody could. Your neighbor even guided us." Mother didn't need to be reminded, but Father was still the best judge of that, and she wished that he had been there to explain to them and make decisions.

"By the way, I haven't seen your little girl--what is her name anyway?" It was Louise again.

"Ruth," Olive answered defensively. "And she's safe. She's out with Nini gathering vegetables."

"Your house girl?"

"A distant relative of Terry's. She was orphaned last year and we took her in. She's not a servant." She added with a slight emphasis.

Chapter IV

"Part of the family, how nice. They're the only ones to be trusted in this society, you know."

Mother shifted her gaze out the window. "Terry should be home soon, then we can discuss what needs to be." She stood suddenly, dismissing the subject.

"And while we're waiting, there's a cake to be decorated."

"Yes, yes!" replied Erle with relief. Louise heartily agreed.

***

The bobbing match reflected in everyone's eyes as it wavered over each candle before going on. Six homemade candles circled the top of the cake. One was a little crooked, but that didn't matter. I missed my friends in town but I had new ones here and that was good.

It was special to me that Doug came, even though I knew that wasn't really the reason he and his parents were here. Doug had talked about war and shooting and people getting killed, and planes flying like birds and dropping bombs and I understood only that it was something to be feared. Doug knew many things and even remembered America. I hoped we would be friends for a long time. I looked around at all the faces, laughing, talking. It was fun noise. So many had crowded in to see the cake. Someone started singing the happy birthday song, but others didn't know it. I didn't know why daddy wasn't home yet, but Mother said he would be soon, so that was okay.

In the middle of singing, some of my friends stopped and looked out the window. The ones in the doorway jumped aside. Some ran. Then Father was up the stairs and standing in the doorway. Mother started to say something, but didn't. Nobody did. There were some men standing behind Father and they all looked scared, but he looked more angry than scared. Everyone was looking at him, waiting. He stared at Mother a long minute without blinking. He didn't even seem to see the candles.

"Iloilo was bombed this morning. We're at war." He said it softly, like a small pebble in still water. And the ripples went out. Mother started to raise her hand, then just picked at a button on her dress. She tipped her head to the side a little waiting for that little wink that would tell her it was one of his jokes, but it didn't come. Erle stared at him, then dropped his head to his chest. Louise had nothing to say.

Mother leaned down, put her arm around me and kissed my cheek. "Make a wish, dear, and blow out your candles."

I blew hard, not wanting to look up at the darkness quickly drawing over my father's face, but I forgot to make a wish. I wondered later if it would have made a difference.

"The news came while we were still in the town meeting." Father turned his back, leaning against the windowsill. His hands gripped the bamboo sill. The

Chapter IV

muscles in his back bunched and rolled under his damp shirt. The laughter and gaiety of a birthday party quickly dissolved. Tension crackled the air. My friends melted out the door and away, urgency and questions in their whispered voices. Some ran toward homes nearby while others, not understanding, huddled together, furtive glances at the door seeking answers.

Louise was at Erle's side gripping his arm. She was the first to speak. "We must go at once." Then turning to Mother she added, "We all must."

"She's right, you know," Erle conceded stepping toward the window. "It won't be safe for any Americans."

"Yes, you must go." Father's face was set. His dark eyes darted, reminding me of a young hawk I had seen, a strong twine about one leg, perched captive on a forked limb, yet no one's servant. Father's eyes settled on Erle, "Maybe your jeep driver becomes nervous at the road and will leave you." Then turning to me, he softened. "But first we must have some birthday cake." With that he spun on his heel and slid up beside me at the table, catching me with my mouth open. I felt the tension ease somewhat and Mother pulled the bench over from beneath the window to make room for all around the table.

"May God give you many more birthdays to celebrate." Erle raised a fork of cake to me then added quickly, "but not like this." A murmur of agreement followed, then a quiet pause as forks tested the cake.

"Delicious!" exclaimed Erle. Heads nodded with mumbled words of agreement but small talk came hard. As if thoughts were scattered, some perhaps of safety half a world away, of families, of war. And some of children eating birthday cake. Father turned aside a moment summoning one of the men lingering outside and sent him to the road to assure the Round's driver that they would not be too long. The conversation painfully returned to the problem at hand.

"It's near Katipunan and about ten kilometers off the road." Erle explained where they were going. "It's quite a hike in but well worth the margin of safety until this thing blows over. It won't be long, but I think we shouldn't take chances."

Louise interjected quickly, "Several families are going to be there. It won't be as if we're out in the bush alone, and Douglas needs a companion." She added. "They say there's a stream where the boys can fish, and waterfalls. It would be like an extended camp-out." Louise made a valiant attempt to smile.

Doug and I exchanged knowing glances, interest growing on our faces. Doug raised a fork of cake toward me. Like a salute. I responded with a smile.

"Maybe it's too soon to go." Father's voice was quiet with a trace of finality in it that only Mother and I noticed. I saw it in her eyes and I turned toward father, disappointed. Doug glanced around at the adults then settled his inquiring gaze at his father. Erle stood and began pacing. He took a moment to gather his logic.

Chapter IV

"We've had absolutely no word from Manila since the bombing of Pearl Harbor on the eighth," he said, and went directly to his next points, "And now Iloilo is bombed. There is no way to know how long it will be before troops are actually landed," he paused for emphasis, "And then it'll be too late to do anything. We must take all possible precautions for our families' sakes." His gaze swept everyone but his words were pointedly at Father.

"You must go if you think it right, but maybe there are too many Americans in one place." Father's answer caused him to ponder.

"Terry, I'm told few people go there." Erle defended his decision. "And Ramon, our evangelist has been there many times. He reports that the people living there are very receptive and to be trusted."

Louise could contain herself no longer. "Olive," her voice pleaded, "How can you possibly think that staying here, just a shout away from the main road, would be safer than out in the bush?"

"These are Terry's people," Mother answered, "He certainly knows them better than I do, and if he trusts them, then I must too."

"You may trust them," Erle countered, "But can you trust the stranger passing through? It only takes one sympathizer."

"Here we are one American among many Filipinos," father answered. "There, you are many

Americans. You will be noticed more and not all can be trusted . . . not anywhere."

Father touched Mother's arm with the back of his hand. "Perhaps everyone would like water."

"Forgive me for being so inconsiderate." She rose and as she turned to retrieve glasses from the shelf, I remembered when Father, in his quiet off-handed way, had once mentioned to her that water should not be served until the meal is ended. In the way of the Philippines it is the signal for the meal to end. A subject change. A decision made.

Erle placed his fork carefully across his plate, resignation on his face. He graciously thanked Mother as he reached for the water offered. "Maybe we should be on our way," he offered, acknowledging nothing more than a cool drink of water. "I'm sure the others have gone ahead and I don't want to keep our driver waiting. Besides it will be getting dark before we get there if we don't get going. It would be difficult hiking the trail after dark."

We watched from the doorway until Doug and his parents were out of sight down the trail toward the road. Mother's shoulders sagged and she stole a glance at Father, perhaps with a slight hope that he would change his mind, or just searching his face for some confirmation that everything was going to be okay. The finality of their good-bye and the difference of opinion as they left hung heavy in the air.

Seldom, however, did mother ever question Father's decisions. Her Midwestern conservative background frowned on independent thinkers among women, as did her church, and even though her spirit rebelled against both, the respect and training of her youth was strong and for the most part her inner feelings remained in check. Here especially, so far from home and the familiar, she was kept in check by her ignorance of what may or may not offend the people, and to offend certainly would go against her gentle spirit.

Father turned slowly, dropping a firm hand on Mother's shoulder, rocking her back and forth several times. It was a familiar gesture. It said, trust me, we're together and it will be okay.

"The place where they are going, it's a good place. I have been there," Father answered the first unasked question, then hurried on to the next. "Today everyone is alert. Everyone is looking and everyone knows who is running, and everyone cannot be trusted to be quiet." He paced a circle on the floor, more of impatience, it seemed, than nervousness. "Maybe tomorrow or the next tomorrow we will go. When everyone is not looking then we will go." His words were for Mother, and for me, but his mind seemed to be running a course much too complex to question.

"Tomorrow we will start the harvest." He stated quietly and in one motion swept an arm around me and turned toward the table and the remaining cake. Mother pulled the chair in across from him.

"I thought it was still a week until harvest."

"A week is too long. By then the rice must be dried and milled. By then we must not be here." He eased his chair back, stood and moved toward the door in one fluid motion.

"Where are you going, dear?" Mother questioned.

"There." His answer was soft but chopped, accompanied by a quick raise of the head and the lower lip pointing. He faced the path that skirted the rice field and clung tightly to the riverbank. "I'll talk to some men about harvest." His footsteps were deliberate and his lean frame quickly disappeared into the afternoon shadows.

Chapter V
ATTACK

A week later the harvest was in and except for the occasional plane flying over which sent us for cover, and Father's increased night meetings, a strained normalcy crept back. But it was not to last.

"Aeroplanos! Aeroplanos!" The now familiar shout came. I jumped up from tussling with my dog and listened. I glanced apprehensively at the door. The sound of an airplane always meant an immediate dash indoors until it had passed. Almost daily now since the bombing, enemy planes flew just above the tree tops following the road that wound from Iloilo City, through our town of Calinog, passed our house and on across the mountains. This time, however, the sound was not approaching but distant and rising and falling in pitch, accompanied by muffled explosions.

"There!" a voice came from above on the vine crowded trellis over the porch. I raced for the porch and in a moment was seated breathless beside my friend, Ramon. He was pointing toward the town three kilometers distant. I shielded my eyes from the noon sun. I could see two, then three planes climbing, diving, then circling to repeat the same crazy pattern.

"What are they doing?" The question went unanswered and we watched, mouths agape. Muffled sounds of explosions reached us. That must have been the bombs that my father had tried to explain to me, but beyond that only my imagination could take me. We watched silently letting the sight and sounds record on our young minds. Abruptly the door opened and Mother stepped out and stopped short. I peered over the edge of the trellis as I heard a stifled cry. She was standing directly below me both hands covering her mouth, her face drained and tight. Her eyes mirrored a fear I had never seen before.

She heard us and looked up startled. "Get down and get inside!" her voice was strained, barely audible. Her gaze snapped back to the scene in the distance. I swung down and dropped beside her. I leaned close feeling her urgency. She placed one arm around my shoulder and pulled hard. I reached for her hand. It shook.

Her voice quivered. "Daddy is there. He went to town this morning for a special meeting." I wondered why Mother was so frightened. Then my mind sorted out the facts. I had been told bombs meant death and pain and I remembered the man that had been brought to us not long before who had fallen off his perch on top of the bus as it lurched past our place. His face was torn and blood oozed from deep gashes, and pieces of gravel were still imbedded in his split and swollen lip. One arm hung at an awkward angle. He choked and vomited blood. I didn't want to think of Father and the bombs.

Chapter V

One hour later the planes made a final circle around the column of smoke rising toward the somber sky and left. Shouts of panic and fear from neighbors shrunk into a tight silence that filtered through the cracks in the walls of our little house. Inside, Mother, Ruth, Nini and I sat until night pushed the sun from view.

Father had told us if there was any sign of trouble not to light any lamps in the evenings. Mother was not one to question his word. The darkness stopped her from reading but her hand still rested on top of the closed Bible. It seemed at times she gained strength from just touching its black cover as she walked past. There had been no news at all from town and only once running footsteps had passed the house.

"He'll wait till after dark to come home." Mother answered the unasked question that must have been whirling through her head. I stepped up behind her chair and let my hand play with a curl that fell across her collar.

"It's dark now, Mama." I said quietly and felt her shoulders tighten. She brought her hand up and touched mine lightly.

"He'll be home soon," she answered, and I wrapped my arms around her neck, closing my eyes to the darkness.

"He may be hungry when he gets in." She spoke into the darkness. "I better warm something up." Nini and Ruth came out of the bedroom to help when they heard Mother in the kitchen. Soon a small fire flickered on the stove throwing darting shadows where it could reach.

Nini pulled out what was left over from the light lunch; rice, strips of beef and a fresh vegetable picked from the garden which Mother insisted tasted like spinach. No one spoke. Each movement seemed a course whisper intruding on our individual thoughts and fears.

A scraping at the doorstep froze us all. Mother quickly set the plates down she was carrying as a familiar voice filtered through the door.

"It's only me." Mother was at the door before it was fully opened. Father stepped through, a quick greeting, a touch on the arm and they turned toward the clay jar together for a refreshing cup of water. Mother pressed close behind, full of questions. She ran her hand up his back, across his shoulders and down his arm as if examining to see if he was all right. His shirt was torn, smeared with mud. It clung damply. The tired muscles in his shoulders gleamed as he turned to her. His eyebrows flickered as they pulled chairs around to the table. Father emptied his cup and handed it to me for refill.

He turned toward the stove and the fire reflected in his eyes. "They bombed and machine gunned for one hour." His voice was quiet, factual, a man recalling a nightmare. "Everyone was in the streets, coming from church. They fell in the ditches. Rolled in the mud to cover their white clothes. The bombs and bullets, you could not see for the dust and smoke." He paused, rubbing at a dark stain on the back of his hand. Mother took his hand and ran her fingers across the dried stain. Father

Chapter V

shook his head slowly as if in answer to an unasked question. "Nobody!"

"Nobody?" Mother's voice trailed off, as if she didn't know exactly what the question should have been.

"Nobody was killed." He finished, a flicker pulled at the corners of his mouth.

I stopped, the ladle clacking against the water jar. Father's voice raised a pitch, "No one."

Mother grabbed his arm. "How can that be?"

He shrugged, dropping his gaze to the table. Then he swept his hand across it slowly. "But the town is leveled. If ten minutes earlier, everyone is in church and many would have been killed. It was hit direct."

"Where were you?" Mother asked, shaking her head slowly.

"We were meeting in the rice mill to discuss what to do if we are attacked."

"A little late." Obvious relief tempered the edge in Mother's voice.

"It has only begun." He paused to pull at his shirt pocket. He tossed a shiny object onto the table. "A sack of rice stopped this right here." He raised his hand, one finger pointing two inches from his head.

I set the cup of water down and carefully touched the object, twice the size of my thumb.

"It's a bullet." Father answered my inquiring glance. "My life is owned by a sack of rice."

I picked up the bullet and turned it over in my hand, pondering the words I knew to be somehow important.

Deliberately father stood and turned toward the bedroom, unbuttoning his shirt.

"I must eat, then I must go. Do I have a clean shirt?" Mother rose slowly, she seemed to hesitate at the rapid change of subjects.

"Yes." But her mind was not on shirts. "Where are you going? You just got back!"

"I must meet with my men. A clean shirt?" he repeated.

"Your men? But the harvest is in, and . . ."

He turned back at the bedroom door, what was left of his shirt now clenched tightly in his left fist. Flickering shadows masked his face. "I am asked to be the one to organize the men."

The confusion on Mother's face only grew. Father let the bunched shirt drop to the floor and in two steps stood in front of her, his hands gently but firmly on her shoulders. His body gleamed with the perspiration of fatigue and his arms and shoulders rippled as he spoke. "To fight," he finished, his voice quiet but firm. The voice of one committed and not to be questioned.

Dinner was four people poking at their plates, glancing expectantly at the fifth for a word of hope, explanation, but none came. Father ate silently and quickly, his mind perhaps reaching ahead to a meeting, the first step in a commitment made.

My mind rolled with pictures of bombs and bullets, of the screams of men, women and children rolling in the mud of the gutters. Of dust and explosions, of a man

Chapter V

carried in, blood and gravel caked to his face, and the food in front of me choked me into sobs I could not hold back.

Father paused. "Soon there may not be so much food. It's good to eat." He never raised his voice but messages were always clear. I tried to spoon another bite to my mouth but the sobs continued.

"I'm not hungry." The words spilled out. I was ordered to my room where I lay on my bed, sobs muffled in my pillow. Through the thin walls I could hear quiet but tense words between them. I felt so alone and longed for an arm around me with comfort and explanations. I heard Mother suggest that I may be homesick. I had not heard that word before, but maybe she was right. I let my sobs grow louder.

The sound of a chair scraping back from the table sifted through the bamboo walls and heavy steps creaked the three stairs up to the bedroom and Father entered. His face was dark and I suddenly knew fear. He ordered me to stop crying but try as I might, the sobs only grew heavier. The last thing I saw was his hand reaching up toward my face, then the blanket I was lying on came around my head and pulled tight across my face. I had no breath left. My lungs burned as I gasped for breath, but there was none. It seemed an eternity, then the blanket was ripped away. I gulped for air and in the midst of a breath stopped. In front of my eyes and barely an inch away swayed the barrel of a pistol. I had never seen what a gun could do, but the meaning was clear. In the darkness

I could not see my father's eyes but I knew fire was there. When my breath came again, Father's voice was subdued and final.

"When I tell you to stop, you stop!" The words burned into my mind, twisting and tearing at pictures and leaving a black space void of thought.

Chapter VI
EVACUATE

The days passed. An endless curtain, ever moving, ever changing, always dark. Father was gone more and more.

One morning at breakfast, Father said with a quiet firmness, "After dark we will leave, but no one can be told."

I glanced up at Mother but could not read her face.

"We must take everything," he continued. "We must leave nothing to say that Americans have been here."

"What about Buddy?" I shifted my eyes hopefully to Father.

"Dogs make noise." was all he said. "I will go now and make arrangements."

Later I sat on the back steps, my arm around the muscular brown neck of the dog some called fierce. I slid my hand down to the jagged scar on his side where no fur grew and I remembered the day Buddy had disappeared. After the third day Father had set out with some men to search for him. Buddy was our best hunting dog and Father counted him valuable. They searched for two days before finding him. His side had been torn open. Intestines trailing, he had crawled a ways until he was too weak. Father said it looked like a wild boar had ripped him. They carried him home where Mother nursed him back to health. Then after gaining strength, Buddy often disappeared to return covered with blood. Rumors soon followed of wild boars found dead, torn by some vicious animal. I buried my face in the neck of the one they called vicious and swallowed the burning lump in my throat.

I was little help in packing, and it seemed Mother didn't really expect me to be. My sister packed and repacked the few clothes she had. Besides Mother, only Nini seemed to grasp the urgency that had shrouded the breakfast table. By early afternoon all the possessions we had left were packed and separated into two piles as Father had instructed: The smaller pile containing only what Mother thought to be necessary for survival.

As evening lowered, Father returned with two men, his favorite horse and a carabao hitched to a carosa that had been fitted with new runners. It was a familiar sight to me. The sled like affair with four bamboo runners pulled by a water buffalo was the common means of hauling anything where there were no roads.

We traveled all night. Often my eyes searched the darkness behind us hoping that Buddy might slip the collar and rope that held him. I knew that by morning neighbors would feed him and soon he would be theirs.

Sometimes riding and sometimes walking, Ruth and I tired quickly and soon slept curled up in the bumping, creaking carosa. We stopped often to rest as no one was accustomed to all night walks, Nini and Mother in particular. They mostly walked beside the carosa holding to the side rail for support. The two trusted men that Father had picked walked, one leading the carabao and the other behind. Father rode ahead and would return from time to time with quiet instructions for the men. As the carosa slid across rice fields, hills and open land, the terrain slowly turned into more forested area. We pushed farther and farther away from the towns and into the hill country. Fatigue overcame me and even the bumping, sliding, scraping of the skids over rocks, fallen branches and everything else hidden by darkness and an untraveled route blurred into nothingness.

The stillness woke me and I raised my head and stretched cramped muscles. I pulled my shoulders in against the chill of morning air. Filtered through bamboo leaves on pencil thin branches, the sky began its coloring on the horizon. The carosa had been pulled up beside a small bamboo house. In front of the house the ground sloped away into darkness, and beyond the darkness it rose into a hill forested with bamboo beginning to catch the color of a new morning. Only the occasional creaking of one bamboo shaft against another broke the stillness of morning.

Back home, father had told me that creaking was the sound of their growing. The next day, with Buddy by my side, I had run to a clump of bamboo near the house, and after finding a new bamboo shoot just a few inches out of the ground, tied a string around the shaft of a bamboo next to it. Each day after that we had run together to tie a new string at its tip and watch it grow, sometimes six inches a day. Soon, it was pushing its way among the mature shafts, some too big for both my hands to reach around. And it creaked and groaned as it pushed for its share of space.

In one of the larger clumps of bamboo away from the house, Father had built a hideout for us if danger came too quickly for us to run. Several feet above his head he had cut off just enough bamboo stems for him to pass between. He had cut them in a way that made them look like they were broken. Then toward the middle of the clump he cut more bamboo four or five feet shorter and made a platform where we could climb in and sit completely out of sight. He had a bamboo ladder to lean against the side which he would pull up after us and hide inside the clump. It would have made a great place to play, but Daddy said that we must not ever go there unless it was an emergency and we didn't dare disobey.

Suddenly I realized I was alone. My first thoughts were of Buddy, who never left my side whenever I was outside. He was not there. For an instant my breath seemed to squeeze from my lungs, then I heard movement in the house.

Father stepped out the door and down the bamboo steps. His face was grim but his eyebrows raised as he saw that I was awake. For the first time I saw the holster strapped to his waist. "Come up. We will stay here for the day." He touched my arm as I clambered out of the cart. "The owners have left . . . here, take this up." He handed me a small bundle of clothes.

Chapter VI

"Where'd they go?" I mumbled as I hefted the bundle.

"Maybe to the mountains." I turned my eyes toward the hills. "These are only hills," Father answered my questioning eyes, "Mountains go to the sky, you will soon see."

***

Not many days later, I peered over the concealing brush to the dizzying scene far, far below. The green valley stretched away to blend into the blue of the horizon. Father's form crouched beside me, arm stretched out pointing to a thin line of smoke moving across the valley. "It's going to Capiz." Father's short statement left more questions than answers.

"What is it?"

"Train," he said, "Left Iloilo, heading for Capiz." His arm swept from right to left. What a train was and even what Capiz was were just words that were to be filed away for future answers. But I did know we were now in the mountains. I stood up to better see and Father's firm hand clamped my shoulder forcing me down. "You might be seen."

Father had chosen a tree-shrouded plateau less than a hundred yards long and protected on three sides by steep cliffs. On the forth side stretched a panoramic view of the valley we had crossed. We had traveled nights and slept days in out of the way bamboo huts and abandoned houses, keeping to the forested lines that divided the fertile valley, skirting all roads. Here we would be safe, he said, and he had started building our house. But soon others on the same desperate journey to safety crowded in and the unfinished house filled.

One evening I looked around the room and through the walls of the unfinished bamboo house with the curiosity of a child that I was, yet blended with indifference born out of futility: The futility of the hunted never being far enough in front of the hunter to be comfortable. It was an air that was fast beating down even the hardest of men. Even my own father. A feeling that soon, not sooner or later, but soon there would be no place to retreat to. The thin blanket under me did little to cushion my bones from the split bamboo floor. I lifted my head enough to see the couple in the next room lying on the sleeping mat. My sleeping mat. My mind absorbed the scene and put it in the ever-growing file titled simply "Why?" I reached out to touch my mother lying beside me, her legs pulled up close in front of her. She opened her eyes and her hand of assurance comforted me.

"Mom, how come they get to stretch out on the pad? It's our house."

"They need more rest, dear." Her smile was reassuring, but the answer went into the same mental file.

Mother stretched the little she could without bothering those around her. Others who couldn't sleep sat with their backs against the unfinished walls. But the roof was complete and superstition said that was all that was

Chapter VI

needed to protect them from the evil spirits that roamed the night.

To many, the Alianza house in the tall wood was the only place high enough in the mountains to provide a measure of safety. The knowledge that Captain Alianza had his guerrilla scouts watching the trails was a magnet that drew even strangers, and the important ones stretched out their legs.

Daylight retreated leaving the small, unfinished house to shrink into the gloom and the night sounds. A cramped leg stretched out beyond the safety of the wall limits and was jerked back quickly. Even sleep did not bring rest.

The chill of first morning light found silhouettes emerging from the house, stretching, and wandering into the brush to relieve themselves. The jungle was still, and somewhere in the brush a wild rooster announced dawn. A practiced ear turned in that direction, thoughts of lunch emerging. Another silhouette stepped down and then sighed, quickly putting away the urge to strike up a fire. In the stillness the smoke would be seen for miles. He turned need fully toward the bushes, then with a fluid motion dove for shadows as the stillness was shattered by a staccato hammering of machine-gun fire.

The sound ricocheted among the stoic tree trunks and jolted a scream from sleeping lips before a firm hand could cover them. Some rushed headlong into the brush while others froze trying to pull the world over their heads. The captain's voice could be heard over the bedlam. In an instant, obedient men disappeared into the shadows to predetermined points of observation. Two more short bursts echoed through the trees as eyes and ears now alert and free from cobwebs of sleep tuned into the sound.

The silhouette of a man emerged from the brush, arm cocked back to throw. An object arched high into the air and drummed harmlessly off a hollow tree trunk. Startled wings beat the air and vanished into the dawn.

"Woodpeckers!" Tense lips repeated the words through the camp and nerves stretched to the limit eased and almost laughed, but the guards held their place in case the scream was heard.

Father had planned escape routes from our little valley and his foresight was not in vein. A few days later, even before our house was completed, a runner arrived with frantic news. Somehow a Japanese patrol had passed one of Father's outposts without being spotted and was on the trail that led directly into our camp.

"No time." There was no mistaking the urgency in Father's course whisper. Mother hesitated only an instant wanting to pick up at least one piece of clothing before leaving. We were single file up the trail leading to the ridgeline and the higher mountains. It was not necessary to express any urgency. It was in the air, every motion, every breath.

Mouths dry, sucking hot air, we topped the ridge. Father's scout continued on up the trail but Father stopped. "This way." He stepped off the trail, leading us carefully around underbrush and trees down the other side away from the ridge. The way grew steep and we picked our way carefully until he stopped us beside a large rock outcropping. He motioned for us to hide underneath. The rock jutted out, overhanging with space under, shielded by low bushes. We huddled close, sitting with our backs to the cliff, the rock above jutting out several feet shielding us from any who might even wander off the trail to search the descending hill. Father disappeared back up the hill.

Nini, pushing herself up tight against the cliff and Ruth and I pulled ourselves close to Mother. Her arms surrounded us protectively. Below us the hill was spotted with trees and thick with shoulder high brush. It was a vast difference from where we had just come with its tall canopy of trees and little underbrush. The remains of rotting stumps scattered about gave evidence that this side of the mountain had been logged off some years past.

Suddenly Mother's grip slipped up from my shoulder and pulled tight across my mouth. It hurt and I wanted to cry out but I froze in silence. A quick hiss from her warned us all and at the same instant movement below caught my eye. Not more than fifty feet below from the right walked a Japanese patrol. They were on an evidently little used trail that would carry them directly below us.

They were talking and laughing, walking with little care or concern. We were exposed, in full view of any who might casually glance our way. I wanted to duck behind the low brush in front of us but Mother's hand tightened. Too late to move it said. Just freeze and pray. The path must have been narrow and perhaps steep as none looked up except to push brush aside as they passed.

It seemed an eternity before they were out of sight and Mother released her grip. I took a deep breath but none moved until we heard Father's reassuring whisper from beside the rock. "Wait." was all he said and the silence hung heavy until he returned moments later.

No one knew why the patrol had chosen to take that obscure path, but Mother was sure it was only God that kept them from looking up. No one argued with her. Our house was not discovered, but Father took no chances and the next day we packed what little we had.

Word soon reached Father that the enemy probes into the mountains had gone back down and our houseguests left too. They, however, went back down, more willing to live in the valleys with risk than the isolation of the mountains. Higher Father led us, hoping to one-day climb above the point where they would pursue, if there were such a place.

Mother's leg was not totally healed from a bad infection and she tired easily. I could see pain in every step and she often bit her lip, but there was a look about her eyes that never dimmed. It had its foundation somewhere deep, where faith is born. It was determination, purpose, a conscious acceptance of an unchosen path, even in the dark. It was not tranquil.

We topped a ridge and my crying muscles and burning lungs welcomed the rest. But it was only long enough for father's scouts to check out the narrow valley before us. We descended, our muscles still knotted and weak from the long pull up, quivered and struggled for control on the near vertical ledge that was called a path. Reaching the relative flatness of the valley, we left the path and found a place to rest on the far side of some thick underbrush, away from prying eyes. Shadows stretched out for the evening and the stillness magnified the sound of a stream or small river somewhere below in the tall trees.

Suddenly a sound exploded our moment of solitude, echoing through the trees to be swallowed again into nothingness. A gunshot. Time froze. And through the silence I could hear only my own thundering heartbeat. The backwash of silence was followed quickly by another sound out of tune with nature. A scream. A woman's scream of anguish that cut to the depth of the soul and snapped knotted muscles into action. With discipline born of fatigue and desperation, we moved as one. Chained together by purpose, beyond fatigue, and fused by Father's strong hand, we silently retraced our steps out of the echoing valley. Not a word was spoken, none was needed. All energy was expended to claw up the trail. Footholds, handholds, and helping hands were all grasped for. No thanks was given. We were all one

A mountain range and a lifetime away we stopped, hoping we were out of range. The scouts reported to

Father as they caught up to us. We were not followed. Air began returning to our seared lungs, and legs long numbed regained feeling, bad feeling. A tear was in Mother's eye and I wondered where her thoughts were.

What few blankets we had left were spread, scouts took up their positions and night gave rest.

Early morning witnessed a guarded conversation between Father and a returning scout. He then waved the scout toward a steaming pot of rice where others squatted. The scout turned toward the welcome aroma and Father sauntered up to where we were going through the motions of preparing for another day.

We watched expectantly as he squatted and pulled idly at a strap. He glanced up and his eyes told of frustration mixed with a touch of humor. Mother read in him that danger had diminished, but something within refused to let the hint of humor touch her.

"It was not a gunshot." he volunteered. "Some fool used a live rock on a fire."

"A live rock? What does that mean?"

An irritated glance told Mother that she should have known. It seemed a millennium ago when he had angrily rebuked her saying that she should never say she doesn't know something.

"A round rock," he explained with control, "cannot be used for a fire tripod. Some are hollow and explode when they get hot."

"And the scream?" she ventured. "Was someone hurt?"

Chapter VI

His eyebrows lowered. "No, not from the rock. The scream was from below at the waterfalls. A woman crossing above the falls slipped and dropped her baby."

Mother gasped, her mouth moved silently as if wanting to cry out, to ask, but she didn't. Instead she diverted her eyes to her tattered dress and wondered about another world, one that seemed so far away at times.

As the enemy searched, so we continued climbing. Another day, another bamboo hut to stay in till night came when we could travel again with reasonable safety. I sat on the ground in front of one of the many huts and let my gaze follow upward at the massive tree in front of the hut, its trunk reaching majestically for the sky, it's few limbs stretched out then up again toward the sky. There was rich foliage and the brown bark of strong limbs, alive, twisting, clinging, encircling . . . encircling nothing. My eyes searched the outline of the tree, so precise, so clear.

A tree had once stood there, tall, meaningful, encroached on by vines that grew around the tree and up, wrapping each limb with tender shoots that grew, clung and eventually strangled the life from the majestic being. The tree had died. Its flesh and bark had rotted and fallen to be absorbed back into the life of the jungle. And the vine, having drawn its strength from the tree, remained and grew on, its limbs still wrapped around the memory of a tree.

Years later, Mother brought this picture back to my mind when she mused how she felt that her very soul had been encroached upon, encircled and crushed in that jungle. It had left her hollow, dead, with only the strength of the encroachment itself keeping her body moving, with only one goal, that of getting her children out.

Still higher we climbed, past the village of the lepers. Mother shared with me later the mix of fears that scrambled through her mind. The lepers walked these same trails, brushed past the same grasses, leaned on the same trees and sat on the same logs beside the trails. The fear of leprosy dwindled with the ever-present danger of capture looming.

On we went, beyond Mount Baloy, one of the Philippine army's last strongholds, on to a little known tribe whose village skirted a concealed lake. There we lived at peace for a time. The people of the tribe were tall, light skinned, gentle and soft-spoken. They were also headhunters.

Prior to the invasion they had hunted the heads of rival tribesmen, not because of tribal rivalries, barbarism or boundary disputes, but for ceremony. It was part it seemed, of the right of puberty, or becoming a man. But as word of their practices reached the government, orders had been given that such practices be stopped or else the tribe would be annihilated. They had complied . . . at least on the surface. Then when the war started, the government eased the restriction with the stipulation that they could hunt only the heads of the Japanese. Patrols

Chapter VI

that wandered into the area never returned and there we lived in safety, among a gentle people whose hunting had become comfortably selective.

Mother and I had both needed the rest. Somewhere along the way an infected *anopheles* mosquito had bitten me and transmitted to my blood stream the dreaded malaria. My strength was completely sapped by the alternating fever and chills and one of Father's men carried me piggyback at all times. On Mother, a tropical ulcer on her leg had not healed as hoped and each step was filled with pain. Father had fashioned a half coconut shell and tied it to her leg, inverted like a cup to keep branches and shrubbery from scraping it. The protection helped, she said, but rest was what she needed to allow healing. The infection was growing and with it a fever that took most of her energy. The only medication left was to place a hot compress on it in the evenings in hopes that the infection would be drawn out. And prayer.

Later she told me of one evening when she doubted if she would live to see home again. She had prayed that God would show her a sign and He did. She turned her fevered head toward the open window of the hut where she lay and clearly outlined against the haze of evening, the face of Jesus looked in at her. The serenity of the face pulled her world into proper focus and at that moment she knew she was going to make it.

Healing was slow, but it was also those gentle people who gathered for us the rare tree root that when processed correctly supplied the life-giving quinine for my malaria. We were told that if not processed correctly it became a deadly poison. Each day I steeled myself to drink the glass of cloudy liquid. The bitterness sent convulsions from head to toe but I was assured the quinine was the only way to stop the fevers and chills. No one could guess what was the proper dosage or even if the processing was correct for that batch, but one glass full twice a day was what these gentle people prescribed. When the fever was high, my mind was not able to focus and it was only mother's calmness that mattered, and her prayers.

Chapter VII
HOPEVALE

I didn't remember time going by, the seasons, the years, all the places we moved, all the lives that touched us and that we touched. Some I remembered. Some I didn't want to. The life of hiding, traveling mostly by night, no plans other than today. Tomorrow might not be. It had become the only life I knew. It was a life void of emotion, of laughter. Those were luxuries to be avoided. They could kill.

Our travels were not planned except to go where the enemy was not. Sometimes we were a step ahead, sometimes behind, ducking into a valley or across mountains they had already searched. Our route took us in a large circle of the island. At one point we returned to Calinog. It had been almost two years as we approached our home from the rear one day. It was barely visible. The flowering vine that mother had planted nearly covered it. Large, yellow bell-shaped flowers dotted the rich green foliage. Mother called it Grandma's vine. Grandma had sent seeds directly from her garden in Pasadena. That was before. Now we dared not stay in the house or even linger. We went on, but mother's desire for American companions was strong and though she held her feelings to herself, father must have known. He never told us where we were going. Safer that way, he said.

Once again our way led us higher, deeper, away from known trails and roads. One foot ahead of the next. The trail had narrowed, winding down into a valley. We had crossed the ridgeline quickly, quietly as usual, no pause to see beyond the next foothold or limb to grasp for balance.

The carosa carrying most of our belongings, the carabao that patiently pulled it and even Captain Alianza's horse had been left behind some time back. I didn't know when. My mind had no reason to keep track of days. The next step was all that counted, although my eyes never missed the flash of a bird's wing or a hint of color hanging from a jungle tree.

On one welcome rest stop, as I wandered a few steps away to relieve myself, I spotted what I thought to be a large blossom protruding from the tree trunk right in front of me. Then it moved. I jerked back, forgetting for a moment what I was doing. Recovering myself, I drew closer to examine it; red, brown and orange bands radiated out from its center in spirals. It moved slowly, a snout protruded in front with two eyes on stalks half the size of my finger. Behind, a glimmering sheath of liquid silk marked its way. At home I had watched garden snails gliding on their paths of silk, but this. I spread my hand out, my fingers barely covering the width of its brilliant shell. So many things to remember.

Chapter VII

Voices intruded, muted, carried on the stillness of the jungle air. Voices from ahead on the trail. I turned, seeking out Father and the quick hand signals that would mean hide, freeze, run, or relax everything's okay. Captain Alianza was not there, only Mother, Ruth and the others, sitting calmly beside the trail. They hadn't heard. My first thought was to scream at them, warn them, but it stuck in my throat and I froze. My eyes shifted to where the trail dissolved into the green of the underbrush and the voices approaching.

"They're just around the corner." The voice was open, disarming. Father's voice, in English.

Another voice, "I'm sure everyone is tired and hungry. Well, tonight you'll rest peacefully." It was an American.

I froze, relief and confusion clashing in my mind. This was the jungle. There were no friends here; only the enemy and the unknown, and if it was unknown, it was assumed to be enemy. Father had used those words, and what the Captain said was to be adhered to.

They emerged, the Captain in the lead followed by an American, carrying himself tall, his eyes quick, sweeping the small group, accepting.

"Welcome to Hopevale," he greeted with warmth. Mother pushed herself up and with surprise and hesitance moved toward him.

"Erle." Her voice choked off and she let her head fall against his chest. He steadied her and she pulled back, still gripping both his hands. She took a breath. "How are Louise and Doug?"

"Fine, just fine. We're all fine. A bit wearied but fine," he added with meaning.

I stepped out from the concealing brush, eagerly scanning the trail behind the man.

"Ah, there you are," his smile and greeting were directed toward me. "Doug was asking about you." He laid a hand on my shoulder as we met. "He's waiting for you at camp. Why don't you run on ahead? Just follow the trail. You can't miss it."

I looked inquiringly at Father and caught the flicker of his eyebrows, then to Mother. "Be careful," she urged and reached a hand to me but I was already on my way.

My bare feet pounded the trail. I didn't know why but I wanted to run. Needed to run. The trail rounded a curve and dropped. I slid to a stop grabbing for support to a vine that clung to a giant of a tree. Ten feet below, a small stream played over its rocky bed, shafts of sunlight splintered on its surface, glancing off the wet rocks. Upstream to my left, an inviting pool had formed where the stream detoured around the tree. I felt like laughing as I lowered myself down the embankment on the well warn footholds and handholds; the exposed roots of the gnarled tree that seemed to hold up the bank.

The water was cool, tingling on my hot feet and legs. I stood for a long moment at the edge of the pool pushing my toes into the sand. Small fish darted from

Chapter VII

shadow to shadow in the depths. I would ask Doug if he ever played here. Reaching down I scooped water splashing my legs and face before turning to the far bank.

The trail followed the stream winding upward into even deeper woods. Sunlight became only brilliant flashes as tree top breezes swayed the leaves. Soon the trail widened and sounds filtered from above. Sounds of conversation and quiet laughter; the familiar slice of machete on bamboo; the clack of a wooden spoon in a pot being stirred, a woman's voice singing softly to herself. This must be Hopevale.

"Carling!" The excited voice rang through the trees as Douglas Rounds, feet flying, jumped off the porch of their house, basket in hand and raced down the hill to where I stood.

"Doug . . . ," was all I got out.

"Come on," he urged slowing to a trot as he passed, "there's crawdads at the stream and we need a bunch for dinner."

He continued on down to the stream without a backward glance and I followed, drawn by the free spontaneity that was somehow foreign to me.

We stood around the table, the family Rounds and the family Alianza, each gripping the hand of the next, the circle unbroken.

"Lord we thank you for the food you so abundantly provide for us and for the abundance of love that is around this table today. May it never cease and may you grant us joy and awareness of yourself in the days to come as we seek you out in this time when we desperately need your presence, guidance and deliverance. We pray this in the name of Jesus our Lord, Amen."

The scrape of chairs and benches on a bamboo floor and we sat facing each other, the strain and fatigue of months of survival in an alien environment washed for a moment from our faces.

"It's been so long since we shared a meal," Erle Rounds said, adding voice to the momentary stillness, his gaze sweeping slowly from left to right then back, settling on Terry, Captain Emiterio Alianza, a title new to Erle but somehow not surprising.

"Two years." Father answered, his eyes locking on to the large bowl of steaming rice being brought in from the kitchen area.

"Not quite," Mother added brightly. "It was on a very special day."

"That's right." Erle leaned back in his chair momentarily. "It was somebody's birthday, wasn't it?" His eyes shifted to me.

"And there were six candles on the cake," Doug added, elbowing me lightly. I glanced around the table then focused on the rice being spooned onto my plate

"And you, the one who never forgets," Louise chided her husband.

"I didn't forget. December . . . December 19, right?" His face widened into a broad grin that he aimed at me. "Birthdays are never to be forgotten, right Carling?"

Chapter VII

A murmur of approval went around the room then dissolved into the sound of two families, somewhat different yet drawn together and knit closely by a mutual desire to survive, enjoying a meal in an atmosphere that had grown quite rare; relative leisure. The meal was built around a massive bowl of freshly harvested rice with its distinct fresh, almost sweet aroma that lasted only a week or so during the harvest time; alogbate, a green spinach like wild vine that I never did grow to like—slimey, I called its slick texture. There was fried chicken and just a few freshly caught crawdads. It seems those responsible for the crawdads spent more time splashing in the pool than hunting. But no one seemed to object.

Doug and I ate heartily and quickly excused ourselves at the first available time. The stream still beckoned, and who knows, there just may be some crawdads left that hadn't been frightened off. "Be back before dark," caught up with us as we leaped from the porch.

"Over there," Erle pointed while everyone's attention was still on the empty doorway. They followed his direction toward a vine-draped tree at the edge of the clearing. "You can build there." Mother straightened, turning slowly, her face mirroring a longing, her eyes eager, searching Erle's face, then Father's. The Captain was thoughtful for a moment, then deliberately reached for his glass of water.

Louise Quickly cut in, "The boys need each other,"
"We all need each other," Erle finished.

Mother nodded.

"Almost two years ago in Calinog," Erle began softly. "You thought we were wrong to come here—sure it's isolated, but we've been safe. The Japanese have been up and down the road, searched every village, and we're still here, and we'll probably stay here until it's over. How much longer can it last anyway? We certainly haven't been abandoned." It was a declarative statement, as if to dispel unvoiced fears.

"We've traveled one large circle," Mother reflected slowly, "keeping just one step ahead. I don't think we've stayed in one place more than a couple of weeks. It does sound nice . . . and I'm so tired," she added almost as an afterthought.

Father set his glass back down without drinking.

"We need you here," Erle said watching father's movements, "your knowledge with the people; your knowledge of the enemy . . . your family."

Father turned the glass slowly, lifting it, setting it down, making circles on the wood planks of the tabletop.

Mother studied his eyes. They didn't seem to move, piercing the tabletop, seeing beyond, perhaps looking forward, perhaps back. She glanced at the glass, the only thing moving in the room, and the battle that raged silently in the Captain unfolded in her eyes. She heard afresh the words he had spoken so long ago now, "To drink water means the end of the meal, a decision made or a subject changed." He was fighting between what he believed to be survival and the relative, if only temporary

Chapter VII

comfort and rest needed by his family. Mother hesitated, then reached for her glass and drank.

"Erle, Louise, I'm sorry, we just can't stay," she said quietly meeting their eyes squarely.

The Captain's eyes never moved as he lifted his glass to drink.

Among the several families at Hopevale, there was not a problem finding room for us while Father and three of his men searched for a place to build that we could hopefully call home for a while. Doug and I were inseparable during those days, spending most of our time at the stream, and we even caught some crawdads too. Ruth was mostly with Nini and the other girls while Mother relished the time with the missionaries, talking laughing, praying together and just being an American again, pushing away the thought of tomorrow.

On the third day Father returned. He had found a place only a half-hours walk where he felt we would be reasonably safe and yet close enough to visit. By way of information he went on to tell how he had needed to check on a rumor that a Japanese patrol was spotted a few kilometers away. That was as close to an explanation as he could come for the three day delay to find a house thirty minutes away.

Mother fought off the desire to glance at his gun belt and count the bullets. It had become ritual with her when he would at times return exhausted from a patrol and collapse into a troubled sleep. She prayed for those that the missing bullets had sped toward. When she had first realized what she was doing, her mind rebelled. Pray for someone's death? No! That the bullet would miss? Again no. For mercy on someone's soul and that the war would be one bullet closer to an end. Amen.

How quickly we rationalize when we are forced to take steps that cross the grain of our convictions. We seek a clean, dry path out of the black pull of the swamp but none can be found. We muddy the path with that which clings to our body and to our souls.

We stayed for two weeks longer soaking in a well-deserved rest while Father and his three men came and went to our new home site, building a house we all hoped would be our last until the war ended.

"You will visit us often?" A sadness tainted the facade of a smile on Louise' face as she gripped Mother's hand.

"Often." Mother replied. Her eyes echoed Louise' feelings. "As often as we can." She turned to go. The rest of the group had already disappeared down the trail toward the stream. Only I had waited, standing quietly with Doug discussing the things of the jungle; of flashing bird's wings and giant snails. Of wily crawdads in cool shaded streams and other important matters.

At the stream we turned upstream, walking in the water when at all possible to leave no trail as Father had earlier cautioned. My eyes caught the footprints in the sandy streambed not yet washed away by the flow and the rocks splashed by passing feet. I knew the rest were

Chapter VII

perhaps only a hundred feet ahead, still hidden by the twists and turns of the gorge.

The walls on either side grew steeper as we proceeded and ferns and moss covered the rocks. Only piercing bright shards of sky could be seen through the canopy above, and though early in the day, a twilight gloom enveloped us and chilled the sweat that clung to our arms and face. Soon we were aware of a mist blowing in waves from ahead bending the fern branches, gathering and dripping from leaf tips.

We rounded a wall of rock and blinked at gleaming rays of sun playing on a large pool. And behind, a curtain of spray and mist cascaded down gleaming rock. And the sound, as of a whispering communion and the applause of watery hands clapping the rock and the laughter of a job well done. A rainbow arched across the pool where mist and sunlight met. On both sides of the cascade the rock walls were all but hidden by tenacious vines and the twisted trunks of dwarfed trees turning back on themselves, clinging to the rock for support.

We stopped at the edge of the pool, Mother, face toward the warming sun, eyes closed, pulled cooling air into her lungs. I let my eyes search the scene before us exploring the gorge walls high above, pushing into the relative gloom where the cliffs met the sand at the water's edge until I spotted the wave of a hand from Father seated on a boulder to the right of the pool. I waved back and touched Mother's arm, pointing toward the group resting in a splash of sun. Mother raised an arm in greeting, then gazing up at the brilliance of the sun splashed waters spreading themselves in a headlong dive from fifty feet above, she stepped forward until the waters lapped above her knees. She seemed drawn into another world by the serenity of the moment until a yell raced across the waters at us from where father sat, "Crocodile!"

Mother jerked out of her reverie, her head snapping toward the voice as the waters split an arm length in front of her. She jumped back, a gasp escaping her throat. Losing her balance she fell back onto the sand feet still in the water. Hands and heels digging into the sand, she pulled herself away from the water, her gaze riveted on the point of the disturbance, now calm except for ripples spreading away and the sound of falling waters which didn't sound like applause anymore.

Then another noise. First low, then rising and echoing from the somber cliffs: laughter.

Captain Alianza stood then, his face quieter now but still bright as the winner of a small game might be. He hefted another rock in his hand.

Mother dropped her knees to the sand pulling her dress tight around her legs. Her face shifted faster than her crawl had. From fear and surprise, her mouth closed and her eyes narrowed into puzzlement and then just a hint of anger before tears overflowed and the corners of her mouth quivered down and she dropped her head to her knees, sobs wrenching her body.

I dropped to the sand touching her shoulder. She didn't seem to notice, her body continuing to shake. I

Chapter VII

remembered sobbing like that once. Once. And then the darkness and the pain, and a gulf formed between me and the one I called Father. The one that a small band of jungle fighters now feared revered and obeyed . . . without hesitation.

    I knew why and I wanted to spread myself over Mother and protect her, to be big enough to stand up to the man that caused this. I looked across at my father now standing arms to his sides, his face unreadable. Then tipping his head back, Captain Alianza let the sun touch him, soften him. Winding up he flung the remaining rock high up the cliff wall and turned, moving slowly toward the two of us on the sand.

    I stood quickly, watching the man approach, his sure, powerful strides closing the distance. A hot, hard stone formed in my chest and I fought for breath watching the captain approach. All I could see was a clenched fist and that gun at his side. I could not breathe. I spun and ran, stopping only when the cold dampness of the rock wall stood before me. The hot stone had climbed to my throat by then and I wanted to sob, to cry out, to vanish but I could not and I leaned my head against the rock wall.

    Silence surrounded me and then slowly, very slowly, everything dissolved into that place in my mind where things are stored for later. For a better time. A splash of water from above ran down my forehead cooling my burning eyes and I looked up blinking and tasting the salt from my eyes. Just out of reach a flower grew from the rock, undaunted by the trickle washing over it, its roots wedged in a crack. Alone, but yet secure in the rock. It had five petals. White with veins of red reaching out from its center. Then a sound returned to my world. The sound of the waterfall and I turned slowly my breath catching once more, not knowing what I would see.

They sat together on the sand. The Captain's strong legs surrounded Mother as she sat, her back to him, shoulders slowly unclenching, her body accepting the apology of his enclosing arms. Quiet murmurs passed between them.

I wanted to run to them, to crawl between and feel the strength of those arms and the warmth of Mother. But I did not.

Chapter VIII
DIAMONDS

"No one can approach without being seen." Father stood casually on the brink of the cliff. He gestured toward the stream below and the cliff we had just climbed. At our feet the lip of rock, like a pitcher spout worn smooth over the millennia, funneled the water clear of the rock wall to plunge into the shimmering pool fifty feet below. All footprints had been carefully swept away by one of Father's men and water splashing up on the sand had erased all sign of human passage.

    I looked for the white flower. Too far away. I let my eyes trace the path we had taken. It started behind a wedge of rock jutting out into the pool. Discernible only to those who knew, a ledge barely the width of a foot angled sharply up the cliff. Roots clinging to the rock, twisting and turning back into small cracks, were solid handholds. Damp. Slippery. Toes gripping. Never release one handhold until another is secured. The mist had gathered and ran down the cliff washing away signs of our passing.

    As we climbed, I had moved ahead a few feet following Father's lead, then turned to show mother where to place her feet, where to grip. Then on a few more feet. Approaching the top, the way had lead up into the tangle of trees, out of sight, then descended above the falls.

Father's voice jarred my thoughts. "Come." He turned, leading the way upstream. We again fell into single file, keeping in the water at the edge of the stream, placing our feet carefully, hands touching the rock walls and boulders for balance. Soon the sound of the waterfall fell away into the distance and only the soft splash of feet in shallow water broke the silence. Even the whispered echoes off the canyon walls dimmed as the canyon opened up to a secluded valley.

Then the Captain stopped, waiting for everyone to catch up. Mother stepped off to the side picking out a large rock to sit on. She massaged her sore leg slowly then raised her head, eyes closed, as she often did. I stepped in front of her as she opened her eyes.

"Look, Mother." She looked beyond me to where the gorge widened. The sun touched the green hillside that climbed steeply, protectively, but not imposing. "No, there." I pointed over her shoulder. She turned. A smaller stream converged from the left. It formed the boundary of a tree shaded, grassy clearing two hundred feet deep and half again as wide. Toward the back, under some trees near the base of the cliff stood a small house nearly completed. A large window divided the front of the split bamboo wall. On the side, to the right, another window and a door. Then another room yet unfinished.

Seated on a log toward the rear of the clearing, two men seemingly oblivious of our presence wove roof

Chapter VIII

thatches from palm leaves. Each leaf was carefully wrapped around a backbone of split bamboo and tied with small strips of vine.

"Welcome home." Father stepped over, took Mother's hand pulling her gently to her feet. A smile tugged at the corner of his mouth. He helped her up the small embankment and, hand in hand, they walked toward the house. And for a moment, a very small moment, he was no longer Captain Alianza, leader of a small, hardened guerrilla force, but just Father. Then he released her hand, motioned her toward the door and stretched his stride toward the two men seated on the log.

Mother hesitated, then placed her hands on either side of the doorway. She pushed at the bamboo doorjambs as if testing their strength. "Welcome home," she repeated as I slid under her arm. She rested her left hand on my shoulder and together we stepped across the threshold. The floor was packed with sand brought up from the streambed. Under the window a slab of wood, looked to be left over from a tree cutting in the distant past, would serve as a counter top. The rest of the furniture I knew would soon be built. Mother looked through the unfinished room to where father now stood in back with the two men. One was pointing with a bamboo stick up to various sectors of the ridgeline. The Captain was once again overseeing his command.

***

Time was not measured in days, weeks or even months. It was measured in distance. Perceived distance from an enemy somewhere out there. And the distance that could be traveled before the camp was discovered. It may be minutes, or maybe not. Father had carefully chipped away foot and handholds in the rock face where the small side stream cascaded down twenty or so feet behind the house. It spilled over the lip of a pool ten feet above and spread out over the rock wall as it splashed downward. Climbing to the pool was wet and slippery, but the constant flow washed away signs of passing. From the pool he had widened a path that bypassed the cataract from above and angled to the right and up. Giant ferns nourished by the stream uncurled toward the sun, their feathery stems concealing even the tallest person. Hidden among the trees at the end of the path, Father built a small shelter where we would retreat to in case the enemy came close. No one was allowed to go beyond the pool for fear of making the trail noticeable.

    One afternoon that small shelter became my hideout from the world. When no one was looking I scampered up to my hideout to lose myself in my own world of imagination and peace. As I scooted between two boxes of our belongings a sharp pain caused me to jump up. Where I had sat, a large scorpion, crippled from my sitting on him, wriggled his last, his long tail still lashing in anger. Carefully I pulled my shorts down. A large welt was already rising on my right cheek. I peeked out to see if anyone watched, pulled my shorts up, and

Chapter VIII

hastily retreated back to the house. My right hip and thigh burned with fire and I wanted to run to Mother. Instead went back up to the pool and sank into the cool waters. If I went to mother for medicine, I knew she would ask me where I had gotten stung and I couldn't lie to her. I suffered quietly for the next several days and never returned to the hideout.

In the peace of the days that followed, Ruth and I often climbed to the pool to laugh, play and splash, and life was as it was intended. Once, as we both leaned back from our play letting the sun warm our faces, I idly brought handfuls of gravel to the surface then watched them glisten back to the bottom. Slowly I sat up, looking more closely as I let another handful drift down. Raising one handful above the surface I stared at it a long moment, then carefully picked out a pebble the size of my fingernail. It shimmered in the late afternoon sun.

"Ruth look! A diamond . . . it's a diamond!" She sat up studying the pebble a moment. Hesitantly at first, then with growing excitement she joined me pulling handfuls to the surface and picking out the diamonds.

Excitedly we scrambled down to rush in and reveal our discovery to Mother, as if the diamonds might melt away if we delayed. We curled into her arms and opened our treasures to her. She smiled, longing it seemed, to escape into our child's world where, for a while, the war was so far away. She then explained as best she could about quartz crystals. "We'll save them," she said, placing them carefully on the windowsill where sunlight would catch them and splinter rainbows across the room.

The mountain people visited at times from where they lived on the ridges. On one occasion, Mother coyly wondered out loud why the evil spirits had not bothered us here in the valley. We had previously been warned that near the streams was the abode of the evil spirits and anyone living there would be either harmed or killed. The answer was obvious, they said: Spirits are afraid of rings, as they observed Mother's ring. And what of Father, he has no ring? Confidently they pointed out that he carried a gun, and so it is gunpowder that saves him.

And the children? A few days later the mountain men returned with two rings beaten out of silver coins for Ruth and me. At times they came with portions of wild boar, deer, chicken or bananas slung over their shoulders. Or something that looked suspiciously like monkey. In exchange they left with silver coins, the denomination mattered none, it was the silver they valued. They were obviously thankful for a piece of broken truck spring that Father had found beside the road. Steel they treasured for their machetes and spearheads.

***

When it rained it didn't just rain—it swept from the sky in torrents. Wind whipped the canyon, lightning bolts split the sky and thunder rocked our little house. The stream would quickly become an impassable cataract and

Chapter VIII

we made a game out of moving things around when streams of rain would slip through the roofing as the wind moved the palm leaf thatches. At times strong gusts of wind would lift the bottom edges of the thatches straight up and rain would pour in unhindered. There was little hope of staying dry, so we enjoyed the excitement of trying to outguess the wind.

The banana plant just outside protested the rising wind. Its leaves, already torn, waved, like green flags in a storm, soon to signal surrender. A lighter shade in its immature stage, the fruit already hung heavy. Below the fruit, the flower clung like an elongated heart the size of a fist. The color of old blood, one petal peeled back revealed the fresh-blood red of its inner, glossy side. Soon we would cut that flower. Grated, it makes a welcome flavor to a stew, rice, or almost anything. With the flower gone, the fruit would mature quicker.

Then the unimaginable. Lightning struck the house. The air hummed, scalp tingled, then a hiss and the bullwhip crack of a million volts of electricity looking for release in the super-charged ground. Blue-white. Searing. Intensity that burns an image into the retina of any eye that just happens to be open in the wrong direction. It's a film negative, white on black with gradients. The shutter snapped and the image was burned into my eye. I closed my eyes too late. It's there: white windowsills around a charred black sky, pinpricks of light circling. I turned to Mother for comfort and the image followed, fading slowly. Mother's eyes were narrowed, shock dampened with curiosity. She held a hand up for shade. The room was scalded in yellow light. A late afternoon type of sunlight. The wind whipped torrents of rain through the open window. The banana made one pass across the window and was gone. And still a squinting bright sunlight within.

Up in the peak of the woven palm leaf roof a brilliant orange ball floated, sparks snapping. Like cold water on a hot grill it sizzled, wavered across the room, diminished from a melon-sized sun down to twink out before reaching the far wall.

Ball lightning, I was told later. A rare phenomenon. Can be harmless, or explode like a cannonball on impact. Scientists still stutter at explanations, but Mother thanked the God who with one hand still creates wonders and with the other holds a shield of protection.

Then as quickly as it started, the storm passed and within a few hours the torrent in the canyon calmed to the quiet stream of before and one more day passed.

***

Mother removed a folded paper from behind the bamboo slat that was part of the wall. She opened it carefully and placed it on the table, smoothing it with her palm. It was penciled off in squares with the word, December, at the top. She picked up a short pencil and ran it down the warn paper. Stopping near the bottom she moved the pencil to

Chapter VIII

the right and placed an X in the next square. "Three more days." She aimed the words quietly to where Father sat leaning against the wall, eyes closed. He was away so much lately she didn't want to miss this chance to bring up the subject. His eyes opened a slit, brows lowering. He was thinking.

"The nineteenth." she filled in the answer, "Carling's birthday. And I think we're expected down at Hopevale. Wouldn't Doug love that?" His eyes opened wider, examining the roof thatches.

"The time is not so good." He rose and stood beside her. He placed his right index finger on the newly formed "X", then slowly, calculating, moved to the right, down one row, then stopped on the square marked 25. "Maybe Christmas. Now the Japanese are going up and down the highway asking many questions and I'm worried for them at Hopevale. Maybe one week they'll go away."

She placed her hand over his, then slowly folded the calendar sliding it back into its place. She knew not to ask questions but to trust his wisdom to keep them safe.

In three days it would be two years since Father had stepped through the door halting my birthday party with that indescribable look on his face. The city had been bombed. The country was at war. The world. Nothing would ever be the same. No person.

And my last birthday was lost somewhere in the jungles. I didn't even remember where. But this one would be different. This one we would remember. The determination in Mother's eyes made me believe it. Even if we didn't get to Hopevale. We would sing, and we would remember what needed to be remembered. The war would be lost. Forgotten. Not mentioned. And we would have a good Christmas too.

The following day Amadore approached carrying a small tree cut from the forest. "This is good?"

Mother eyed it, head cocked. "It's good. Thank you, Amadore." Father had left early morning but promised to be back for my birthday. Perhaps he wouldn't, but Mother would not let the day be spoiled.

Ruth and I gathered around helping Mother strip the leaves off the tree. Then with green crepe paper scavenged from somewhere on one of Father's forays, we wrapped each branch carefully. "There, that's what Christmas trees look like." Mother said, tipping her head from side to side, trying perhaps to get a more believable perspective on what stood before her.

Chapter IX
MASSACRE

Dawn of December 19th, Mother went down to the stream to sit on what had become her favorite resting place. Perhaps shattered down from somewhere above when this island was still volcano hot, her rock had been formed, scooped and rounded by the ceaseless chitterings of water and sand. Now it rested beside the stream, leaning back slightly, facing downstream and the deep "V" of the canyon walls below the falls.

She lowered herself into the scooped seat and leaned back on the curve of cool stone. From there she could watch the brilliance of the tropical sun edge down the west wall of the canyon turning the darkened trees into uncountable shades of green. Sparks of color here and there never ceased to amaze her. Flowers, birds, or something special just for her. It didn't matter. Nothing was without its own beauty.

These moments were few and fleeting and she used them to cleanse her mind. To skim away the dark scum. To look to the God who created it all and pray for the day when life would be back the way it was meant to be. Maybe today. She said it often. Maybe tomorrow. And any more her prayers seemed to rise just so far, hang, then sink back empty. An oppressive, spiritual darkness, she called it. But God was still there. She knew that. She knew.

This was one of those dark times. The Captain had not returned. She told herself she should be accustomed to it by now, but was never able to completely pull her mind away from the thought of him someday not returning. She would circle protective arms around her children, then what? No picture ever formed. No next step came to her mind if that time should ever come.

Her thoughts returned to that evening—had it been a year now? —When Father handed her that gun. And the three bullets. She had taken the gun, slid the three bullets into the cylinder as he instructed, then asked, why three?

"For the children and for you if there is no escape . . . it's better than capture."

They were words she would never forget. But even now could not fully comprehend. Life was too precious. Nothing, her mind said, could ever justify that. Capture could not be worse.

She woke, heat of the sun on her face. How long had she dozed? She squinted up at the sun. Two hours. Maybe three. A column of smoke smudged the morning sky. It rose straight in the still air from downstream. The direction of Hopevale. With bamboo houses and only wood to cook with, there was always the danger of a fire getting out of control. She sent up a quick prayer that no one was hurt and turned toward the happy sounds coming from the house. She climbed the small embankment then turned back, still troubled by the smoke. Movement caught her eye.

Across the stream, from the trail the mountain people used, a lone figure approached. Sunlight caught the familiar lean frame as the Captain strode toward her and splashed across the stream. She waved, then faltered. His walk was not the casual stride she had become accustomed to, nor were they the footsteps of one returning from a wearied patrol, perhaps days without sleep. They were purposeful steps, legs strong, sculpted by adrenaline.

They touched hands as he pushed easily up the bank and stood a moment. His eyes deeply showed the fatigue that his stride did not. His gaze steeled toward the house and the happy sounds, then dropped quickly to the ground, meeting her questioning eyes for only an instant. She wrapped both hands around his and waited. Hopevale? The smoke? Someone was hurt. Or worse?

Father raised his head, his eyes sweeping across, stopping on the plume of smoke, seeing, trying to erase. His voice low, flat, "Hopevale. *Napatay tanan.*"

The captain reverted to his mother tongue. The one we all use when words come hard.

Mother's mind could not comprehend. Would not. The words spilled out of him faster than she could pick up, but she knew her friends were dead. All of them. Friends who wanted nothing more than to be left alone to do the work they came for: to live in peace and explain to anyone that would listen who the author of that peace is. They were gone.

It seemed only yesterday they had sat on the porch in the quiet of morning as the first slivers of sunlight penetrated the upper foliage at Hopevale. Louise, in her quiet yet straightforward manner, best expressed the hearts of all: "Someday we'll wake to the real sunrise and this darkness will be just a passing moment, swallowed by the light."

Mother's heart was a burning stone in her chest and the thought of sunrise would never again be the same.

"They are taken to the high hill above the valley so all can see and they are killed." Father's voice faltered.

Mother's legs crumbled under her and Father eased her down to the sand. She sat silent, unable to move, to speak. She turned toward the pillar of smoke from the valley, the only thing in focus. "How did . . ." she started.

"One man talked with soldiers. Maybe pleading with them. Then it's as if they all prayed then they are made to kneel, one by one, and the soldier with the sword . . . he did it." Father's voice broke.

Mother's head jerked up then buried in her hands.

Father continued, his voice barely audible. "But not the children."

A trace of hope glimmered in Mother's eyes.

"For them it is the bayonet."

"No! No . . ." Mother reached for his arm. "How do you know? Are you sure?"

Chapter IX

"Some from the village are near. They are allowed to go free so they can tell others who are hiding that they cannot escape."

Mother stood suddenly, pulling herself to her feet on Father's arm. "We have to go now!"

Father took a deep breath, then with a gentle hand turned Mother toward the house. "Come, we must have a birthday party."

She stood, a swirl of contradictions in her head. Less than an hour down the trail her friends had just been slaughtered. She must have not understood. "Shouldn't we be leaving?"

"Maybe tomorrow, or the next tomorrow."

"But . . ." She hurried to catch his pace.

"They will not follow." His tone was final. Change of subject.

She resisted the temptation to count the remaining bullets in his belt.

Chapter X
RIVER CROSSING

One evening in a rare moment of rest, Father leaned back on the bamboo bench and gazed out the window for a long moment. His profile was dark against the afternoon sun filtering through the tall trees. Weariness masked his face. It had hardened, weighted down by the tension and pressures of war. And even closer in, concern for a wife and two small children of American blood, the prime enemy of the Japanese. He was fighting the enemy with one hand, the other held protectively about his family.

He glanced at Mother's gray eyes. They too, were focused in the distance, perhaps half a world away; a world she may never see again. "The American submarine that brings us these guns to fight with is taking refugees away."

Mother turned to meet his eyes, recognizing in the quiet tone that a decision had already been made. He turned back to the near horizontal streams of sunlight and the sounds of the deep forest.

"American citizens are allowed to go," he went on, "but it is far to where the submarine comes and even I don't know when it comes. Only a few days before it arrives does anyone know. You must go."

Mother's eyes searched him briefly then joined his gaze into the forest, which seemed suddenly to fall silent in anticipation.

"You won't be going with us, will you?" Mother's voice was hesitant.

"My place is here until my country is free."

Mother's fingers twisted the gold band on her finger. "When?"

"Maybe tomorrow, or the next tomorrow. Amadore will guide you to the ocean. He will take care of you."

Lieutenant Amadore Lucero was Father's right-hand man and had been with us from the beginning of the war. Many times he had stepped in as a buffer between the harsh discipline demanded by the captain of a guerrilla force, and the family whose only immediate goal was to stay alive.

***

Slivers of sunlight filtered through the green canopy, dancing brightly in counterpoint to heavy air that pushed among the shadowed tree trunks. Intense flashes spotlighted an unmarked jungle trail. Leaves stirred in the sultry moisture. A band of long tailed monkeys paused in their eating and grooming routine and eyed our small group with cautious indifference. Their leader leaned over his limb challenging the balance point, his tail wrapped tightly around an adjacent limb. He barked defiance; it seemed more for the sake of impressing his band than us. Unseen birds signaled our passing and small things scurried in the underbrush. In this world, we were the intruders.

At a curve in the trail, a Banyan tree loomed majestically skyward, oblivious to the tangle of vines clutching, reaching. Its top branches, hidden from view by the lower growth, reached beyond the green canopy. Leaves turned toward the life giving sun. I pictured myself up there above the darkness, laughing, the wind cool on my face, an unending horizon beckoning.

Suddenly I was yanked back to reality as my toe snagged a rock at the edge of the trail. Pain flashed up my leg. I caught my breath and glanced quickly at Father a few steps ahead. He didn't turn. I let my breath out slowly and stopped for a second to examine my right foot. Only some skin missing. I glanced again at Father's lean back. His shoulders were bowed a little, not a heaviness of fatigue, but a crouching, an awareness that could explode into action in an instant.

He walked with authority even on the jungle trail, and if anyone doubted, they just needed to look into his eyes. They were eyes that seldom laughed anymore, firm, and gave a clear signal of who was in charge. His steps were light but sure. His head turned constantly letting nothing pass unnoticed.

He stopped, a hand raised in signal. We froze. Instant obedience had become an unquestioned reflex. Turning his head slightly, he listened, his eyes intent on piercing the undergrowth hiding the trail around the curve. In the stillness of that moment, I felt a rumble through the ground, penetrating my callused feet. Leaves shivered without wind. We stood unmoving, waiting. My foot ached but I dared not move. Then Father straightened and lowered his arm. Only then did I notice the gun in his other hand. He slid it back into its holster as a familiar figure eased around the curve. It was Amadore.

"The river is flooded, Captain. We cannot cross."

"We will cross," Father said quietly. When he spoke with that tone in his voice, I knew we would cross. "We have little time. We might be followed, and we're not going to be trapped here." His eyes swept a circle around us, then ahead.

"How far to the river?"

"Maybe one hundred meters, but we can't . . . ." Father's head came up just a little and he snapped a look that said, if you're smart you won't say any more. Lieutenant Amadore Lucero was smart.

After a few pointed instructions, Father sent him ahead to the river with the other three scouts. As he turned back to us, he shot a glance down the trail. In the shadows at the last curve stood one of the tribal men who had been accompanying us. He was short and dark, and blended well with the jungle. The tip of his spear stood well over his head and his machete scabbard almost dragged the ground. I knew that machete was razor sharp. It was a matter of pride with them, Father had said. A weapon, a tool, a person, should never be allowed to become less than it was created for. I was sure no one could approach us unnoticed from that side.

"Wait there." Father pointed to the Banyan tree a ways off the trail. "And leave the trail the way I told you. Wait behind the tree roots. The Banyan tree will hide you. You will be safe there. I'll send for you when we're ready to cross. I don't want you waiting out in the open . . . Go!" He spun and disappeared toward the river.

I carefully stepped off the trail leaving no footprints or broken brush, then pointed to a good spot for Mother and the others to leave the trail. Mother took my hand as we wound our way down to the tree. Her leg was still quite sore from the infection, and although I never heard her complain, I knew the going was tough. Ruth followed with Nini and the two men carrying our belongings . . . all we owned in the world.

"Do you think we can cross?" I asked Mother as she eased herself down on a tree root and began loosening the bandage on her leg.

"If Daddy says we can cross, we'll cross." Her eyes tightened as the bandage unwound.

I took my eyes off the dark tangle on the jungle floor and looked around. The Banyan tree's massive roots thrust out from the trunk far above my head and angled away, each root a wall, a living curtain extending out to anchor deeply into the soil twenty feet distant. Roots branched off roots, crossed and interlocked into a veritable labyrinth.

We had edged through a fold in the root curtain barely two feet wide and were in a three-sided room with walls stretching above our heads. Curtains of living wood reached down for the life offered up by black jungle soil. Soil that gained its richness from countless generations of plants, animals and insects that in death had found one last purpose. Dead but yet living, the stillness crawled with sounds. The rank, heavy odor of decay invaded my nostrils and clung to damp skin.

A rustling, a movement at my feet and a foot long armor plated body edged out from beneath rotting leaves, gliding, gleaming like burnished steel. Propelled by a hundred legs on each side rising and stepping in perfect sequence, it moved as a fluid wave. Pausing, it tested the air with its antenna, then turned its segmented body seeking darkness.

My toes curled away although I knew it to be harmless and indifferent. This giant cousin to the centipede's only defense was to roll into a tight ball and emit an eye-burning odor.

I leaned against the root curtain and let my back feel the coolness of the moss-covered bark. Slowly I lowered myself to my haunches and rolled my head back. High above, a breeze I could only imagine bent a limb and a flash of sunlight found me. I let my eyes trace the ray on its downward slant through the crowded air; its path marked by leaf tips it brushed, leaving them as glowing emeralds.

Flying things buzzed and fluttered in the column of light, flashing brilliant reds, blues and greens. And on its way to where it splashed at my feet, the column of light found and lingered on a twisted limb cradling an orchid that drank in life and shook out a shower of beauty. Shades of dark purple edged in gold, a halo of light surrounded it protectively.

It seemed so alone, yet complete in itself. Held high above the decay of the jungle floor in the arm of a king, this crown might only last a few days, but it would bloom forever, in a special place in my mind.

It was a place I had discovered where I could store special moments of color, of sound. Of a green turtle peering from beneath a fallen leaf at the base of a whispering waterfall; the brilliant flash of wings as a parrot measures the tapestry of vines high above; a cluster of unknown white flowers twenty feet away announcing its presence with a fragrance, clinging, lingering. In this growing corner of my mind nothing is questioned, just recorded and retreated into. It is a corner where hope grows without asking how or when.

I turned to Mother to share the moment. She saw it too. She seldom missed anything of beauty. It was one of those times when words would only detract from a deeper communication. Serenity on her face had wiped away lines of fatigue etched by days, months, of total commitment to survival in an alien setting, of fear of capture and mercifully a quicker death than Doug and our missionary friends had met at Hopevale. Wiped away for a brief moment were the truths that she lived with, that we all lived with, that a cough at the wrong time, a misplaced word, an instant's delay in obedience could bring to a close this book we call life. Or at least bring down the slashing wrath of a man obsessed with escape. Escape which seemed more to him than just survival, but a victory, a clenched fist slamming through darkness into the light, as this giant of a tree had done pushing upward, beyond the reach of darkness.

"You are as the Banyan tree of the deep forest, my son." The words swirled down from that place in my mind. From the time long ago when laughter was a guidepost in life and danger was only a word. Words from a father whose strong arm was a pillow for my head and the cool grass tickled my back as clouds silently slid across a blue eternity. He talked of the wisdom of his father, Amay, the Grandfather I never knew who died as I was being born a half a world away. "Your arms spread wide giving comfort to many. Your roots are strong, spread wide for many to see. Do not hide your roots, my son. They are your strength." The picture receded and I dug my fingers into the black soil.

Mother's eyes were on me, her smile faint, soft, a transparency making me want to curl up on her lap and be absorbed, protected from all that was not love. I turned away instead, examining the rough bark on the living wall of protection surrounding me and to glance once more at the halo of color high on the limb. The spotlight of sun had moved away now, leaving the blossom to itself until tomorrow, but it was still there.

My mind, still young and accepting, struggled to understand the growing darkness that was separating the warm loving protection that was Mother, and the cold discipline that was Gather; the razor sharp machete slash that commanded authority, the Captain Alianza that my father had become.

That too was protection. The protection of a captain over his command. I yearned to cry out to him, to feel his strong hand on my shoulder, the exhilaration when he would swing me over his head, but that was all past. That was no longer in the world of Captain Alianza.

A silent shadow touched me. "We will go now." It was Amadore. He turned, leading at a quick pace, and in a few moments we stood gazing in awe at an angry brown river clawing at its banks. Father said we would cross and I knew we would. Father knew how to cross rivers.

Brush, ripped away from somewhere upriver, swept past. I stared open-mouthed as a large tree went by, tumbled over and over by the boiling current. A wet and very scared monkey leapt from one broken limb to another, trying to keep on top. We stood on an outcropping of rock that challenged the onslaught. It quivered under the pounding, carrying through my bare feet the message that nothing was secure.

Amadore led us down river, winding in and out of the brush along the bank until we rounded a curve where the river widened and slowed from its wild plunge. There Father and the three men were putting the final ties on a bamboo raft. A dozen bamboo chutes six inches around had been cut to about fifteen feet and lashed together with vines. I'd never seen a raft before but Father made it, so it looked okay to me. He motioned toward the river and two

Chapter X

men stepped into the swirling waters holding the raft while the others lifted the other end sliding it into the water. As it pitched and bobbed in the current, I couldn't help wondering why it wasn't bigger.

"Get on. We must hurry." Father said, quietly grabbing hold of my arm. "We'll have to make two or three trips. You and Mother first, then Ruth and the luggage on the next."

I stepped on and dropped to my knees as the raft rocked. Looking up, the other shore tipped crazily and seemed so far away.

Father's voice jolted me. "Move up to the front! You won't sink...Move!"

I moved, hesitation not even an option. The raft bounced sharply and I turned around to see Mother on her hands and knees crawling onto the raft. She looked up at me and smiled, though biting her lip. I knew she was trying to encourage me, but it didn't help much. Father pushed us off and we joined the swirling waters, one man on each corner swimming valiantly, but we were moving more down river than across. My father's voice echoed in my mind, "We will cross!"

As the raft approached mid-stream, the stronger current spun the raft and I looked up facing the bank we had left what seemed a long time ago. I searched the bank for Father but there was no sign of him, only the dark silhouette of a man of the jungle, spear lifted point upward in salute. Quickly he faded back into the brush and I could once again feel Father's grip, firm, almost fierce, and his last words to me, "You won't sink . . . move!"

I shivered. I thought of that wet, darting monkey on the tree, the tree larger than our raft. I didn't care to linger on that thought. I turned instead to thoughts of God and the many guardian angels that mother said always surrounded us. I wondered if they were scared too. I turned again to Mother but her eyes were closed tight. Probably praying. I closed mine too. It was the natural thing to do in prayer, but the dizziness returned. I needed to see what was happening even though I had no control.

A warning shout and the raft tipped dangerously as it struck something. It spun wildly, one corner held firm and the other dipped, cascades of foaming brown water covering my hands that gripped the vine ropes and swirled up to my elbows. It tore at my knees and my toes slipped on the wet bamboo. My fingers were numb, wrapped wire like around the vines. If the raft had turned over, I most likely would have remained that way until the raft and my body were discovered somewhere down river. The raft righted itself however, and I wrenched my eyes from my whitened fingers to see, inches away, a tangle of roots, gaunt, reaching into the wind.

We were at the other side. The floodwaters had undercut the bank and the men were pushing desperately to free us from the roots that held us. As we were freed, the current grabbed us once more spinning us away. Another shout came and the men pulled the raft in to where a small stream feeding the river had cut away the bank. Strong hands held the raft against the sucking current and I scrambled ashore reaching back to help Mother up. She was shaking badly and blood stained the corner of her mouth.

"Dad said we would cross." I said, gulping a great breath.

There was a long pause as she turned back toward the angry river. "Yes . . ." she answered, her voice fading out as another thought seemed to push its way in. "He never kissed me goodbye, but he's a fine man. You must never forget that."

I wouldn't. Neither would I forget the touch of sadness, a reaching, in her voice that was beyond my understanding. I followed her somewhat mistful gaze across the river to the green wall of jungle, vibrant, alive yet passive, growing yet ever dying. Gaping holes opened dark in the banks as now being ripped, it slid little by little into the angry brown force, emotionless, surging toward the sea and its own end.

The four men who had brought us over fought the raft up river. Three scrambled along the bank pulling it with a large vine secured to one corner. Amador rode the raft pushing it away from the bank with his feet, keeping it free of the rocks and debris along the edge. When they were well upstream of their starting point on the far bank, they swam the raft across then made a second trip for Ruth, Nini and the few belongings we owned.

The three men soon had our belongings shouldered with makeshift packs and with Amadore leading the way, we turned away from the river. I stole a final glance across the river. A lone figure stood on the far bank, then blended back into the shadows.

I never saw him again.

I looked up to Mother sensing a need for an explanation, a warm touch, an assurance, but her eyes were closed, her head lifted. This time I was sure she was praying.

Chapter XI
RESPITE

We crossed mountains, rivers and virgin forests, widely skirting all roads and well-used trails until nine days later we arrived at a small village on the coast somewhere near where the submarine would surface.

A distant smile hinted across Mother's face as one afternoon we sat on the beach facing the sea. She had told me that home was out that way and it seemed her thoughts were more and more out that way too, across the sea. High in the mountains she had confided to my sister and me that she didn't know if we would see Grandma first or Grandpa. Grandma was in America and Grandpa had been in heaven for many years now, the result of a motorcycle accident. Heaven, she said, is a place where everything is perfect and whatever we wish will be there.

"Will Buddy be there?" My mind saw the orange face, stiff, short fur and the jagged scar that angled down the side of my dog. It had been a long time now yet fresh in my mind since I last saw him, tied to the house, straining at the rope as we left that night. *Dogs make noise* was all Daddy had said.

"If you want him there, he'll be there." Mother said, and in a way that only nine-year-olds can understand, that was more important than seeing Grandpa, but then, maybe Mother understood too.

I scooted myself down on the pebbled beach and laid my head on Mother's lap. The sun began its evening ritual behind us, behind the mountains. We knew the colors of sunset would stretch to each horizon. They always did, although here facing east they would be muted softened, more peaceful. That peacefulness was mirrored in Mother's face and filtered down to me through touch, through a communication difficult to describe.

Ruth strolled back and forth at the water's edge, her bare feet dragging through the marble-size pebbles of the beach. Head down, she seemed intent on each pebble as the slight surf rolled them clicking against each other. Watching but not seeing, she too was distant, but I felt her distance was not eastward and the possible escape to America, but rather somewhere behind. Somewhere back with Daddy. She was often pensive, restless since the river.

"Listen," Mother said. I listened. The clicking of pebbles rolled by the surf was all there was to hear. Then it came from the left, and then the right, all around. I looked to Ruth, kicking pebbles as she walked, but she was seated now, knees drawn up. Waves had not changed, but the sound still grew. "There." Mother pointed a few feet away where something moved.

"The rock is moving," I whispered. "And there's another . . . and another one." I looked out across the beach. They were everywhere, moving, the clicking surrounded us. I rolled over to examine one as it clicked against the pebbles as it passed. Bright orange stripes circled it. A seashell . . . with feet.

Mother reached out to pick it up and as she touched it, the feet vanished. A moment later the feet reappeared, then legs, followed by two eyes on stalks, waving to and fro. "Hermit crabs," Mother explained. "During the day they sleep, then come out to search for food as they feel the coolness of evening." I touched one and it withdrew, only to peer out again and click away. "As they grow," she said, "they search for another larger shell then slip out and wiggle into their new home."

The sun was now gone and all the world had been dipped in orange, which was slowly deepening and would blend into the purple of royalty and then sleep. We would not be moving in the coolness of this evening. For nine days we had traveled nights and slept days, hurried across open places and roads, wiggled into new homes before sunrise, to begin all over again the next evening.

This was a whole new world. We were just resting. Waiting. Amadore had safely led us here, and here we would wait for escape he said. We had reached the sea and this small fishing village a week ago. Far from the road and even any trail, we were told we would be safe here for a while

It was nighttime when we had arrived. As the village slept, Amadore quietly slipped up to the door of the largest house and called softly. The two men who had been carrying our belongings had vanished somewhere. Sleep probably, or maybe home. As was custom, men in any house or village we passed were obligated to carry our baggage for us until we came to the next place where someone was available. I don't know if this was a normal custom or just adapted by courtesy because of the emergency of the times. I noted too that Amadore always paid the men at the end of their turn. That, I knew, was a courtesy.

The owners of the house where we stayed were somehow connected with the resistance force, but we asked no questions. They owned a large parrot that was kept in a cage under the house. Often I stood and admired it. Its feathers brilliant green, orange and red. I wondered how they could be so bright, so different, yet side by side. They seemed to change colors as the bird moved in the shifting light. Its long talons wrapped around the limb it perched on. When I would stick a small twig into the cage, it easily snapped it in two with its beak. I knew that was no place for my fingers.

We adjusted easily to the different foods. The sweetness of ripe mangoes, papaya, and pineapple caused pain in the back of my mouth and made the saliva flow. In the mountains and forests seldom did we have ripe fruit. It was picked green before the bats and birds tasted it. We never knew if we would be in one place long enough to wait for it to ripen.

At times Mother gave us small sips of *tuba'*, a sweet drink made from catching the sap from coconut trees. It was the only thing sweet available. Mother said she didn't want us to forget the taste of sweet. Only small sips were allowed, as it was also intoxicating.

Men who harvested the *tuba'* would cut notches in the towering coconut tree trunks with their ever-present machetes. They would set one bare foot in the notch and cut another in the other side and on and on until the top. There they would choose a young bunch of coconuts and chop the stem just above the bunch, which would fall like an oversize bunch of grapes. They'd hit the ground and shatter throwing water everywhere. The kids told me to stay back till they hit the ground then we'd run and grab one that had shattered open and scoop the soft, white meat out with our fingers or a wooden spoon. If we found any that had not completely shattered and still had some of the water, we'd enthusiastically tip it up and drink the sweet liquid.

As soon as the stem was cut, the gatherer would stick a section of bamboo he had carried up with him over the stem and catch the dripping sap and fasten it in place with a string like a handle on a bucket. Then every morning up he'd go with another bamboo fitted with a wooden handle that fit over his shoulder. He also carried with him a large bamboo brush like a gigantic bottlebrush strapped to his waist. At the top he'd carefully take the tube off that he had hung the day before, pour the gathered liquid into the carrier on his back. Then with his brush, he'd clean out the tube before returning it to the tree. The brush swished in and out then two taps on the tree trunk to clean it. It was always the same rhythm: swish, swish, tap tap. Swish, swish, tap, tap. Then on to the next tree. When his gathering tube was filled, home he'd go and the men would sit around and drink and talk. The more they drank, the more they talked. If any *tuba'* was left over, it was poured into a large clay jar and capped for two or three weeks. There it would become a spicy, strong vinegar that Mother used on our *alogbate* and *tancon,* which she said tasted like spinach. I didn't really know what spinach tasted like so it didn't matter.

The villagers were friendly and anxious to show us their particular way of living. One day Ruth and I went with Eming, one of the fishermen, out to the fish traps. We climbed into his small boat carved from the trunk of a tree. Near the front and the back bamboo poles were secured with vines and extended out the left side farther than my arms could reach. There a larger bamboo was attached that connected the two and rested in the water. That kept the boat from tipping over. As he paddled out toward the traps, I dipped my fingers over the edge slicing a groove in the crystal water. The boat seemed to be floating on air the water was so clear. We passed over multi-colored rocks, which I learned later were the homes of small animals. Coral, Mother called it.

As we approached the traps, which from where we were looked like low walls of stones piled up, Eming lowered his paddle into the water and tipped it a little. The boat turned toward the stone traps, then he slipped his paddle sideways and the boat slowed, the front sliding

Chapter XI

between two rocks. Ruth and I scrambled out and he followed, picking up a rock from in the front of the boat. It was bigger than his hand and had a hole in it. Through the hole was tied a rope, the other end secured around the bamboo pole. He wedged the rock between two bigger rocks on the traps so the boat wouldn't drift away.

The tops of the traps were a foot above the water and from there I could better see how they were made. Like dams built of large rocks, they stretched straight out from the beach to two-hundred yards or more, then turned at a right angle to intersect with other dams farther down the beach. There were six large, square areas enclosed by the dams. Eming said this one belonged to his family. When the tide came in it would rise three or four feet over the tops of the dams, fish would swim in and be trapped when the tide went out again.

We walked carefully, stepping from rock to rock until we came to the farthest corner of the trap. There a hole in the dam was covered with what looked like a large basket made of bamboo. The water rushed out through the bamboo basket as the tide receded. This is where the fish would swim, trying to get out. Smaller fish were able to swim through the basket and only the larger ones would be trapped. There were no larger ones though. We watched until Ruth and I both got bored.

Suddenly a dark shadow flashed across in front of the basket. I wasn't sure I had seen it at first, then it came across again. Eming didn't see it. "There!" I shouted, pointing toward the shadow. Then he saw it and drew his machete from its scabbard and stepped down to the water's edge where the shadow was flitting back and forth. He waited, machete held high. As the fish darted past, he sliced down. Missed. Again he tried. And again. Finally he hit, and the fish stopped instantly, flipped a couple of times, blood flowing from its back nearly severed. Quickly Eming stepped into the water, grabbed the fish by the tail and pulled it out. It was as long as his arm, gray and slender, unlike most of the smaller, colorful ones that swam around the coral. He smiled at me, his eyes pleased. I thumped my bare feet on the rock, happy with myself and Ruth just stood, sort of uneasy, staring at the fish dripping blood into the sea. We would eat well this evening.

So many new things to learn. The day after we arrived, Mother and I walked a long way down the curve of the beach. I think Mother just liked the sun in her face and not having to walk in the shadows and hide. We walked until we heard laughter and fun. The beach ended at the base of a cliff that jutted out into the sea and there a stream swept along the base of the cliff. The laughter came from several boys who were floating down the stream to the surf then racing up the beach to do it again. I waded into the stream wanting to be part of the fun. Then turned back to mother expectantly, "Go ahead." she urged. I watched a moment then came back to her side.

"I can't swim." I said quietly.

Chapter XI

"Come, let's learn." Taking my hand, we walked to the surf. "Let's take your pants off so they don't get wet."

I'd never done that before when others were around, but then, the other boys had nothing at all on. I hadn't noticed. Quickly I stripped off my shorts and looked to Mother. "It's all right for boys, but adults don't do that." she said, and we walked into the surf together.

Later, maybe it was the next day, I don't remember, days seemed to flow together into a time made for spreading our arms in the sun and laughing. Then Amadore felt it good that we know about something special. He and another man took us to where the stream fed into the sea at the edge of the cliff. We followed the stream a little ways away from the sea to where it didn't flow so fast and there he waded across. It was almost waist deep to him, so Amadore suggested we hold hands to cross. He then took my hand and I reached back for Mother's and she took Ruth's and we carefully crossed. The village man then led the way behind trees growing on the side of the cliff and up to where, hidden by thick bushes, a dark hole opened into the side of the cliff.

He carried with him a tree branch the size of my arm that had a familiar odor. I had remembered that odor from when we stayed with the headhunters in the mountains, pungent yet sweet; it was sap from a special tree. They would cut V shapes in the bark and catch the sap as it oozed out, so thick it wouldn't drip. A stick or branch would be pushed into the glob of sap and turned so the sap formed a ball on the end. When lit, it made a long lasting, sweet smelling torch. He lit a match and touched it to the ball of sap. Instantly it puffed into that familiar orange ball of flame. We stooped down and followed him into the cave.

Inside, the flickering torch cast wavering shadows as we walked. The floor of the cave was soft and a damp, acrid odor was in the air, definitely not sweet. High-pitched chirps echoed off the walls and roof and flying shadows flicked in and out of the torchlight. I had never been inside a mountain before and the darkness, the echoes, smells and the flying things opened new feelings in me. I wasn't scared. If it was safe for him, it was safe for me, but I could feel my heart pounding and I wanted to touch, to see, to learn. We followed the passageway that began climbing and made a turn to the left and the brilliance of daylight flashed. As we approached the opening, I saw we were high above the ocean on the side of a cliff. A narrow ledge angled down to a different beach and another village. The cave had gone clear through the cliff that jutted out into the sea.

Amadore and the villager talked quietly together for a few moments, then Amadore returned to where we stood to the side. "This place was used before by some to hide when the Japanese came through. It's good to know it is here just in case."

We then turned and retraced our steps to where we had entered. At one point our guide stopped and held the torch high. Hundreds of black furry animals hanging from the cave roof. Intense, black eyes seemed to glare at our presence and at times one would drop toward us, spread its wings and flash away. "Bats." Mother said.

"But how do they see in the dark?"

"They see with their ears." That thought seemed to dissolve into nothing and I waited for more. "When they screech, the sound bounces off the walls and they can hear how close the walls are." I understood. I would have to try that sometime.

Two weeks passed. Two weeks of resting, playing, swimming—I had learned to dog paddle—and walking the beach. One day Amadore walked with us the other way down the beach, passed the fish traps and around a curve. There trees grew right down into the sea and out for perhaps a hundred yards. I learned later they were Cypress trees and we had to walk carefully as their roots grew back up through the silty beach sand like sharp spikes.

We quickly saw why Amadore had taken us there. In the quiet waters under the trees, away from the waves and pebbles, seashells floated in undamaged. Some still alive, slid through the shallow water leaving their track in the soft sand. Amadore showed us one shell, reddish-brown stripes circled it. He nudged it carefully with his foot, then seeing that the shell was empty, picked it up, "Be careful of this one if it is alive," he warned, "it has a needle that can stab you and some have died."

The sun all too soon told us it was noon and we turned to head back toward the village, our arms loaded with unbelievably colored and shaped seashells—empty ones. Mother and Amadore let us go on ahead and I turned once to see them stopped and talking intently.

The next morning we climbed into two boats with bamboo outriggers and were rowed out past the fish traps to where a large boat with a sail waited. On the side of the boat was painted the name, *Romeo*. We took nothing with us.

Chapter XII
ESCAPE

The wind smelled of salt. Fresh, soft, puffing in from the open sea to the east. It filled the large sail and pushed us to the northwest, paralleling the coast. I laid, belly down at the rail, head over the side, watching the bow chop through the clear blue water. At times a wave would slap the wood siding sending spray and mist up the side, cold against my face. I turned as Mother called out.

"Be careful, son." She was sitting, leaning against the wall of the small cabin. Beside her, Ruth huddled under a corner of a large gray cloth. The morning chill always felt good to me. I wanted to soak it in because I knew it would be hot later. The mast creaked and groaned as a gust pushed at it. I rolled onto my back and watched the gray, patched sail strain against its ropes. The deck pitched slowly until I could see the blue water on the other side, and beyond where the dark green of coconut trees lined the shore, and the seashells, the cave, bats, a huge green parrot. I had learned to swim there. To live.

Gradually the shore turned from coconut tree lined beach to gray towering cliffs and above the cliffs, the always present shades of green. Trees twisted and gnarled by the wind and sea gripped the rock wall, their roots probing deep into the cracks of the cliff.

I let myself go and rolled across the sloping deck, thumping up against Mother's curled legs. I closed my eyes.

I recognized the sound even before the scurry of bare feet on the deck and the darkness enveloped me. My heart thumped as a canvas was thrown over us and Mother gripped me tightly. I didn't need another warning. I froze as the sound of the airplane grew. The canvas over our heads shook and my mind filled with pictures I didn't want to remember. I had never heard an airplane so close. Then the crewman pulled the canvas away as the dreaded sound diminished toward the land.

"Japs Ma'am. We must be careful," Amadore said as he helped the crewman roll the canvas up and dropped it to the deck beside us.

"He's flying so low." Mother still gripped my shoulder, her hand shaking.

Chapter XII

"They are using Caticlan for landing," he said. Mother's questioning gaze prompted a reply. "At Caticlan is a dirt landing place built by Americans before, but now Japanese use it. It was nice place before." Amadore shook his head slowly

"Isn't it dangerous for the sub to come in so close to the airstrip?" Mother questioned.

"Submarine will be on other side. Water is deeper there."

The sky shimmered cloudless in the late afternoon as the Romeo ghosted around the northern tip of Panay Island and turned south, heading toward the rendezvous site and hoping somewhere beneath the surface was a submarine on the same journey.

The wind had slacked to a point that starting the single cylinder diesel engine became a topic of discussion, but the decision was quickly made not to unless the wind ceased entirely. There was plenty of time left and the sound would most likely arouse suspicions if any Japanese patrols were nearby.

Darkness had long settled when we were helped down the side of the Romeo on a wooden ladder to an outrigger canoe and rowed to shore. There we would wait.

Chapter XIII
SUBMARINE

Silently its rounded shoulders pushed up from the depths of the South China Sea. Drifting slowly toward the shore, its ponderous movement gave no indication of the power that lay within, nor the authority it demanded as it prowled the gloom of the depths. Under the cover of darkness it was only a black silhouette easily mistaken for a native fishing boat.

It was September 29, 1944, and the U.S.S. Nautilus, America's largest submarine, was on a silent mission in the midst of war's clamor. On the side of the gray conning tower amid ship was its designation SS168. Above, and shielded by chest high armor, a small platform served as lookout station. Towering ten feet above that, the periscope was first to break the surface, then as the conning tower emerged and the water drained away from the platform, a hatch in the floor was flung open and the Captain emerged followed by his lookout man. Even before the deck broke surface, from the conning tower they were able to scan the horizon.

Commander George A. Sharp stood on his platform pulling the freshness of the salt air deep into his lungs. It was a welcome relief from the confining gray walls and recirculated air below. As forward movement

Chapter XIII

slowed, the sub's phosphorescent wake dwindled and only the sea draining off its deck showed the faint glow. Captain Sharp knew that an alert enemy lookout could at times spot the glow of even a submerged craft.

Though almost mystical in beauty, the glow caused by disturbed plankton floating in the warm sea, or even the coral in the shallows could give away their position as readily as any light. He strained his eyes into the darkness. Beside him, the seaman scanned the dark shore with his binoculars. Not a light shone. No moon. Only the stars: a million blazing pinpoints scattered haphazardly against a defused radiance belted diagonally across the sky. Below that, where the stars ended, the horizon and a beach where hopefully, men waited. The right men.

A beleaguered guerrilla force somewhere in the central Philippines was in desperate need of reinforcements and orders were given to slide undetected beneath enemy lines to deliver guns and ammunition. Then before the waking sun once more stretched its searching rays across the dark sky, it would have hopefully taken on board a few remaining American civilians who had somehow been overlooked in the evacuation, and glide away beneath the protective waters, its mission completed.

A hatch swung open on the deck below and two men swiftly climbed out. Disciplined hands prepared the 50-caliber machine gun and swung the barrel toward shore. They weren't expecting danger, but Commander

Sharp was not one to take chances. Discipline, awareness and, on this mission, silence were top priority, but never a guarantee of success.

This would be their last rendezvous with the resistance forces. Although the time, date, and even the place were changed often and only a chosen few were given the vital information, the High Command felt the risk was getting too great. Commander Sharp wondered if the Americans were indeed out there on the darkened shore, or if they were even alive. If they were alive, how they managed the trek through enemy held territory to this remote beach . . . that is, if they even received the message to come.

Beside him, the seaman touched his arm and pointed into the darkness off the starboard bow. At the same instant, the gun crew swept the barrel toward the area. Commander Sharp made a mental note of their alertness.

A moment later, a dark shadow formed out of the blackness. Only the creaking of woven vine ropes against bamboo outriggers and the quiet sound of oars slipping rough water could be heard. The two men, naked but for scant loincloths, dragged their oars slowing the dugout canoe. Carved from a single tree trunk, it lay low in the water, a mere three inches of freeboard showing above the ocean chop. The front man shipped his oar laying it carefully in the boat in front of him. Picking up a long bamboo pole, he pushed it forward to fend off the impact

Chapter XIII

as the man in the rear levered his oar steering them into a bow to hull position.

Whispered passwords were exchanged along with simple directions. Then they pushed off, bronzed backs gleaming in the starlight. Their oars dug deep. And as they blended back into the darkness the lead man stood and cupped his hands to his mouth. A single syllable rode the silence ahead of them and seconds later the muffled thump of a one cylinder diesel motor echoed its response.

Within minutes a larger shadow appeared, its planked sides riding high in the water. It showed no lights. On the bow, up high, its name hand painted in deep orange, "Romeo". A single mast sails furled, punched through the top of the small cabin. The thumping engine eased back and stopped as it ghosted closer to the sub. One man could be seen holding a bamboo pole waiting to ease them together. A second man leaned against the beam of the sail, a narrow gangplank hanging beneath. As they slid alongside, bamboo pole bending, a line whipped through the air, was caught and secured. The boom was then swung out and the gangplank lowered onto the bulging gray steel of America's largest submarine.

Soon the long task of unloading the precious cargo would begin. Commander Sharp checked his watch and calculated how many hours they had before dawn. They were on schedule.

"I understand we have some refugees to take aboard, sir," The seaman broke the silence.

"That's what they say." The Commander was distant, his thoughts probing the darkness.

"Everybody wants out." The seaman's eyes never left his binoculars, scanning the gloom. "Pretty tough out there," he added. "Are these people special?" He turned to the commander.

"Wives and families of the men we're handing the guns to."

The seaman's eyes held his commander. An unspoken question.

"If they're caught, they're killed," Commander Sharp answered, "and I don't have to remind you the Japs have ways of killing we never heard of. Spies are everywhere, Hanson, and chances are the enemy knows the names of every one of those people out there."

"I hate spies. It's beyond me, Sir, how anyone can spy on his own people."

"Have you ever been tortured, Seaman Hanson?"

"No sir." It was an apology and Seaman Hanson retreated from the subject.

"There might be an American woman out there too." The commander spoke softly into the night.

"Sir?"

"With two small children. Wife and family of one of the leaders . . . if they made it this far."

"An American leads these jungle crazies?"

The Commander's mouth twitched. "Crazy they are, but the Japs are scared to death of them and I salute them. But no, he's Filipino, from what I understand." he

Chapter XIII

answered the seaman's question. "I don't think an American would have the heart to lead a bunch like them. Guts yes, but not heart. It's something else when you're fighting in your own back yard. And your neighbor, or maybe your own cousin might be the one to turn you in, sign your death warrant."

"Hope we never have to do that, sir."

"You got that right."

"How long has this woman and kids been out there . . . from the beginning?"

"From the beginning."

"That's guts . . . Sir."

A lot of heart out there too, the Commander thought, and in his mind he could hear the laughter and the smiles of his own family, a world away. Safe.

Perhaps, just perhaps those out there could also be brought into that security. If they were out there. He squinted into the darkness, glad for the cover but wishing somehow he could cut through it and know if they were there.

"Shall we begin the transfer, Sir?"

He nodded, stealing another glance at his watch.

***

Below where the stars ended, on a beach of black volcanic sand a line of men, eager, lean, waded chest deep to where the Romeo moved slowly with the roll of the easy surf. Muscles strained, some staggered as the heavy load pushed bare feet deep into the black sand. Nobody complained. Determination and hope drove them as they waded out to the heavily loaded boat, turned, laid a piece of burlap or a banana leaf as a cushion on their bare shoulder as another box was swung on. Then back, laying the boxes in rows high up on the black sand.

***

Watching from a fallen coconut tree where I sat with my mother and sister, I lifted my eyes toward where the horizon should be. I thought I could see the outline of a submarine, whatever that was. I didn't understand it all, but the fear and anticipation hanging in the air made me breathe cautiously. Fear had long since become a natural part of my life. It was as natural as sitting quietly while within, a thousand questions and feelings waited for answers. But the anticipation that tonight might be the night of escape was too much for me to comprehend. I was only eight-years-old and my head was burning with fever.

    Mother adjusted the blanket around my shoulders and pulled me close. There had been so many false hopes and rumors. Some even fabricated just to keep the spark of hope alive. But now this was real. It was happening. Soon, before sunrise, we would be on board that submarine sliding away to safety. That beautiful, gray submarine.

Chapter XIII

I fingered the rough patches of dress that fell across Mother's knees. The only dress she had left. It had been a year since her shoes had fallen apart and the tenderness in her feet had long been torn, ground and tortured into calluses that only the sharpest of rocks could penetrate. Two and a half years of existence in the jungles had left her with little but the prayer that God would somehow let her see us get out.

I longed to be there at the water's edge, cooling my feet and legs, or striding the rows of boxes and guns, counting. But I could do little more than lift my head. The fever of malaria came and went as it willed, leaving me completely drained.

In the jungles the mountain people knew the rare and sought after tree and carefully followed the complex preparation of its roots into raw quinine. They knew that a wrong step would produce a poison instead of the treasured healing qualities of quinine. Its bitterness always sent convulsions down the length of my body, but it was the only remedy. Here though, on this beach, there was not the wisdom of the mountain people, nor the wonder of medical science. Maybe there would be better medicine on the submarine.

Mother reached out to lay a comforting hand on my sister. Though already ten, Ruth could remember nothing of America. She was only three when we left. Mother's touch brought no response and she withdrew her hand reluctantly. Ruth seemed torn between returning to

America, the country she didn't remember, and staying with Daddy.

Ruth had asked why Daddy couldn't come with us to America, or even on this last nine-day trek across the island to the rendezvous. Mother tried to gently explain the importance of Father's position. She agonized over the explanation, finally telling us that he had sent us on this last desperate grasp for safety because of his love for us. But even as she had explained, the words echoed hollow.

Sensing someone approach in the darkness, she turned. It was Amadore.

"Ma'am, it is good to see so much guns for us, no?" He began in his broken English. "Soon all will be unloaded and maybe God will let you to leave. Your prayers are answered, Ma'am."

"Yes, Amadore," Mother's eyes were distant, focused somewhere beyond the horizon. "It's been a nightmare, but now it's ended."

"Maybe, Ma'am." Amadore turned away into the darkness.

"There's no maybe, Amadore, the sub is here." She looked up at Amadore, his face turned politely away. "What could ever happen now?"

His face was only a dark silhouette as was the voice intonation which Mother had never learned to master; where a yes may mean no, and a twitched eyebrow meant more than either.

"Amadore?" she probed apprehensively. "You're not telling me everything."

Amadore continued hesitantly. "The tide is going out, Ma'am, and if it does not come back before the sun rises . . . ," His voice trailed off.

"Amadore, please!" she mustered all the forcefulness she could at the moment.

"Ma'am, the submarine is stuck up on the reef and will be destroyed if the tide does not lift it before the sun rises, Ma'am." He pushed his words out, his courage faltering.

"Destroyed?" She questioned, knowing that a Filipino's use of the word could mean anything from a paint scratch to total oblivion.

"So it will not be captured by Japanese, Ma'am," he paused as if searching for the right word. "The Captain will explode it, Ma'am." But Amadore had not a glimpse of an idea what that entailed.

Trained hands would expertly place pre-packaged explosives in strategic locations. Locations that would destroy engines, guns and controls, but most importantly in at least one of the loaded torpedo tubes. Safety pins would be pulled from all their torpedoes and when all the crew except one had safely left the sub, that one would set the fuse and quickly join his crewmembers somewhere out of harm's way on the beach.

The explosion would not only destroy America's largest sub, but would most likely alert the Japanese. The precious arms and ammunition carefully unloaded earlier would be at risk as enemy soldiers would quickly converge on the area. And what of one hapless American woman clutching tightly to her two children?

My fever somehow kept the message from registering. Ruth looked up, as if hearing good news. Mother pulled me closer and I felt her breath, hot, close against my cheek.

Wavelets lapped at the black sand and hope receded with the tide. And the darkness deepened.

Time passed all too quickly for the men unloading the cargo. Knotted and tired muscles dared not slacken and anxious eyes glanced eastward searching for the first hints of dawn. Many hands grasped for the precious cargo, removing it into the darkness—young hands, old hands, all who valued freedom.

The last of the cargo was unloaded and the Romeo rested.

Mother's breath came in jagged chops. Perhaps shaken by pictures she could no longer keep pushed out of sight. Pictures of men, women and children, her friends, who for no other reason than they were fortunate enough to have been born in America, were bound, thrown to their knees and whose last sight was of a two handed ceremonial sword being unsheathed and of the blood-stained grass of a jungle hill half a world from home. And the hiss of the blade as light, eternal light overcame the darkness. A sunrise that would never fade.

And the picture of her husband, my father, standing tall on the far side of a swollen river, then

Chapter XIII

blending back to be swallowed into the jungle. No one waved. Mother had turned then toward the trail that she was told would eventually lead to this dark beach—and freedom.

Amadore walked to the water's edge. Quiet words were exchanged with the boatmen who squatted there. He returned and without a word sat a discreet distance away on the fallen tree.

The chill that enveloped was more than just from the night air. It was the last fragment of hope balancing on the turn of the tide. The wavelets lapping the beach reminded us that freedom was still no closer than the shrouded horizon. The Romeo rolled lightly with the sea and sent a wash across the feet of the two men at the water's edge. Without a word, they moved back a step. An eternity later, it seemed, they moved back another step. And again. Whispered words were exchanged between them and the Lieutenant echoed it.

"The tide is coming in, Ma'am. We can go now. But we must hurry. Soon comes sunrise."

A tear slid down Mother's cheek and dampened a patch on her dress.

Chapter XIV
FREEDOM

Through my fever, the sub seemed to be of another world. Gray, clean walls, immense wheels and rows of gauges wavered passed my eyes. Clanking metal doors, men hurrying through narrow passageways, clipped words and the deep drumming of powerful engines. We were guided into a room which I learned later was the forward torpedo room. Mattresses lay on the floor covered with crisp sheets. A pillow and blanket were also new to my world. This would be home for the next seven days.

I lay on my mattress, pillow soft, the smell of clean. I tucked the blanket tight under my chin. It too was soft, warm, protection from the strangeness around me. Pipes and wires criss-crossed the ceiling above me. I followed each one with my eyes, wondering what use they could be. On the front wall more gauges, handles and valves. On each side of the front wall, one over the other, two round lids as large as a truck tire. In the middle of each was a shiny brass wheel with brass spokes.

Each day two men came in and rolled a cart directly in back of the lids, then turned a valve. A new sound smashed at my ears. Air hissed out and one man spun the wheel and swung the lid back on its hinges. A large, shiny object slid out and the men guided it onto the

Chapter XIV

cart. It was round and longer than a man was tall. On the back end four fins surrounded a propeller which they spun with their hands and oiled. Then after checking other parts, they pushed it back into the tube, closed the lid and turned the valve. I never got used to that penetrating hiss of air.

At times men hung a white sheet on the front wall, put the lights out and they made us watch movies. Huge buildings and streets crowded with cars, people, new sounds. Airplanes, which had always meant danger, flashed noisily across the sheet. I always pulled close to Mother and was glad when they ended. I longed for the green and the quiet of the jungles and mountains but knew, because I was told, that this was freedom.

Suddenly the drum of the engines stopped and the room tilted. I clamped my hands over my ears as pressure threatened to collapse my head. We were diving and I reached for mother's comforting arm and her smile told me it was all right, but her eyes were troubled. Or maybe it was just my fever.

Meals were served in another room toward the rear of the sub. While at dinner one day, the alarm sounded to dive. Men scurried back and forth and a tenseness filled the air that I had not felt before. From that time on, we ate meals in shifts. A Japanese plane had been spotted and the command was given to crash dive, but with the added weight toward the rear, the dive was agonizingly slow.

Another time a man came through the doorway and told us not to be alarmed. We had barely missed a floating mine. The captain had given orders to explode the mine when we were at a safe distance so no ship would hit it. Minutes later the sub shook with the repeated whump, whump, whump of machine gun fire. Then the room shuddered and pressure slammed at my ears as the mine exploded. I glanced at the ceiling and walls but everything was still in place. I hoped that wouldn't happen again.

On the seventh day the sub arrived at an undisclosed port in New Guinea. My fever had come and gone throughout the trip leaving me almost too weak to walk. As we climbed out on deck, sunshine blazed in our eyes. The brilliance was blinding after living in the gloom of the sub for a week, but fresh air and a breeze on my face more than made up for it. All around us gray ships, larger than I had ever seen, rested at anchor. New sights, new places, new memories.

For one week we lived in Red Cross tents under a cluster of trees at the foot of a cliff. As I began feeling stronger, curiosity urged me to climb the cliff to better see the airplanes that I heard coming and going above. My mother's warning not to climb was lost on my nine-year-old mind. I crouched in the brush at the top of the cliff watching airplanes land and take off from the dirt airstrip. The larger planes sped down the length of the strip before lifting into the sky a few feet above my head. I held my breath as a smaller fighter plane, one engine billowing smoke, circled from the right and struggled for enough altitude to clear the end of the runway where I lay

Chapter XIV

watching. It bounced hard and slid to a stop as men with equipment rushed out to put out the fire. I learned later that was a P-38 Lightning and it became my favorite plane.

At the end of that week we boarded a truck that took us the roundabout way up to that airstrip. There we boarded one of the larger planes. I watched as the large propellers spun slowly then faster until they seemed to disappear. Soon we were on our way to Australia. Miles of green jungle slid by under the wings. My sister Ruth and I amused ourselves by tearing small bits of paper napkin and pushing them out the round, finger size hole in each window. She sat in the seat in front of me and I tried to see the bits of paper fly past my window as she pushed them out. Unable to see them go by, I stuck my finger out in hopes of feeling them whiz past. I never did, but was amazed at the force of the wind pushing my finger. Then we crossed more water, and finally Australia.

Brisbane was hot, a barren desert compared to the Philippines. Three months went by while we lived in steel huts, ate wonderful food and swallowed varieties of medicines. Mother said they were to cure us of any possible diseases we could have picked up. The medicine would also kill the intestinal worms which had long since become a part of life. For the past two and a half years, going to the toilet was an act we all dreaded. We knew we would pass the large pink worms, and I hated when one would come only part way out. Then it was necessary to reach back and pull the squirming thing the rest of the way out and drop it into the mass below.

By chance, a young man that Mother had known in California before I was even born had joined the army and was stationed in Brisbane. He visited often and once took us in an army amphibious jeep to an outing at the zoo. Kangaroos, wallabies and other strange animals brought moments of long awaited laughter.

On December 6, 1944, we boarded the S.S. Monterey, a troop ship carrying wounded soldiers back to America. Three weeks on the ocean, seeing nothing but water slip past seemed more than I could comprehend. Whenever on deck we wore life jackets. We were told that enemy submarines prowled everywhere. Mother said the captain was pushing extra hard to arrive on New Year's Day, and each day I strained forward to get a glimpse of America.

January 2, 1945, Mother woke us early in the morning. "We'll be going under the Golden Gate soon." She was as excited as I had ever seen her. She dressed us and with life jackets on and we stumbled up onto deck. The wind was biting cold and brought tears to my sleepy eyes. Mother pointed to some lights low on the horizon. "There it is," was all she said as she pulled us close to her. The ship had slowed and it seemed forever as we approached. The lights grew and finally became recognizable as a string of golden lights across a bridge that stretched away into the darkness on both sides.

Chapter XIV

I looked up into Mother's face as we slid slowly under the lights. Tears streamed down her face and her lips moved, trembled. I wanted to join her in the excitement because this was freedom, she said. This was America.

Chapter XV
SECOND LETTER

Nineteen years passed. Along with the Marine Corps and college, I married, had two children and owned a three-bedroom home on a hill in the Kansas City suburbs. The American dream.

It was nineteen-sixty-four and a great year. Our second child was born. A boy, Michael Scott. It was also the year of the second letter. My heart took an extra thump as I turned the letter over. Upper left corner in small, neat print was the familiar name of my father, Emiterio Alianza, Philippines. After ten years with not a word, there it was.

My mind swept back to that first letter ten years past and the explosion of nightmare memories. An explosion that dislocated and relocated my memories and perceptions and altered many decisions in the years that followed.

The first letter had caught me in the midst of Marine Corps training. We were being taught how to stay alive. How to kill. While being pounded, thrashed, formed and disciplined into a "fighting machine," my mind often returned to the cruel disciplines ground into me by my father. With one strong arm he controlled a small band of guerrilla fighters who knew nothing of the

Chapter XV

rules of war as outlined in the Geneva Convention. They struggled for their lives and country against a highly disciplined Japanese army. An army that vastly outnumbered them and didn't care about rules of war. The other arm he held protectively around an American wife and two small children, the prime enemy of the Japanese.

As the Marine Corps training sculpted my actions and reactions, it also reformed my mind and with that, my priorities. It was then I began to understand the complexity of the decisions and actions that weighted my father's shoulders. My eyes were opened to the overlapping and contradictory emotions that at times collided in him. Slowly I recognized that his shoulders were broader than mine would ever be.

When the second letter arrived, it was most welcomed although I wondered why there was so many years between. As I turned the letter over to open it, my eyes caught two small letters after my father's name, Emiterio Alianza. Two very small letters suddenly became large . . . Jr.

This letter was not from my father. This was his son . . . my half-brother? Another explosion rocked my mind.

Late fall clouds bothered the Kansas City sky and leaves danced in circles on the driveway of our newly purchased home on Scenic Drive, southeast of the city. Pauline, my wife of five years, appeared at the open garage door. Carla, our three-year-old bundle of sunshine, had her in tow by her little finger. Seeing me ambling up the driveway, Carla turned her loose to find her own way and ran toward me, taking time to kick at the swirling leaves as she passed. I swung her up and she wrapped an arm around my neck.

"You got a letter, Papa," she said, reaching for the envelope.

"Who's it from, Hon?" Pauline rolled an arm around my waist as together we turned into the garage and away from the snap of the afternoon breeze.

"My half-brother," I answered, still trying to fit the image into a life from long ago and far outside the normal life we had built.

"Half-brother? I didn't know you had a brother. Half or otherwise"

"I didn't either."

I sat on the edge of the kitchen chair and carefully slid the point of a knife under the flap of the envelope.

"Dear Brother,
I am sad to tell you the news that Father has died. I would have written to you before but only when going through his personal belongings did I find your address. When are you coming back home . . . ?"

The letter went on to explain details that took my mind into areas totally foreign. Father had remarried after not hearing from us for some time. He had married Nini, the young lady who had become part of the family

Chapter XV

throughout the hiding years and had been a trusted friend and helper to Mother as well as a companion to my sister Ruth and me. They then moved to Mindanao, the southern and second largest island of the Philippines, purchased a farm and had prospered. When Father died mysteriously, somehow Aunt Patricia, the one who had stolen his inheritance nearly thirty years ago, was involved. And now she owned this farm, too. Emiterio Jr. along with his brother, sister and mother were destitute. I pushed the letter aside and slid down in my chair. I felt my eyebrows tighten.

Pauline reached for the letter, hesitated, then when I didn't object, read it carefully. She looked up. "Can we do anything?"

"I'll write and find out, but I'm not going back there. That's not home."

Not long after, I sat in the same chair, wrote and rewrote a letter seeking to fill in blanks where I didn't know blanks existed while keeping an arm's length from anything that could be construed as a commitment. There was no hiding my curiosity, but this was not my responsibility and I wanted that to remain clear.

Two months passed and then the answer.

"Please do not try to do anything. Others have tried and have been killed."

In a few pages the whole story unfolded. It was a story that started nearly thirty years ago. Of Father's younger sister, Patricia, who stole his inheritance when I was being born in 1935. The Japanese invasion and occupation in 1941 destroyed what remained of the plantation. Then two years after my mother, sister and I escaped back to America and were struggling to build a new life, Patricia successfully stopped all communication by coercing her husband, the town mayor, to stop letters my father was trying to send to mother. And with a stamp marked DECEASED, he sent incoming mail back to Mother with the dreaded message.

Father then married Nini, assuming it was Mother's desire to end the communication and also the relationship. And now, in 1964 as he lay in the hospital with bleeding ulcers, Aunt Patricia once again succeeded in convincing him that she would take care of the family should Father die. She convinced him that Emiterio Jr. at fourteen, was too young to handle the responsibility of the farm. Father then made her beneficiary with the stipulation that she would take care of the family in the event of his death. She was true to her word, allowing them only enough money to survive while she took over the farm.

When Father had gone into the hospital, Terry Jr. had taken over the responsibilities of the farm. Each morning he peddled his bicycle to the hospital, then on to the farm for the day. On his way home in the afternoon he would again stop by the hospital. On one such afternoon, one of the hospital staff informed him that Father had died and had been buried.

The family was enraged. A quick burial like that was uncalled for in the culture. The hospital staff

Chapter XV

explained that it was standard procedure when the patient's bill was not paid, and the attending doctor would not comment. Terry had persisted however, until it was finally leaked out by one staff member that Aunt Patricia and her husband had visited the hospital just before Father died. From information Terry could gather, and also from what he was not being told, he came to the conclusion that foul play had indeed occurred. And Aunt Patricia owned the farm.

I read and reread the letter, trying to absorb the complexity. Pauline sat across the table from me, not being very successful in hiding her curiosity. To make clearer sense in my own mind, I read the letter out loud to her, slowly, pausing after each sentence to allow it time to settle into a logical spot in my mind.

"So why did this aunt of yours want to stop all contact? Did she not like Americans?" Was she—?"

I waved away her words. "I've got to think a minute." I stood and turned toward the kitchen window. The sky promised snow and thoughts of Christmas were in the air. I needed fresh air. I walked to the back door, pulling my coat from the hook as I passed.

"Where you going?"

"Fresh air." Pauline picked up the pages scattered on the kitchen table as I opened the back door and stepped out. I pulled the icy air deep into my lungs. It seemed to send fresh blood to my brain, cleansing, enriching. This was not the season to be thinking about the troubles of a family a world away that two months ago I didn't know existed.

It was Christmas and I had my own family, right here. Carla's birthday was in two days and mine next week. With that thought, other birthdays slipped into my mind. Of Japanese planes bombing on a Sunday morning. Of Doug and his family massacred. I shook the pictures from my head, zipped my jacket up and shoved fists deep into my pockets. That was then and this is now and I owed them nothing.

That was my plan, but God had another.

Chapter XVI
RETURN

"Attention all passengers. We'll be arriving in Hawaii tomorrow morning at six. We'll be having a pre-arrival orientation, so would all passengers please gather in the game room after dinner at seven p.m. Thank you."

It was our first of four stops on our way back to the Philippines. We gathered for the meeting, anticipating the one-day layover. The meeting was informative and interesting; telling docking time, departure time, where to rent cars for the day, good hotels, sights, restaurants, and ended with an up-shot. "Have a marvelous time and don't forget to be back on board by 0700 hours—that's seven in the morning to any land-lubbers that may be here." Laughs rang out mingled with a few remarks in sea-slang. We then broke up into small groups eagerly planning the next day's excitement. Some wandered into the bar, others strolled the decks, or leaned on the rail lifting faces to the salted breeze.

Behind us were four years of intense training. On the snow-swept plains of Alberta, Canada, at Prairie Bible Institute, we learned the necessity of separating ourselves from the things of the world to wholly dedicate our minds and hearts on the task ahead. In a remote, wooded camp in Pennsylvania it was the sweat and strained muscles of building an existence in a foreign environment. There at one of the New Tribes Mission boot-camps, we also learned the basics of communicating with a people whose thought patterns ran counter to what we were born and raised with. This created challenges that we would soon find indispensable.

It was April 10, 1972 when we left for our first term as missionaries in the Philippines. At that time, a cruise ship was far less expensive than flying, especially considering the mountains of baggage we piled on. Well meaning friends had told us that the particular area of the Philippines we were heading for was quite primitive so we better take along everything we could conceivably need in the next year. So we did, including mosquito netting and a machete, as if a tropical country wouldn't have mosquito netting available. Machetes were probably invented there, for Pete's sake.

Chapter XVI

For Carla and Mike, eleven and seven years respectively, it was all adventure, new places, new people. Pauline, my wife of thirteen years, shared the excitement with the children, but with an adult's perspective that this was going to be work. I had been there before and had more of the mind-set of a workhorse: It's work, but that's what I'm here for.

None of us had any doubt that this was where God wanted us, and held equal assurance that there were hardships ahead. "But God enables those He sends," we encouraged each other when those hardships did come.

Once aboard ship and on the way out of Los Angeles harbor, we had scanned brochures with the ship's itinerary for on-board activities, then begrudgingly forked out what we thought were horrendous tips to our baggage handlers.

Our first stop was Hawaii. We had met another first-term missionary on board and had agreed to share expenses and rent a car for the day. We drove around Oahu and with every curve in the road new vistas opened. Surf pounded on cliffs and hissed up through blowholes before settling back in cooling mist. Black beaches, soft as powder, giant fern forests arched over the road, and always the blue, blue of sky and sea.

"Is the Philippines like this, Papa?" Carla's quiet eyes took it all in and stored it away in her eleven-year-old mind.

Old memories, dimmed by time, hidden under the brambles and underbrush of growing up were once again pushing to the front. Yes, I remembered, explained and pointed out details most people would miss which kept my little audience attentive.

Next stop, Tokyo. Most memorable was the heart-stopping taxi ride to a recommended restaurant. Pauline's hands were a vise around my arm as the driver, one hand on the horn and the other on the gearshift, somehow found space between cars, and at times even on the sidewalk. I laughed as memories of taxi rides during my military time in Japan swerved onto the screen of my mind. The thrill of the day would be in offering the driver an extra 50 yen if he would hurry. Not a sport for the faint-hearted.

Hong Kong and the memory we came away with was a rickshaw ride around the city. Pauline questioned if we had to, I mean really had to, and Carla shrunk into the seat cushion in embarrassment. After all, four people sitting in a two-wheeled cart, being pulled down the street by a diminutive man with no more on than a torn pair of brown shorts with a hole in the back. Really, Papa! "It'll make a good memory," was my reply. It did.

Taiwan came next. We wanted to see what the real people lived like so we hopped a train to a small village where English seemed unknown and was certainly unknown to the ones who printed street signs and directions. We managed lunch in a restaurant by pointing to beautiful displays of food while hoping it would not be something raw.

Chapter XVI

Whatever it was, it gave Pauline instant diarrhea. Bathroom? Restroom? How about toilet? Someone finally caught on and pointed across the street to a small building where men and women were coming and going. Problem: only one door. She went in hoping to discern a divider of sorts. Women were definitely on the right and men on the left, but divider? None. There are times when life's little necessities leave no time for procrastination. Another memory.

Next stop, Manila, capital city of the archipelago of seven-thousand-one-hundred-six islands called Philippines. This was our destination. Our ears perked at the voice from the intercom.

"Attention all passengers. We'll be arriving in Manila Bay tomorrow morning at six a.m. . . . ."

That evening we crowded into the game room anticipating the travel-wise suggestions of the one who would know. After his usual cheery greetings, he glanced somberly at his cheat-sheet. "If Manila is not your destination port, we suggest that you do not leave the ship." He looked up to see if he was connecting with us. "If you do decide to leave the ship, please do your utmost to return before dark, do not drink the water, and here is a list of areas to avoid . . . ."

I glanced around the room, then waited, as it appeared everyone else was, for the punch line. It didn't come. We were dismissed.

I thought I heard God say, "Welcome," but I wasn't sure.

***

It was a long walk down the gangplank the next morning. From an air-conditioned cruise ship to the stifling, choking swelter of Manila in the summer.

Passports and sheaves of paperwork in hand, we were ushered into the immigration office. That consisted of a large tin roofed warehouse type building with dozens of desks scattered about. There was no air conditioning and heat radiated through the tin roof. Numerous fans aimed at the officials lounging behind the desks didn't seem to help. We were shuffled from one desk to another, answered questions and waited for the thump of the rubber stamp on yet another form. It seemed an eternity before we emerged at the other end, still not sure where our baggage had landed or if indeed it had.

At last, after endless questions, we were guided to where our luggage sat at the far end of an adjoining warehouse. Unbelievably, we were able to account for all of it: eight fifty-five gallon steel drums securely locked, four wood crates measuring three feet square, the maximum allowed, and one two-door refrigerator jammed full of non-perishable food-stuffs. We were told we would need to hire a truck to haul our cargo before they would release it. I assured them that it would be taken care of and picked up our numerous suitcases that we had kept in our cabin. We made our way out of the immigration area, eager to catch a glimpse of Mr.

Chapter XVI

Dalisay, the mission director, who was to meet us and escort us to the mission house. There was no waiting area and we stood on the sidewalk trying to find shade from the noon sun.

We looked around and hoped the place we would eventually be settled into would be different, somehow cleaner, more civilized. The waters of Manila Bay swam black with floating garbage. Garbage caked the gutters and overflowed onto the sidewalks. It stuck to the bottom of our shoes and steamed up abusing our nostrils. Brightly painted passenger jeeps and motorcycles with sidecars scrambled in an effort to solicit passengers. There seemed to be no particular traffic pattern, whoever got there first, occupied.

We waited. Mr. Dalisay was nowhere to be seen. Eagerly we watched every mode of transportation that pulled to the curb. We had never seen him or even a picture so we were completely in the dark as to what he looked like. Two hours later he sauntered up and introduced himself. He had the definite advantage, as we were the only Americans there. After the customary introductions and pleasantries and without a mention of his being two hours late, he made the necessary arrangements to have our big baggage picked up then flagged down an empty *jeepney* (as the brightly colored jeeps were called). The bodies and frames had been stretched so they would accommodate as many as fifteen to twenty Filipino sized passengers. As we drove through Manila traffic Mr. Dalisay talked nonstop. The most noteworthy statement that caught my ear was, "Oh yes, we decided to place you on a different island."

    His original plan for us was to be located on the island of Mindoro, in a tribal area that was known to be hostile toward outsiders. Our new destination was the next island south: Panay. A friend of his lived in a small town on the northwest tip of the island. In the foothills and mountains behind the town lived a little known tribe. That was to be our destination. I had spent seven years of my childhood on that island, that same area, but at the moment I didn't care much. It was hot, clinging hot, and my eyes and nose were burning from the polluted air and my ears rang from the noise of traffic. It seemed that in Manila traffic the most useful item on any vehicle was the horn.

    An hour later we pulled up in front of a two-story, unpainted cement block building on the outskirts of Manila. In back stretched rice fields. They were flooded this time of year and the odor of stagnant water hung heavy in the air. Mr. Dalisay led the way upstairs to our room. We followed, dragging our suitcases with us. The room contained one Filipine size double bed with foot and headboards, a small dresser and one chair. Nothing else would fit. The bathroom was down the hall. Carla and Mike's room was similar.

    After we were left to ourselves, Pauline flopped down on the bed to rest. She lay a moment, eyes wide open, then slowly sat up and pulled the bedspread down. Solid wood. No sheets or blanket. Just a bedspread over wood planks. We did have pillows though. Later as I stretched out on the bed, I found it to be about three inches shorter than I was and with sturdy footboard, I could only sleep on my side with legs curled up. Which didn't leave much room for my wife as the bed was little more than single size wide. We managed to procure a sheet of sorts to cover the wood.

That first evening, tired, confused and sweltering hot, I reached for the light switch, but before I could reach it, Pauline's voice, with a touch of alarm stopped me,

"What's that?" I followed her wide eyes and pointing finger to the far corner of the ceiling where a scaly head protruded from a crack between the ceiling and the walls. From its mouth protruded the body of a cockroach. As it kicked out the last of its life, the head disappeared back into the crack, meal in mouth.

"It's a gecko, hon. Harmless. They help control the cockroaches." She wasn't convinced they were harmless or that they could control the large population of cockroaches that began emerging from the cracks.

"You sleep by the wall," she said quickly scooting away from the wall.

"Okay," I relented, clambering over her, "but you'll have to get the light." After a last visual survey of the enemy she reached gingerly for the switch and was quickly snuggled close. It didn't feel like a romantic snuggle, but rather of fear as the room sank into absolute darkness. After a few attempts to find a soft board in the bed, exhaustion overtook me.

Suddenly I was wide awake, a scurrying and rustling in my hair. "The light. Turn on the light." I tried to keep my voice low as I grabbed for my head and yanked something from my hair and flung it viciously against the wall. When the light finally came on it revealed Pauline standing as far as possible from the wall with one finger successfully on the switch without touching the wall. She scrambled back for the bed jerking her feet off the floor where a severely maimed cockroach close to two inches long skittered in a small circle on the floor. "Step on it!" She just looked at me incredulously as she pulled her bare feet as close to her as she could. I grabbed a shoe and finished the job, then attempted to comfort a trembling wife. The rest of the night we spent with the light on as the flying cockroaches preferred darkness.

The following week a decision was made to fly down to the island of Mindanao to pay a visit to my half-brother, Terry and family. The town of Digos where they lived was over five hundred miles from Manila and there was no airport in Digos. The closest airport was in Davao City, fifty miles away, and no direct flight. It was necessary for us to make a plane change in Zamboanga City, a culturally Muslim city known for its beautiful woven fabrics, tapestries, seashells and brass statuary. We decided to spend a day there on our return flight and act like tourists. I sent a telegram telling of our expected arrival date.

Chapter XVI

The overcrowded bus from Davao to Digos was not unpleasant, however passing through small towns on the two lane road at speeds that would have made it impossible to stop if a pedestrian, dog or other animal wandered across, was uncomfortable. There were no lane markings, sidewalks or stop signs. Pedestrians and animals seemed to have equal rights and access to the street and it was only survival instinct that prompted them to move . . . and the continued blare of the bus horn.

As we approached Digos, I made my way to the front of the lurching bus and showed the driver my scrap of paper with Terry's address on it. He glanced at it and turned back to his job of driving and blowing his horn. I waited a moment then decided it was too distracting for the driver and went back to my seat. I was sure there was some form of bus station and we could grab a taxi from there.

A couple turns and lurches later he stopped the bus and waited. I didn't see anything resembling a bus station and no one was moving to get off. I glanced in the rearview mirror and the driver's eyes were on me with just a hint of impatience. Two other passengers turned casually my way and I realized this must be my clue. The driver glanced at the house where he had stopped, and then back at my puzzled face in the mirror. I pointed at the house and caught the slightest flick of the driver's eyebrows. We got off with a profound thank you to the driver and he was gone without an acknowledgment. So much to learn.

As we stood suitcases in hand at the side of the road, we became aware that every window in the unpainted two-story wooden house was filled with faces that quickly turned away as we returned their gaze. We were being expected and inspected.

I glanced at Pauline and I received the distinct impression that she, along with Carla and Mike were glad to let me take the lead up to the door. It didn't take a trained eye to see that the house was seriously leaning toward the left. A glance in that direction revealed a number of timbers braced bravely against the lean. It was somewhat comforting. The door opened as we approached and a diminutive woman emerged, the look on her sunken face as one welcoming long awaited rescuers from a life of hell. She rushed out with an unconcealed cry and wrapped arms around my waist, burying her head in my stomach. Then she looked up at me with another wail, which seemed to contradict her dry eyes. Then with my arm gripped tightly, she led us into the house.

This was Nini, the woman I remembered to be much taller when I was eight-years-old, who taught me how to spot little green turtles hiding under floating leaves. This was the one whose unquestioning loyalty throughout the war years had been a strong arm for Mother. She was also the one who accompanied Father on his sometimes days long forays with the small group of guerrillas. This was now Father's widow and the

Chapter XVI

mother of the other family I didn't know existed until that letter eight years ago.

We were treated as royalty in a home that was obviously on the verge of collapse in more ways than one. Terry Jr. was away at Bible College at the time, but we met the younger sister Marylou, and the youngest brother Herbert. We learned also that in Filipino families seldom does anyone go by their given name. Terry was known as *Toto,* Marylou as *Bing* and Herbert was *Bobot.* I also learned of a younger brother who died as a baby in a tragic accident. Bing had been carrying him and as often happens when a baby is angry, he lurched backwards. Bing threw her other arm around his waist to keep him from falling and his backward momentum carried his upper body back and broke his back, severing the spinal cord. Silent tears slid down Bing's face as Nini told the story.

My questions about Aunt Patricia were answered with pleas to not get involved. The rest of our visit consisted of drawn out talks of family and happenings and introductions into cultural differences that needed to be learned sooner or later. From our jarring bus ride we were all in need of a bathroom. I quietly inquired where the bathroom was and was guided outside to a cement block enclosure about five feet high. It had three sides, the open side facing away from the house toward the neighbor's house. The cement floor had one small hole in the corner. My furtive visual search revealed nothing else, so I assumed the small hole was where I was to direct my urine. Back in the house, I discreetly told my family of my discovery. Mike, with equal discretion said, "No Dad, that's the bathroom . . . the toilet is on the other side." Words that we take for granted suddenly took on more definite meanings.

It was insisted that we take the only spring bed in the house. We were thankful to not have to sleep on the floor or on wood slats, but that evening we discovered that the spring bed did not include a mattress. One thin blanket separated our tired bodies from scraps of cardboard that covered metal springs. Carla and Mike slept better on the woven mats on the floor. The next morning we told our hostess that regrettably we needed to get back to Manila that day as there was much to do before proceeding to Panay. Much to do.

The next day we took that same bus ride back to Davao then a flight back to Zamboanga City where we spent a day looking like tourists. We bargained over the colorful Muslim weavings and clothing in the marketplace. The intricate brass statuary and castings done in their exclusive Lost Wax process, which we were told was a secret Muslim technique, intrigued us. In addition, we marveled at the variety of seashells. After a decent nights rest in a modern hotel—modern being with running water and a bare electric bulb hanging from the ceiling—we packed up our treasured purchases and headed for the airport.

During the next week in Manila we purchased language-learning tapes in *Ilongo,* the language spoken

Chapter XVI

on the island of Panay. Preparations were made for our trip down to the island we would call home for the next several years and we did some repacking. Mr. Dalisay suggested we leave our refrigerator with him. Perhaps we wouldn't need it, he said, and anyway it was much bigger than his. We politely declined

Chapter XVII
INTERISLAND TRAVEL

We boarded the *M.V. Aklan* two weeks later for our twenty-four hour trip down to Panay. Carrying mostly cargo and about 150 passengers, we classified it generally as a tramp steamer. We slept on folding cots on deck with a canvas over our heads. The cots were tight against each other and the only way to get on was to crawl from one end. Most passengers had carried their own food and water. Mr. Dalisay had not advised us of that particular survival tactic.

Pauline was still recovering from a type of flu and spent most of the trip on the cot, but Carla, Mike and I roamed the ship, enjoying the sea and fresh air. Often dolphins raced, leaped and seemed to enjoy the company of the rusted steel hull. Lifeboats were securely padlocked down as were the lockers containing the life vests. Gaping holes in the lifeboats made me wonder at the seaworthiness of the rest of the ship. It shook and vibrated, but nevertheless carried us uneventfully to our destination.

The port of New Washington, Aklan province, introduced us further into the life-style we would soon call home. Outrigger boats with single cylinder motors spitting out their unmuffled exhaust competed with colorful painted fishing boats, sails floating limp in the stillness. Along the shore, fishermen mending their nets and children playing naked in the shallow waters pulled me back into another time. Not much had changed in thirty years.

Even before we crossed the swaying wooden gangplank to the dock, we spotted Mr. Araiza waving to us. A welcome sight indeed. We were praying that the welcome here would be more encouraging than in Manila. He was short and lean, even by Filipine standards. He probably did not reach the five-foot mark but he stood straight, proud of every inch, which made him appear taller. He strode quickly to meet us as we stepped onto the deck. An eager handshake and ready smile stood in sharp contrast to our Manila meeting with Mr. Dalisay. We later learned that he had trained with New Tribes Mission and knew what to expect of Americans.

He helped us with our bags and ushered us to a waiting jeepney. "I have a nice house for you in Kalibo," he said in well-learned English. "It is big for you."

The eight miles into Kalibo, the provincial capital was all paved road and I was silently thankful for the lack of traffic. The terrain was all flat, coconut palms planted in straight lines filled our view. Bamboo houses on stilts with walls made of leaves from a type of palm pressed into place with bamboo strips lined the road.

As we neared Kalibo, Mr. Araiza tapped the driver on the arm and made a circle with his finger. The driver lifted an eyebrow and turned toward the middle of town. He was taking us on a tour of town and all we wanted to do was get "home" and rest. The town itself consisted of about four square blocks lined with stores of all types and styles. The two main cross streets in town were blocked off. It was Wednesday. Market day. Everyone who had anything to sell or barter brought it to town, laid a cloth down on the cement street, placed their wares down and waited for buyers. They strung colorful cloths of sorts overhead for shade. Many of the merchants who owned the stores along the street brought their wares out to display too. Strings and ropes stretched across the streets holding a mosaic of patterned cloth, all hung Filipino height.

    The driver circled the town then headed out on one of the main streets. He slowed and stopped at a cement block building about six blocks from town. An outside cement stairway led to the second floor and from the second floor a balcony opened up to the street. On the opposite end of the building, another stairway and another balcony. Obviously a duplex. The first floor was taken up entirely by two sagging doors that looked to be large enough for a small car. Downstairs in back, a bamboo lean-to held the washhouse complete with hand-pump. Wash water came from a shallow well, but water for the small sink in the one bathroom upstairs came from town water. The toilet was flushed with a pail of water drawn in the sink. And it had electricity. There was one bedroom large enough for a double bed . . . Filipine size, and one small bedroom with a cot size bed. The kitchen consisted of a cement counter five feet long with a sink to one end.

"What's downstairs?" I asked.

"Only upstairs is yours."

"Can we rent the downstairs also?"

Mr. Araiza seemed taken aback that we wanted more room. "Maybe," he replied, then added that he had hired a good Christian that owned a trucking company and our barrels, crates and refrigerator would be delivered in three days. Then he left, throwing in that he'd see us in church on Sunday.

Sunday morning arrived, but our cargo had not. Perhaps Monday. We dressed and with Bibles in hand, waited for Mr. Araiza to pick us up for church. He never showed and we had no idea where the church was. So in the quiet of our little home we had our own church service and gave praise to the God who knows all about it.

Monday our cargo arrived. Every bit of it. It was only a little late, delivered on an open bed truck with a name painted boldly on the side of the faded blue cab in black lettering, Ezekiel Laguna, Laguna Trucking Co.

I shook the eager hand of a smiling mister Ezekiel Laguna and listened speechless as he recalled being introduced to Christianity by his high school teacher in his hometown of Calinog in 1937. An American woman. A Mrs. Olive Alianza. Just another little tweak thrown in by God to add strength to our sometimes-wavering spirits.

As the cargo began being unloaded from the truck, it was obvious that it was very wet. Salt water. The cargo hold of the little tramp steamer that wallowed down to the province from Manila had been flooded. Our books, clothes, everything that was not sealed in metal drums was lost. Ever try to dry out a book soaked for three days in salt water? As soon as you take it out of the sunlight, the humidity of the tropics is drawn back by the salt. They had to be tossed. Now what did I say about those wavering spirits? They got flared up again, but not the kind of flare up God would be proud of.

So there we were in this strange town, the provincial capital of a province that didn't exist a few years ago, trying to learn a language from self-help tapes that our mission director suggested we use. Then part way through this huge series of self-help language tapes, we began realizing this was a language that was not used here. We tried to decide whether we should go get our money back or just pitch them. We pitched them.

We contacted a schoolteacher who was glad to spend her spare time teaching us the provincial language. Then began months of struggle learning a language not only strange to the American ear, but vastly different from the regional language which I had learned as a child.

Chapter XVIII
MALAY

Six months passed before we had the opportunity to travel into the tribal area that we would eventually call home. In the meantime, we were able to purchase an old Jeep left over from World War Two. Complete with a bullet hole in one wheel. It had been painted red, as if we needed that to announce the arrival of "white eyes", as the Ati tribal folks first called us. We christened it JJ, for junk jeep. We all agreed it was fitting. Mr. Araiza drew a rough map to the home of a believer that lived not far from the tribe. He would provide a guide for us, we were told. "The road only goes there." he said as he waved us off. "You can't miss it," I felt that same feeling in the pit of my stomach every time someone used that phrase.

    Mr. Araiza neglected to mention that there were places where the road skirted the seashore and it was impossible to pass at high tide. But then, anyone planning to travel in the area should have known that and scheduled their trip accordingly. At times bridges were out and a wait of two or more days could be counted on. Time after time we needed to stop as herds of sway-backed pigs calmly rooted out holes in the dirt roadway. We then wound up and through a pine forest that took us all by surprise. Down the other side, the road again hugged the seashore.

As we passed through one village, the road gradually narrowed into a pathway that wound between coconut trees. Pauline looked at me cautiously. "It only goes there," I repeated mockingly. "You can't miss it." I heard snickers from Carla and Mike in the back seat as I stopped and searched for reverse. As I backtracked, I noted a wide spot between two bamboo houses. A man standing casually beside one of the houses flicked an eyebrow and his eyes turned for an instant in that direction. It was the cultural equivalent of a policeman with a windmilling arm and a whistle clenched between his teeth.

With that turn the road led up through a pass away from the sea. Then as we topped a rise, to our surprise, there below us was the ocean again. We had crossed over a narrow neck of land and from there on the sea would be to our left.

We approached another village where a massive tree straddled the road. Branches spread out from a trunk that appeared to be a forest of trunks coming together into one trunk thirty feet from the forest floor. At intervals, roots dropped down from the limbs to touch the ground and grow into more trunks for support as the limbs reached farther and farther. The road wandered under one large limb with its natural supports on either side of the road. Chickens fluttered out of the way and curious eyes peered from propped open windows.

Chapter XVIII

Once again the road wound up through thick forests. The terrain changed and dark lava outcroppings stretched out, at times overhanging the road. Fallen coconut tree trunks had been used to form bridges over some of the deeper ravines. Two trunks laid side by side formed one side of the bridge, a two-foot gap between, then two trunks for the other two wheels. I stopped and measured the distance between before proceeding. Then leaning out the side so I could watch the position of the wheel, I proceeded with utmost caution. The left wheel had to be directly on the tree trunk for the right wheel to also be on the trunk on the right side. Three inches one way or the other and the wheel would be in mid air and that air extended down some thirty feet.

At a later time our hearts were tested on one such bridge. As we bounced down the hill toward the bridge I reached for the brake to stop before crossing. I had made that a habit, as coconut tree trunks were not a reliable bridge material and rotted quickly. If there were any visible sign of deterioration I would walk the bridge before venturing on it with our ancient Jeep loaded with family.

The brake pedal sank straight to the floor. I had barely enough time to pump it once—again to the floor—before we bounced wildly onto the bridge. I gripped the wheel, my eyes focused over the hood to the logs, trying to keep both hood and logs lined up. With several inches of slop in the steering wheel, it was necessary for constant twitches on the wheel in order to keep those other four wheels on top of the rounded tree trunk. Wheels don't like to stay on top of a rounded surface anyway so it was a very long forty feet of constant reactionary twitches to cross the bridge. Reactionary was the primal word as there was no time to think; no time to pray, just use what is already ingrained in the head. Moments like that when we are forced into depending on our primal reactions is when we are confronted with the solidity of who we are and what we rely on. Or not. No time to dig up the instruction manual of life or dusty sermon notes. Just do what has been implanted in memory storage.

After a thankful stop back on terra-firma to investigate the rotten, ruptured brake hose, we proceeded on through seven small villages and towns before arriving in Kalibo where there was any kind of vehicle repair available. The trip went much slower as each slow-down meant double clutching into the next lower gear and if complete stop was necessary it was simply a matter of

Chapter XVIII

turning off the key. Not the normal procedure, but it had worked.

Constant switchbacks around the lava outcroppings began taking a toll on my tired arms. We were cutting through the rugged northwest tip of the island. This was the area we later learned was called, *Palhi*, the enchanted land. It was so called for the numerous volcanic caves where clouds of bats flew at dusk and where the wind moaned through the passageways. The homes of the witches, they said. This portion of the road was not traveled at night.

Then down, through a grove of coconut trees and another town with its traditional plaza in the center and the landmark Catholic Church. Its construction of black lava blocks chipped from the cliffs, held together with mortar made of ground seashells and sand, was showing its two hundred years of age. This was Malay, our home, although our eventual home would be five miles beyond. We drove slower now, the road leading out of town and along the seashore. Pauline searched the hand-made map, trying to locate mentioned landmarks. Houses lined the seaward side of the road and rice fields the other. Ahead, a lone man strolled out from one house. He waved casually. Pauline, eyes on the map, said, "It's close now."

"There it is." I said. She looked up surprised that I would know. Then seeing the man wave, she put on her best smile, which came out with a tired twist to it.

As we pulled ourselves out of the Jeep and stretched from six hours of dirt road, he introduced himself as Mario Ocson, friend of Mr. Dalisay of Manila. His handshake was firm and smile warm. Through the cracked right lens of his glasses I could tell that he meant it.

"Come," he said. "The food is ready." He led us into his house where introductions to his wife and children were passed around, then on out the back door. The soft sound of the surf was almost lost in the murmur and quiet laughter of two dozen voices. A banquet had been prepared in our honor. I never knew, nor did I ask how they all knew when we were coming.

Two wooden tables along with two sawhorse type platforms with rough wood planks stretched across them caught our eye. Banana leaves served as tablecloths. Such were the banquet tables, but who could tell with the mountains of food spread across them: meats and fish of infinite variety, and center stage, a *lechon,* roasted pig, reclined. The top of its head had been hacked open and the back neatly sliced into bite-sized morsels. No apple in the mouth. And of course mounds of steaming rice.

Our first real Philippine banquet since our arrival. As guests of honor, plates were pushed into our hands and we were escorted to the tables.

Oh good, first in line. Along with lessons we had already learned, I fitfully searched my memory for identification labels for much of what lay before us. Pauline was pushed to the front and I followed, then Carla and Mike. Mike's eyes were taking it all in, urged by an empty stomach. Carla glanced apprehensively at the feast then at me. Through my plastered on smile I urged them to follow my lead. I leaned down pushing closely into Pauline so I could whisper directions if need be.

"I don't recognize anything except the pig." she said quietly but with enough animation and smile to appear as a compliment.

"Goat," I stabbed a chunk of dark fried meat. "It's good." She followed suit, carefully choosing a smaller piece. She shuffled down the table, stopping in front of a platter brimming with large, flat, noodle-like pieces floating in a thick black secretion. "Oh yummy," I whispered. "*dinago-ong,* pig intestines boiled in blood." As discreetly as possible she passed on to the next. I followed suit. Glancing back, I saw Carla's plate still empty except for a healthy pile of rice. Mike forked a second piece of goat, a bite-size chunk already missing on the first piece.

"Here, Carla," I reached across to a plate in back. "Fried chicken . . . honest." She gave me a, "Yeah, right!" kind of look and held her plate out.

"*Bago-ong,*" I whispered to Pauline as she hovered in front of a plate of what appeared to be purple oatmeal. "Rotten, salted fish. It tastes like it smells." I explained. Raw, sardine-size fish were packed in salt and left to ripen in the sun. She bent low until a whiff reached her nose, then with a visible quiver, she moved on.

"Try that one." I pointed to small chunks of fried, white meat. She hesitated. "Just try it. It's good." It really was, and I'd explain later about iguana.

As we both reached for slices of the main entree, Pauline leaned toward me, "Do they really eat that?" Her finger lifted slightly off the plate she carried and pointed toward the pig's head laying open.

"Brains are a delicacy," I said, "but I wouldn't. They don't look very done." I doubted if she would have anyway.

Chicken and pork *adobo* were a familiar and welcome dish. Tasting much like sweet-and-sour pork with a salty overtone, we piled it on.

Shrimp the size of small lobsters didn't need any explanation. Neither did the slices of pineapple, papaya and steamed rice cakes, which we had learned to love in Kalibo. There in the provincial capital vendors walked the streets early each morning, their cries ringing through the yet quiet streets, "*Putoh! Putoh!*" Baskets filled with the muffin-sized sweet rice cakes wrapped in banana leaves. Another vendor favorite was *shiopao,* steamed rice wrapped around sweetened, shredded meat of sorts. In some regions of the country the meat was cat, in others dog.

Conspicuously missing were vegetables, as were, thankfully, the country delicacy of *balut,* boiled duck eggs. Taken one week before hatching, the fertilized eggs when boiled were soft enough to bite through, bones, feathers and all. On occasion the beak proved a bit much though.

We sat on wooden benches under the coconut trees, plates balanced on our knees and thoughts of

Sunday dinners back home in Kansas City. We chewed carefully.

After dinner our tiredness showed, conversations lagged and we were soon shown to our room. The thin, cotton like mattress on the bamboo bed did little to ease our tired bodies, but the sound of the gentle surf helped and sleep did come.

***

Morning we awoke to the aroma of fried eggs, *chorizos*, a spicy local sausage, and fried rice. After breakfast, Mario insisted that his son, Bobot, would accompany us to visit the Ati tribal village. We decided to walk as it was only a mile or so up the road then half mile inland. We were anxious to get a glimpse of these first inhabitants of the Philippines, the people we were to spend a few years with.

It had not been easy getting accurate information about the people. Myth and truth intermingle. These were the first inhabitants of Panay who, legend has it, came over from Borneo. When the lighter skinned people, mostly of a Polynesian race came, they bargained with the Ati and bought the island for a golden hat and a basket of trinkets. The bargain was that the Ati would have the mountains and the Polynesians, later known as Visayans, would occupy the lowlands. As the Visayans multiplied, the Ati were pushed further back until they now lived on only the land the Visayans didn't want and worked for the Visayans for their food. Other than that, fishing and hunting provided them with their food. Their story reminded me much of the original inhabitants of America.

The path led inland, skirting the bank of a small river, around the side of a hill, then ups the hill to end at the village of Cogon. The small village consisted of seven houses scattered under some large trees on a flat area. In the center cleared area grew a large mango tree, its bare roots spreading wide. The village was empty. Smoke still curled up from the remains of a fire in the center of the clearing.

Then I spotted a lone occupant, naked but for a ragged pair of shorts, his dark body blended well with the tree root that he squatted on. He looked to be middle aged, black, curly hair and black eyes that seemed to be unfocused. He did not acknowledge our presence but continued stroking the flat stone in front of him with the gleaming blade of his machete. From time to time he splashed water on the stone from a half coconut shell by his side.

Chapter XVIII

Bobot said he was drunk on *tuba*, that slightly intoxicating drink made from coconut sap and lime. Bobot translated a continual somewhat annoying running account. "His name is Rostico. He comes from the other side of the island but has lived here for many years now." Apparently the others had hidden when they heard of our approach. Few had ever seen white people before, but Rostico considered himself well traveled and was not afraid. Perhaps his state of intoxication helped give him courage.

Other than that, the most we could get out of the lone occupant was a wave of the hand toward the brush when asked where everyone was. We left him to his task and peered around the village. He rose unsteadily to his feet at one point in our wandering and peering around the village, but slid down to perch rather precariously on the root again, either deciding not to do whatever it was, or in his state, forgetting what he started up to do.

Before hand I had cautioned Pauline not to display any negative feelings, but she wasn't very good at that game and the shock of the poverty and filth tore at her. Cautiously she approached one house. "Oh I, it's worse than I had imagined." Placing fingertips timidly on a windowsill layered with grime to steady herself, she leaned in. "Look at the roof, how can they stay dry when it rains?"

I shook my head in dismay. In a corner of the lone room a black cooking pot balanced atop three stones imbedded in a clay platform built up on the bamboo floor.

Underneath the floor was tied the family pig. He looked up through the bamboo slats and grunted in anticipation of some morsel being dropped through. Three rolled up sleeping mats leaned against one wall. Higher up the wall several rolls of clothing were stuffed behind bamboo wall supports. Above that yet, in the corner, a basket woven of coconut leaves was secured. Over the edge, one baleful orange eye glared suspiciously at us. A mother hen sat her eggs.

    I glanced back at the loner sitting listlessly on the roots. He had turned slightly to keep us in view but his eyes seemed unfocused and betrayed nothing. I wondered how drunk he really was. He splashed more water on the stone and took two careful passes across it with the steel, then thumbed the keen edge carefully before sliding it back into its scabbard. He rose mechanically from the tree root. His fingers fumbled with the string on his scabbard before successfully slipping the knotted end around his waist and through the looped other end. He angled toward us, a curious eye glancing at Carla and Mike. Carla edged closer to me and Mike stabbed at the ground with a stick he had picked up along the way.

    "*Imong unga?*" Rostico asked.

    "*Ngani,*" I answered in the affirmative, they were my children.

    He responded with a grunt, which I took to mean that he approved. He went on to explain more about his people, although I missed most of it. Bobot translated that Rostico was not from this place but from the other side of the island, in fact he had been all over the island and he was switching from one local dialect to another. This seemed to be a form of telling us that he was a well-traveled man. I noted that he had sobered up quickly.

On our hike back to Mario's, I mentioned that we wanted to build our house somewhere near the village and Bobot pointed out a piece of land on the side of the gentle hill. It belonged to his uncle, he said, and maybe it could be bought. It contained one and a half acres that stretched from the flat rice fields up the hill and a large flat section above ideal for a garden. At the top of the hill stood two large mango trees and a small stand of bamboo. I asked him to look into the purchase of the land.

That afternoon Mario took us to town where he introduced us to the mayor and other dignitaries which was proper etiquette. The next day we returned to Kalibo, encouraged to continue our language study and with the assurance that the land we looked at could be bought.

Chapter XIX
RETURN TO HOPEVALE

"I'd like to visit Hopevale," I said one evening as we leaned back for a well-earned rest.

"Weren't we told that area is communist controlled now?"

"NPA are strong there, but I still want to try at least."

"The who?"

"NPA. It stands for New People's Army. That's what the militant ones like to be called. They don't want to be known as communists and be labeled as anti-American, just anti-Marcos."

That started the wheels rolling and plans unfolding. I didn't know exactly how to get there but thought we could find someone that would know in Calinog where I lived as a child.

"I don't think we should take the children," Pauline advised.

"Too dangerous," I finished her thought.

A week later we had made all arrangements. Our language teacher, who had become a trusted friend, gladly agreed to stay with the children while we were gone. We loaded hiking clothes, water and some sandwiches in J J, as we had fondly christened our junk jeep, and headed for Calinog. The road was mostly mountainous, paved, but filled with potholes that could swallow a vehicle like ours. Each turn was a caution as there were no road markings, warning signs or speed limits. Large trucks and buses took their share of the road out of the middle and little else was left.

Three hours later we arrived in Calinog. I drove slowly through the town, trying vainly to pull landmarks from my memory. The one place I did know lay through town and across the bridge. It was on the right. Thirty years had not dimmed that memory. The new bridge was cement but I doubted if the road had been paved since 1941 when we left. There was no house on the property but there was a lone orange tree, planted by Mother from a seed brought from Pasadena, California in 1937. I walked the land, noting that the large hill where a kite once flew now seemed much smaller and the spring where turtles hid and where we took our baths was littered with debris.

Back across the bridge, I located the town police station. A few questions led us to the chief's office where, feet on desk, he advised us not to go to Hopevale. After explaining who I was, he relented, warning us that he would not be responsible.

"After kilometer marker 72," he said, "there will be a road on the right. That will take you to Katipunan. From there maybe someone will guide you. Please do not stay after dark," he warned. We thanked him and assured him we would take the utmost precaution.

We backtracked down the same road keeping aware of the kilometer markers. Not all the markers were in place or underbrush had claimed them back so we drove slowly. "There!" Pauline said and pointed to the marker with 71 painted on it. When I thought one kilometer had passed, I turned out into a wide spot that had been cleared. It looked to be regularly used, like a bus stop. No road though, only a trail through the brush. I swung back to the road and drove on.

Soon appeared another kilometer marker, 73. "That had to be it back there, Hon." I swung back to the clearing and the trail, parked the Jeep and prayed it would still be there when we got back.

The trail took us through brush and tree covered hills for about three miles. The hills got higher and the trees denser as we walked, then underneath the trees, in a small valley, were a dozen houses.

We were greeted rather coolly, until we explained who we were and where we wanted to go. The one who seemed to be in charge motioned us into a small bamboo house that had one wooden bench. He closed the door behind him and we waited about an hour and a half.

In our short time in the country we had discovered that Philippine clocks all run about one and a half hours slow. If you plan a meeting for 9, expect it to start at 11. If you understand their time system you might try announcing the meeting for 7, then you can start at 9 . . . that is, unless they discover what you're doing. Then they will drift in at noon because they know you really want

Chapter XIX

the meeting to start at 9 and you know they won't be coming in until 11. So they think that's actually when you expect the meeting to start, so noon is a good time, but then that's lunch time and you should be considerate enough to have lunch for them, and then, of course it's siesta time. It's an all day affair. A wonderful challenge.

An hour and a half later a man walked in, about my age, wearing ragged shorts, a wide brimmed woven hat and a machete. Barefoot, of course, and the first thing I noticed was half his right foot was missing—only a big toe and diagonally cut to middle of the foot. As if a machete chop had glanced off target. My first thought, *A cripple is going to lead us?* He did not introduce himself, but as I told him where we wanted to go, he turned and walked out. We followed. We couldn't keep up with him.

We walked three or four miles, climbing into the foothills, passed small rice terraces, banana groves, into the forest. The trail finally topped a wooded hill. From there I could see two small houses on a facing hill. Our guide took off his large hat and waved it over his head twice. A signal. I didn't know whether to feel good because he signaled, or worse because he needed to signal. He then led the way down the hill into the valley called Hopevale.

Brush and trees all but hid the winding trail. At the bottom of the hill he stopped, slid his machete from its wooden scabbard and began cutting a trail to the right and up a rise toward a large banyan tree. From there we descended into the Grotto where the missionaries had worshipped thirty years ago.

Layers of decaying leaves covered the area, but still visible was the semi-circle of smooth rocks on a built up terrace facing the pulpit to our left. A pile of rocks was all that was left of the pulpit. The Grotto had been lovingly cleared and formed by one of the elder missionaries when they had first arrived. Behind the pulpit rose the majestic banyan tree, its branches covering and completely hiding their chapel in the Grotto. Only at midday could a few stray beams of light penetrate. To the right a vertical cliff covered with vines and small brush rose out of sight, its top hidden by overhanging tree branches. To the left, a cliff also, but not as steep, covered with underbrush and trees then down the other side to a small stream where two little boys used to play.

Doug Rounds was eight, I was seven and there we had splashed and played. There he taught me how to catch crawdads and splash away thoughts of war.

Here in the Grotto they had all worshipped the Lord until the day they met Him face to face.

Our guide approached, interrupting my thoughts. In his right hand, his unsheathed machete, in his left, a staff he had just cut from the cliff. He had trimmed the branches and leaves and cut it to a little over six feet. Straight, with one end curved into a hook, it looked like a shepherd's staff.

His eyes had softened with a look I had not recognized before. "Give this to your mother," he said.

Chapter XIX

Then he told me who he was. His family name was Gayas, the name mentioned by Mother as someone we owed our lives to. Thirty years ago he was seven, he said, and at times he was sent by his father with sacks of food up to a spot beyond this valley to where we had lived in hiding. The Japanese patrols had never bothered to question a seven-year-old where he was going or what he was carrying.

Mother had wanted to live with the missionaries in Hopevale, but Father said, "No, too many Americans in one place." So we had gone farther up the valley about a mile and built a small house. It was from there that on my eighth birthday, December 19, 1943, we watched smoke rise from their burning houses.

My newfound friend then guided us out of the Grotto, across the small stream and up a high hill. At the crown of the hill stood a large memorial: a concrete cross ten feet high with a plaque at its base. On the bronze plaque, the names of those killed on that spot. Doug's name was there.

As we stood in the shadow of the cross, he told me his version of the story. All the Americans that were captured were led to the summit where we stood. From there, anyone in hiding could observe what happens to those who do not surrender.

Mr. Covell, who had previously been a missionary in Japan and spoke fluent Japanese, stepped forward. He pleaded eloquently for their lives. The soldiers were affected by the pleas but told him orders had to be carried out. The missionaries then asked for a time for prayer and were given about an hour. At the end they came forward. "We are ready," they said.

They were executed: beheaded with the traditional Japanese two-handed sword. The three children, Doug Rounds and two boys, sons of one of the miners, were not counted worthy of the executioner's sword and were instead bayoneted in the back. Identification was later difficult until witnesses hiding in the brush and forest were able to locate their heads, which had been rolled down the hill into a gully. Only a few of the miners who had built their houses several hundred yards away had escaped.

We left Hopevale with another link to the past secured, and a staff that would forever remind us of a shepherd and his flock.

***

The next six months were crowded with language study, home schooling for the kids and many trips to Malay for land purchase and home building. Mario found three lots for sale. One by the sea, one by the road and the third was his cousin's near the Ati.

We searched our hearts and minds for the right choice. By the sea was certainly the first choice. By the road was most convenient and near the Ati, the best for building relationships. By the sea was healthiest, the road dustiest and by the Ati most prone to disease. The decision came hard but we knew we were not here for the beauty or for the convenience.

Mario wanted us to build a large wood and concrete house but I felt a house made of the local materials would better suit our purpose. Soon bamboo and nipa, the leaves of a particular palm that were waxy and did not shrivel with age, began to be gathered. These would be woven and used for siding and roofing. Cement for the post footings and the posts themselves along with most lumber were purchased in Kalibo and trucked in. Most of the labor was done by Ati men who slowly became accustomed to the white people. We learned later that they began trusting us quickly because we brought our children with us. No one who meant harm would do that.

I designed two bathrooms and in the process of digging the septic tank, one man asked me cautiously what the hole was for. I pointed out the toilets, the large black pipe leading to the hole and explained that the waste would travel into the hole, which would be covered with a concrete lid. He nodded in understanding then asked, "But why do you want to save all that?" My lesson in hygiene was wasted and might as well be flushed also.

In typical style, the house was elevated for cooling air circulation and the bamboo strip floor allowed further circulation through the floor. It also allowed free access to bugs and any form that could squeeze their bodies through one-half inch cracks.

The house also had three bedrooms, kitchen and a large *sala,* or living room, knowing that we'd most likely be having many guests.

Digging the well caused some anxieties and explanations. While one man was at the bottom digging, filling a bucket on a long rope with the dirt to be hauled out, the ground began shaking. He covered his head as rocks and gravel shaken loose from the sides tumbled in on him. He was not injured, but my heart did a double thump as I imagined the consequences of a more severe earthquake collapsing the hole and burying him thirty feet down.

I had chosen the dry season to dig the well and when we were three feet below the water level I decided that was deep enough. It was then I realized I had no sealer for the sections of pipe that were to go down the well. I did have a small can of enamel paint. That would make a passable substitute so I opened it and painted the threads before screwing the sections together. I didn't know until the next day when no workers showed up that I needed to do a bit of explaining. One of their superstitions was that in order to have a successful water supply, a child must be sacrificed and the blood thrown in the new well. Unfortunately the paint I had chosen was bright red.

Even the location of the house caused hesitation in some. Beside the location for the house stood a large termite mound and in their local beliefs, that was the home of evil spirits. Eventually that turned to our benefit as they observed that we were not afraid of those spirits.

In March of 1973 our house was completed and we made the final move. Each trip to Malay we had brought a little more with us, so the final move was not as strenuous. We were able to trade our refrigerator for one powered by kerosene. After all, what good was it where there was no electricity?

Our House

Chapter XX
HOUSE MOVING

Six months passed and we were deeply entrenched in cultural living along with its struggles, challenges, and victories, which too often come to us in the forms of struggles and challenges. Every morning.

One such morning I reluctantly opened my eyes as early morning breezes riffled the torn plastic over the hole in the roof we called our skylight. Everything decays fast in the tropics. Maybe that was what woke me. Or maybe it was the hushed voices drifting up from the front of the house. People were arriving for clinic as they did every day. Pauline lay beside me in deep sleep. I turned slowly toward the edge of the bed, trying not to disturb her. My legs protested; an uncountable number of twisted, aching muscles reminding me which day this was.

It was the day after an eleven-hour hike through virgin forests and mountain land to survey a possible resettlement site for the Ati, the tribal folks that we came to live with. Some of them were at this moment seating themselves quietly on the living room floor to wait for "Mom" to wake up and with loving care, tend to their numerous diseases and ailments. She was "Mom" to them because that's what our kids called her and so it must be right. Of course then that made me "Dad." I pulled my legs over the edge of the bed and sat for a moment rubbing sore muscles and letting my mind wander back.

"Why don't we make it a family affair?" Pauline had asked two days ago. "I want to be sure the Ati don't get cheated. Besides," she hurried on, "you've told us what a great view it is from up on the mountain, and I need to see something great."

"Yeah, Dad, let's do it," came from Mike with the uncheckable enthusiasm of a nine-year-old. Carla wasn't as eager, but also needed a break in the routine. Her help in the medical part of the work was immeasurable. She often stepped far beyond anything that could be expected of a thirteen-year-old.

I couldn't deny that, and even though I knew it would be hard for Pauline and the kids, I wanted them to see it too. From the top of the mountain five other islands could be seen. From the sparkling white sands of Boracay, the nearest island just off the coast, to the blue-gray mountains of Mindoro on the northern horizon. To the east stretched the three Romblon Islands. They were only five of the over 7,000 islands that comprised the scattered island nation called Philippines. From a distance they were as a handful of multi-faceted turquoise flung casually across an azure South China Sea. It was often necessary to distance ourselves to see the sparkle of the gems. Up close the sparkle too often twisted into the glint of a machete, or a tear coursing down the dark cheek of a young mother for her child, now hidden forever under a row of shiny nails in a small coffin, or a well worn shovel digging yet another grave.

That next morning, the four of us set out, accompanied by six of the tribal leaders. As expected, the going was much slower than when I had gone alone with the men. When alone with "Dad" on the trail, they would often pour on the steam to test the old man, the "Cano," as all Americans—in fact anyone light skinned—was called. I took it in stride, trying not to let the pain of stretched muscles show. I had to prove myself. My big four-o birthday was galloping up on me and if that wasn't enough, how could I relate to the people if I couldn't even keep up with them?

On my last hike to the land we had taken the ridgeline up to the peak, the proposed boundary of the resettlement land, and then returned. Pauline however, wanted to plant her feet on the actual land where the people would settle. For that we needed to angle down from the ridge, cross a deep gorge where springs flowed year around to reach the relatively level plateau. They had selected that spot because of the water. It was a good choice, but until a trail was established we had to hack through virgin forests on a slope too steep to stand on until we could find a place to cross the gorge.

Two men went ahead cutting away clinging vines and underbrush, sometimes digging out footholds with the tips of their machetes. I followed then Pauline and Carla. Mike scurried back and forth proving his young muscles to whoever could be impressed, yelling back all too quick positive replies whenever asked to be careful. I wasn't much worried about him. Seldom have I seen monkeys or cats fall.

We were traversing a difficult section where rocks kicked loose rolled twenty feet down the slope before free falling to the gorge below. I heard a yell behind me and turned to see Carla sliding feet first toward the gorge. Her foothold had crumbled. I leaped toward her, trying desperately to reach her and grab brush or anything that would hold. I was sliding, scrambling to intercept her course. She had turned on her stomach, hands wildly grasping but everything was sliding. I lunged.

"Papa!" she cried as I clamped her wrist. We slid together. Our slide carried us down the slope past a small tree. I reached and wound one arm around the tree. It held. Rocks and dirt tumbled past to scatter into the gorge below as I pulled Carla up to me. She gripped my shirt and buried her face in my chest.

"I've told you before about trying to take shortcuts," I mumbled into her dust laden brown hair, the feel of it against my lips, gritty, sweet.

She tightened her grip. "I didn't mean to, Papa." Then she looked up and a grin that matched mine smoothed her face and caught the tear that slid down.

More rocks rolled past as Nilo and another Ati man scrambled down. Strong hands reached for her and pulled her up. "Thanks," I muttered and clawed my way up behind them. Until we reached safe ground again, Carla's feet barely touched the earth as the two men, one in front and the other behind, never released their grip on her hands.

On reaching the land, the tribal men with us all agreed it was adequate for them. Without much effort, the small stream could be diverted for irrigation and they talked on about the many possibilities. We then decided to return by a different route. Easier, they said. It led straight down the mountain to the river, then across to home.

Evening began settling as we descended the last foothill above the river. I turned as I heard a call from behind. Mike sat on the side of the hill, arms locked around his knees, head down. As I approached he looked up and I could see he was crying. "My legs hurt, Dad." I sat beside him and we rested. I didn't think it necessary to remind him of the energy he wasted earlier.

It was well after dark when we finally crossed the river and the last rice paddy dike to home. After quick showers and muscle relaxants, we rolled into bed, hoping there would be no emergencies that night. There weren't and we slept.

A quiet whisper at the bedroom door pulled me back to the present, "Papa?"

I stood, tested my legs and walked quietly to the bedroom door and opened it, a finger to my lips. Carla turned and walked down the four steps to the living room before another word was spoken, and then only in hushed tones.

"Nilo and Mercedes are having a *bayanihan* and remembered that you had said you wanted to take pictures next time someone moved their house, so . . ."

"Where are they moving to?" I asked quickly, hoping they were not moving far.

"They're coming down stream to be nearer, Papa. They'll be right here in Cogon."

I turned back to the bedroom and wakened Pauline just enough to tell her our plans and grab my camera. As I closed the bedroom door behind me, Mike was already at the foot of the steps slipping into his rubber sandals. Never go barefoot in the tropics, we had been told. We were by no means ignorant of the list of diseases that could be picked up through bare feet, but couldn't help wondering what good the flip-flop slippers did when we were usually up beyond our ankles in either mud or dust. But rules were rules and, as so many rules are, it's often easier to just follow than to analyze them and modify to fit particular situations.

"How you feeling, Mike?" I noted that some of the enthusiasm of the day before was gone. Carla sported a few abrasions, but was none the worse.

Fifteen minutes later we approached the little bamboo house upstream, obscured by trees and brush. "We'll pass that way," Nilo said quietly in his dialect, pointing his chin up the slight hill behind the house.

I turned facing down stream and the rice field beyond. As had become custom, I paused to mentally phrase my reply before opening my mouth and risk offending or be culturally misunderstood and provoking a reply equivalent to, "If you say so." Pointing my lower lip toward the rice field and the obviously easier route, I answered in the dialect, "It might be very difficult going that way." I tried to make my reply even toned and free from judgment or implication.

Nilo's answer was what I wanted to hear, not the content, but the fact that I was trusted enough to be given a little more insight into the local culture. His reply, however, troubled me. "The owner of that field killed himself," he said carefully. "His spirit is still wandering the field and will not allow."

I nodded and turned back to watch the men as they continued digging out the posts of the house. However, his statements recorded on my brain. Nilo was one of the strongest professing believers in the tribe, yet his everyday actions were still based, even though unconsciously, on the existence and control of the spirit world.

"Ta?" It came from one of the workers, a single syllable with a multitude of meanings depending on the context. In other situations it could mean, "I got it," "Let's go," "It's your turn," "I finished my work," or "Let's eat, I'm hungry and if you don't join me that's your problem." But there and then it meant, "Let's get underneath this house and see if we can't lift this baby." Without another syllable, twelve men rolled their shoulders under the bamboo poles previously tied under the raised house and with the command, *"Isa, daiwa, hay*

tatlo-o-o," a few grunts were heard, dark shoulders strained and the ten by fifteen foot house lifted. Again the command, *"Ta."* And they lowered it, the poles settling back into their holes. Shoulders readjusted under the load and again the count, *"Isa, daiwa, tatlo-o-o,"* and the house lifted, turned and started up the cleared way over the hill.

My camera shutter snapped several times as I moved up behind the house, watching the small, quick, tight steps as the bare feet struggled up the hill. The unsure burden swayed as each man stepped over, around, and sometimes stumbled on the rocks and pointed stubs of chopped off vegetation on the side of the hill.

Then it happened. One man stumbled and went down. The house tipped and dropped, settling on the exposed back of the one who stumbled. A cry of pain went up accompanied by confused commands. I dropped

Chapter XX

my camera and let it swing on its strap. Quickly I slipped beside the man under the load. I curled both arms under the pole, now no more than knee high, and lifted. It was enough and the man rolled out from under. He stood, and with an embarrassed smile, set his shoulder again to the task. I knew that questioning him would only add to the embarrassment, so I relayed the load back to him, the house lifted and all was well again—except for my back.

A pain, sharp and icy, pulled the breath from my lungs. It was all I could do to move my legs, but move I did, and carefully followed the progress of the house over the hill, down the valley and into the village where the posts were lowered into the pre-dug holes. Then with a tight, locked grin, I turned toward home with Carla and Mike running on ahead, aware only of a successful house moving. I willed my legs down the five hundred yards of trail to the house. I felt sure that a splinter of bone was somewhere in my back gouging enormous strips from nerves that I surely would need again. Up the two steps into the living room, across the living room to the four steps leading up to the bedroom where I sank to my knees by the bed. Not to pray, I had been doing that for some time by then, but because it was all I could do. Then the pain began. Pain like I had never felt before.

I had seen pain of many types and intensities in the past several years in others and felt a bit myself. I had watched a man bite quietly on his shirtsleeves as Pauline cleaned out a tropical ulcer, the white bone a stark contrast to the black of rotted tissue. Another man had walked in smiling and asked for an aspirin, his right hand bound with a dirty rag. I asked what happened. He said his water buffalo bolted, the rope tangled around his index finger. It was missing. I had seen pain of a different kind as a young mother watched nails being driven into a tiny coffin.

    Suddenly it was different. It was me. I was supposed to be the strong one. The one everyone leaned on when the air twisted and grew dark. True, there were times when Pauline disagreed, growled and mentally shook a fist in my face, but I had my role, and now I couldn't play it. This was a new game and I didn't like it. I didn't even know the rules.

    Through the pain I felt a gentle hand on my shoulder, then Pauline's worried face down beside mine as I tried to explain through clenched teeth what had happened. I reasoned that the hard bamboo bed in the spare bedroom might be better. She agreed, but even with that and the strongest painkillers she had, the pain didn't subside. It came in waves, exploding in my lower back and slamming the air from my lungs in bursts that I couldn't control. I cried out.

    She was beside me again. How much time had passed, I didn't know. Time had no meaning. "Here, this should help." I opened my eyes as she swabbed a spot on my arm and pushed the tip of the syringe into the small vial.

    "What is it?"

Chapter XX

"It's from Doctor Prado. Mike bicycled to town and picked it up."

I closed my eyes again as the painkiller began its sweet job. I could feel it course through my veins, cooling as it passed. It settled on the hot coal that sizzled somewhere in my lower back. It cooled, softened, and sent the message back to knotted muscles that they could relax. For the first time I felt the fatigue of muscles and tendons pulled tight for too long, trying to compensate for something gone really wrong.

Pauline still sat beside me. Her soft touch up and down my arm told me so. "The Ati say there's a telegraph relay station in the mountains that could relay a telegram for us."

Her words seemed to come through a long tunnel and I nodded. "They are saying it's an eight hour hike up there but several men have volunteered to go." I was still nodding. "I'm going to send a telegram to S.I.L. and to the embassy." Nod.

I had taken my linguistic training with the Summer Institute of Linguistics and flown in their small planes to several almost inaccessible landing strips. I knew they could easily land on the grass strip a few miles down the coast and I knew they would do all they could.

The message was sent with two men along with twice the money to cover any irregularity in service that the men manning the station might possibly conceive of. American with a dislocated back, sounded like an adequate emergency situation to Pauline. I nodded again.

It seemed only minutes later that I awoke, sweat rolling off me soaking the thin *kapok* mattress between me and the bamboo slats of the bed. The hot coal was back and I must have cried out, as the door opened and Pauline stepped quickly in.

"Mike went back to get some more injectable pain killer. The doctor can't give out more than one vial at a time . . . some stupid law," she added.

It was three miles to town and three back, on a gravel road, in the steaming oppression of a tropical summer. Mike had never seen his father in such pain before, let alone to cry out. If I had a choice, I never would have let him exert himself like that. But at the time I was aware only of the pain. Before the day ended Mike raced into town three times on his bicycle.

The clinic, however, had to go on and patients arrived with complaints, small or large to be treated. But many came to just sit on the living room floor or on the porch only to say that they were there for "Dad." To do whatever he needed. Word spread that eggs were good for healing broken bones. They came with eggs. Dozens of them. Pauline thanked them profusely for the precious gifts, for precious they were. The Ati seldom ate eggs. Better, they said, to let them hatch and increase the flock.

The second day started with little promise of improvement. I found that by pulling my legs up into a near fetal position, with legs at the edge of the bed, I could lock my back and legs in that position and by using only my arms, pull myself into a sitting position. That only lasted for a few moments before the pain became too great. It was during one of those times when I was working up the courage to sit up that I heard a vehicle approach. The murmur of voices at the door was not intelligible and I decided this was not the time to put myself through the pain of trying to sit up for a few brief moments. My eyes were clamped shut as if trying to shut out the pain when I heard soft footsteps on the stairs. I opened them as Pauline stepped through the door and closed it behind her.

"Honey, you have a visitor." She paused for a reply then went on. "It's a Raphael Ong."

"Oh? Maybe I'll just come down and visit a while—"

"No you don't!" she said, quickly stepping up to the bed with a gentle but firm hand on my shoulder. "If he wants to see you he can come up here."

I knew it was useless to argue with her when that tone of voice hung in the air, but I did anyway. "It's not culturally correct to have visitors in the bedroom ... not even in our culture—" I added before a spasm of pain cut me off.

"Sure you're going to get up .. Just as soon as it snows. You're going to wait right there," she pushed a finger against my shoulder, " and I'll send him up." With that she turned and was out the door.

I closed my eyes and tried to gather thoughts, took a deep breath but it was cut off. Somehow deep breaths were linked with the lower back.

I had met Raphael Ong only once that I could remember. We had exchanged waves once or twice as we passed on the road, but I knew Raphael—Paing as he was known to his friends, more by reputation. I would have preferred to keep our relationship friendly but somewhat distant.

Raphael was the youngest son of the man who, in spite of numerous taunts and against the better advice of the elders of a generation earlier, settled and claimed the rocky, mountainous northern peninsula of the island a generation ago. Nothing would grow there but coconuts, they said. At that time coconuts were not thought of by the general populace as a harvest crop. They were worthless except for a cool drink on a hot day and food for the sway-backed domesticated hogs. But Tatay Ong was one who saw past today and its local needs.

He had worked with the volcanic soil and found it rich. He tested various vegetables and found them to thrive. Bananas, however, were the main crop which he traded for much needed rice that would not grow well among the rocks and mountains. Then as the country struggled to its feet after the war, and the international market began opening, coconut oil became a sought after commodity for shampoo and soaps as well as a lubricant and the base for many processed foods. The coconut brought Tatay Ong wealth and power. Wealth from the forests of coconuts that thrived on the wild, rocky, volcanic peninsula and power from the many he employed to harvest his crop. They were loyal to the man with wisdom and foresight and in time an entire village grew on the rocky, almost inaccessible upper regions of the peninsula.

All his children eventually left the nest to produce successes of their own, but Raphael the youngest, the favored, remained to inherit *Palhi,* the enchanted place, the place where the spirits dwell. With *Palhi,* he also inherited the power because the wisdom and foresight of his father had fallen on him. He gave loyalty for loyalty and often fought for the rights of the people. And in the days when every man who had anything worth fighting for carried a gun, his gun spoke often. It was said that those who crossed him never did it more than twice.

It was only natural then, that when the oppression of the Ferdinand Marcos regime became heavy, Raphael stood against it and all it represented. Others who sought power but in a much broader arena, looked up the man who held the local power that they might have in him an ally.

Footsteps stopped at the bedroom door. Opening my eyes, I looked into the face of one that was open and friendly, reflecting its Chinese ancestry, not only in feature, but in a quiet confidence that whispered of something more than appeared. Raphael Ong was the undisputed local leader of the New People's Army, known as the NPA, the militant arm of the country's Communist party.

"My fishermen had a good catch so I brought some for my friend." His voice was quiet, deep and with warmth that caught me by surprise.

"Thank you, Raphael—"

"My friends call me Paing," said the young Communist leader.

"Thank you very much ... Paing." Feeling uncomfortable on my back in front of company, I tried to lift up on my elbows and was thrown down by a spasm that choked off my breath.

The young leader shifted his eyes away quickly and turned to Pauline standing behind him in the doorway.

"He must be taken to Manila quickly, Mrs."

"He can't be moved yet, Mr.—"

"Paing." He cut in. "Excuse me, but call me Paing, please. I must go now and he must rest. I will come back tomorrow, Mrs.—"

"Pauline . . . please call me Pauline." She stretched out a welcome hand to a man she had just met and knew nothing about.

Chapter XXI
PARALYSIS

Carla walked out of the spare bedroom where I lay twisted in pain. Swiftly she descended the stairs to where Pauline talked quietly with an obviously ill woman.

"Mother, I think Papa needs more pain medicine. He's really hurting, Mama." She spoke low and in English to keep from alarming any of the patients and a half smile played on her face. She had learned through observation more than teaching that here in this world facial expressions were read more than words, but her eyes reflected her Papa's pain.

"Pasentia, Nay." Pauline excused herself. *"Pero may pasiente pa ako sa ibabao,"* and tilting her head toward the bedroom explained that she had another patient above.

"See if you can find Mike, sweetheart, and have him get another vial from doctor Prado." With that she turned toward the stairs leading to the bedrooms. Pulling on the rail for support, she climbed the stairs, into the main bedroom and the bath. There she scrubbed her hands thoroughly before splashing water on her face, forehead and running a hand across the back of her neck. She straightened, rolling her head back to loosen cramped muscles.

It was barely after noon and the constant stream of patients and others just coming to see if they could help "Dad" was taking its toll on her strength. How far away was help, and where in the world were those men who so quickly volunteered to send the telegram? Under her breath she cursed the lackadaisical, fatalistic air of the people. *Bahala sa Dios . . . Bahala sa Dios.* She had heard it so many times it was all she could do to keep from grabbing someone by the neck and screaming, "It's not up to God! He gave you a brain and strong hands, now get out there and do something about your situation." But she didn't . . . At least she hadn't up to now.

She heard someone behind her. It was Carla. Her voice too, was heavy with fatigue and strangely apologetic. "Mama, Mike's not feeling well and laying down. Maybe I'll just go into town for the—"

Pauline's voice spilled out, "I've been up all night and I need you to help with the patients down there and I've got a husband in the other room that I don't know will ever walk again and Mike has to take a nap? I—"

"Mama". There was an urgency in her voice that would have stopped Pauline even if it hadn't been for her daughter's outstretched arms, palms forward. "I think he has a fever." Carla always spoke quietly when it was important, and this was only loud enough for Pauline to hear. She stepped back as her mother hurried passed her and into the next room where Mike lay, his head rolling slowly back and forth. Her hand went professionally to the side of his neck, then to his forehead.

Chapter XXI

"How are you feeling, son?" Her voice was calm again.

Mike's eyes snapped open, wild, then settled as realization came back to him. Hastily he pulled himself up to his elbows. "Dad needs more medicine," he mumbled.

"Don't worry, I've already sent someone for it," she lied. "Just rest awhile. I'll get you a couple of aspirin," she said, turning to Carla standing at the foot of the bed. Carla quietly left.

Two hours later, when the aspirin didn't help and the fever was still rising, Pauline's concern grew. A cold sponge bath did little to stop the fever and with no other symptoms to give a clue as to what was going on, Pauline and Carla kept a closer watch than normal.

Four hours passed and Mike's fever continued to rise. Pauline then made the decision to give him an antipyretic injection to lower the fever. Her prayers were quickly answered as the fever dropped dramatically, only to return again, only higher. Another injection and the cycle repeated, rising even higher than before. And again the injection and repeated cycle. The fever was now climbing to dangerous degrees and Pauline began questioning how many injections were safe for a nine-year-old.

"How are you, son?' she asked at one point when the fever was lowest.

"I don't know, Mom," his voice slow, "just so tired."

"It's only normal, son. Fighting a fever takes lots of energy." She sat for a moment in silent prayer and exhaustion, her hand wrapped protectively around his hot body. Suddenly she felt his body tighten, his eyes widened, searching.

"Mom, I can't move my legs!"

"Sure you can, son. You're just tired." She ran her hand down across his hot leg. Her mind, already straining for any clue toward unknown fevers with no other symptoms, was alerted to several possibilities. The most prominent being polio.

Poliomyelitis, the definition seemed to jump into her mind; an acute infectious viral disease especially of children that is characterized by fever, motor paralysis and atrophy of skeletal muscles, often with permanent disability and deformity. Her heart was in her throat as her mind saw her active, eager, always running son—her only son, an invalid. She swallowed hard and once again tried to be the professional nurse. The one who made decisions that often saved lives. Or sometimes forced into choosing who would live and who would not when there was not enough medicine. That was called triage. But this time there was no decision to be made; no choice, no medicine.

"You'll be all right," she said, forcing calmness into her voice. "I'll be right back, son. I'm going to look in on your dad."

She slipped from the room but turned instead to the right into her bedroom, reached for the desk and her

Chapter XXI

medical books. A moment passed and Carla was at her side, a silent question in her eyes. Pauline slid her fingers down the page of her open medical book, then stopped, her eyes skimming the section. Then they lost their focus and drifted to where Carla's hand rested on the desk. She cupped her own hand over it before answering.

"It could be polio, Carla." Carla folded her knees, sitting on her heels. She looked up into her mother's face. "He's paralyzed from the waist down."

Carla slowly laid her head to rest on her mother's arm. Then again looked up. "Mother, we both had our polio shots." It was a statement, but yet a question.

"Yes, and we all had typhoid shots too, but I got typhoid, remember?"

Carla remembered.

***

Days merged into nights that stretched endlessly. I ate when I should, knowing that nourishment was my ally, and slept when the white-hot coal in my back would let me. My mind crowded with the things I should be doing instead of laying on a sweat soaked mattress waiting for my next injection of painkiller.

Voices from below intruded into my thoughts. Perhaps Paing was back. Footsteps on the stairs and the door opened. Pauline stepped through followed by Mayor Socapaño and the Chief of Police. Words of greetings, explanations, and sympathy were courteously handed around. With the authority carried by his office, the Mayor then authorized the Chief to send a telegram on the private police line to Manila explaining the situation. He made it sound quite official and a large kind-hearted step away from protocol, but we all knew that "official business" was open to a quite broad interpretation. Pauline and I thanked them profusely as they left and assured them that their kindness and concern that allowed access to the official line would not be forgotten.

We had met the mayor on our first arrival in Malay. It was cultural for newcomers to pay a respect visit to the mayor. During our coffee and hot rice cake visit, by way of history he mentioned how during the time of war his father's sailboat, the *Romeo,* had helped shuttle guns and ammunition from a submarine to shore. He also mentioned an American family that his father had picked up at the village of *Po-ok* and taken around the point, past Palhi to where a submarine picked them up. I had then told him of our family's escape, and in so doing, silently acknowledged his father's life-saving aid. I was indebted to him from a generation ago.

Pauline sat on the edge of the bed. "I didn't want to tell you earlier, but the men came back from the relay station on the mountain."

Even through the pain, I could sense that all was not well. "They couldn't send the telegram," she continued. "Not enough money, they said—but it's okay because now the Chief will send it." She forced enthusiasm into her voice. It helped take the edge off of the frustration for both of us.

"How's Mike?" I probed, knowing only the few snatches that I heard through the thin walls.

"He's lying down. He came down with a slight fever two days ago and I thought it best if he rested some. Everyone is fine though, we just need to get you up."

"Two days ago? How long have I been here?"

"Three days."

With extreme caution, and with Carla and Pauline on either side, I was by then able to make my way to the bathroom and back. It was a big move for me. Faithfully, Paing came every day, or sent one of his men. One day he carried with him a freshly caught squid, its tentacles still dragging the ground as he held it over his head. A delicacy to be sure. After he left, Pauline gave it to one of the Ati families knowing that the whole village would get a taste.

The evening of the fifth day, Pauline and Carla knelt beside the bed where Mike lay, his legs paralyzed. His fever raged and, when conscious, he stared wide-eyed at objects floating over his bed. He raised a weak arm trying to pluck his hallucinations from the air.

With hearts on the brink of explosion, Pauline offered up a simple prayer, "You gave him to us and we commit him back to You." Then Mike slept.

The next day, they sat on the side of my bed trying to make small talk. Mike was still resting from his "slight fever," as Pauline put it. My mind was capable of only the most surface of thoughts and the fact that Mike's slight fever had dragged into the fifth day was not registering any alarm.

Chapter XXII
HELICOPTERS

The breeze coming through the open window behind my head was cooling and brought with it sounds almost foreign to our little world. The sounds grew and finally registered.

"Get towels," I said almost shouting, raising my head from the pillow until that knife somewhere in my back again twisted me to silence. With what was left of my breath I continued hoarsely, "Get in the rice field and wave them down." The sound was now unmistakable. Helicopters and more than one. Pauline and Carla ran from the room. The choppers were approaching from over the hill behind the house.

I turned my head—had to see them. Reaching over my left shoulder, I grabbed the windowsill and with both hands pulled, twisting myself toward the window as the two beautiful choppers skimmed the mango trees on the hill and toward the house. The house shivered and the air-squeezing drum of twin military choppers a hundred feet overhead obliterated the small thud in my back.

I waited, listening for the telltale sound of their turning to circle back as they surely saw two white-women crazily jumping about in an empty rice field waving white towels. They didn't, and a feeling of utter abandonment swept in on me even before the backwash of silence.

Then another feeling registered . . . or lack of it.

As if being shaken awake from a nightmare, it took a moment for me to orient myself. I was standing beside the bed, hands still gripping the windowsill.

I felt no pain. I held my grip on the windowsill, expecting the sharp stab that I knew would hammer me to the floor. It didn't come. Carefully I twisted to the left. Then right. Nothing. Still careful, I released my grip and stood. Slowly I sat on the edge of the bed, rolled onto my back and then I laughed. The twisting and pulling had somehow realigned something in my back.

"Thank you, God." And again I laughed. I felt, perhaps, as a kitten would, lying in a ray of morning sunlight. I think I even purred.

Then footsteps, and Pauline and Carla stepped through the door, white towels clutched, faces drawn. Pauline, a tear standing in her eye, stepped to the bed. "They didn't stop."

"It's all right," I said and slowly swung my legs off the bed. I stood and took her hands in mine. "It's all right."

Her mouth opened, lips forming silent questions, eyes scanning me up and down, searching for answers. I eased her to the bed and we both sat. Carla joined us and together we acknowledged that God does have His own way of doing things, and a sense of humor that at times seems just a bit off center. But then, we're not viewing it from where He is.

"But where'd the helicopters come from?"

"We've never had choppers over here before."

"They had Philippine markings."

"Then they weren't from the embassy."

"There's no military base anywhere close."

We laughed softly. Then a faint voice from down the hall. "Mom?"

Carla was first out the door, Pauline following. Though free from pain, I was acutely aware of weakness in my back and moved slow, carefully.

The door to Mike's room stood open and they both were kneeling beside the bed. Pauline's hand stroked his forehead. Even from the doorway, the sweat soaked bed told me that his fever had broken. Pauline's glance up at me verified it, her face almost aglow.

"I'm hungry." His voice drifted up. "Do we have any eggs?"

"You bet we do."

"Lots of salt," he mumbled.

***

Paing returned the next day, glad for the recovery but anxious that we get proper check-ups. "You must go to Manila," he said "I'll take you in my Jeep. Maybe you're not strong enough to drive yet, and soon comes the *habagat*."

"You're right." With the monsoon winds would come the rain then no one would leave. "Maybe tomorrow I'll be able."

"I'll return when the sun rises."

Morning found us packed and waiting as Paing in his stretch-bodied Jeep topped the hill under the mango trees and bounced down the hill toward us. Pauline, Carla and Mike along with our two suitcases crowded into the two side seats in the back and I braced myself in the front passenger seat. Mike was still weak, but his paralysis had gradually left along with the fever and we repeatedly thanked God because our resources amounted to naught. I prayed the makeshift back brace that Pauline rigged up would serve its purpose.

The five-hour dirt road trip out to the provincial capital was trying in the best of situations. Most of the trip I gripped the edge of the seat with my left hand to take some weight off of my spine, while my right wrapped around the windshield post. Paing drove slower for my sake and the trip stretched long and painful.

Paing chose to lodge us in the *Ati-Atihan* hotel, the newest and best hotel in Kalibo, the Provincial capital. The hotel squatted on a slight rise in the flat Aklan River delta near the sea. It sported a swimming pool, half filled with ominously green water alive with bloated toads vainly trying to climb the slippery sides. Hearing it had a pool, Carla and Mike hurried to check it out. They decided not to swim.

Chapter XXII

Paing appeared anxious and glanced at the darkening sky. "I'll go back tomorrow," he said, choosing, for my sake, to stay the night.

"Maybe tomorrow you can't cross the river," I suggested. I too had noticed the sky. The western horizon, sculpted by the mountain range that divided the island, was now curtained in black. Paing hesitated, then conceded. We both knew what the dark western sky signaled this time of year. It was the beginning of the *habagat*, the southwestern winds that ushered in the torrential, and sometimes violent, storms that often lasted for days before settling into the seasonal monsoon rains. Paing left within fifteen minutes and we settled into our rooms with the hope that the night would bring well-needed rest.

Chapter XXIII
FLOOD

The drumming woke me. I opened my eyes in the pre-dawn darkness. My waking ears turned the drumming into a violent pounding that rattled the door. Someone wanted our attention.

"Sir, you must get up! *May problema kita!*"

What kind of problem could we have now, I thought. Then I remembered my own problem. I pulled my knees up and locked them before pulling myself to a sitting position and lowering my feet off the bed . . . into ankle deep cold water.

"Honey, you awake?"

"Mm-hmm."

"Be careful when you—" A small splash and a gasp.

I groped for the flashlight. The beam of light scattered about the room, glancing off the muddy torrent boiling up under the door. Pauline sat on the edge of the bed, wet feet pulled up, toes curled. Out of habit, I had set our suitcase on the table—less chance of any crawling or slithering visitors that way. Our clothes hung over the bedpost. As Pauline fumbled for her clothes, I slipped my pants on and opened the door. The scared little hostess

Chapter XXIII

stood in the swirling floodwaters, robe pulled tight around her bare legs.

"Baha," she uttered, announcing the obvious, but her eyes said so much more. Panic. An emotion rarely seen on the face of a Filipino. She hurried on to wake other guests, dragging her feet through the water, now half way to her knees. One step down from the room level, the courtyard was a restless brown tide. Darkness still hid anything beyond but I knew what to expect. We were on high ground, perhaps only six or seven feet, but I was quickly thankful for Paing's choice of hotels. Carla and Mike were soon up and joined us to stand helpless and gaze, almost entranced, at the water, heavy with mud as it swept around our legs. The few other guests chose to retreat back to their rooms, perhaps in hopes they would wake from this nightmare. We too, soon retreated and sat on our beds and aired our varied thoughts.

"What do we do if it gets deeper?"

"Obviously the airport will be closed for days until the gravel runway dries out."

"Then we'll go on to Roxas City and catch a flight there. At least they have a paved runway."

"Right, but how do we get there?"

"Do you think your back can take the road trip?"

"At least the toads got out of the pool."

"But what *do* we do if it gets deeper?"

"I think it stopped rising."

"But it hasn't even rained here yet, only in the mountains."

With that, we all dropped our gazes to the swirl around our legs.

"I think it *has* stopped rising." I sloshed to the door and opened it. It was mid-morning and the skies pressed down. The waters appeared to be receding. Hungry by then, we started across the courtyard toward the kitchen and dining area.

From the shrubbery at the side of the courtyard, movement, and something cut through the waters angling to the other side leaving behind a wandering wake.

"Look, Dad, a fish!" Mike said.

I studied the wake. "Nope. That was a snake."

After the briefest pause, Carla and Pauline, with tall, hesitant steps, returned to wait in the room. Mike and I were left to continue our quest for food, stepping briskly to the side as another wake slithered past. We were indeed on the high ground and every surviving snake in the area had headed this way.

Soon the kitchen was back in action and for the next two days, with pant-legs rolled up, we sloshed and squished our way to meals and back. On the third day, floodwaters had receded enough for a few vehicles to venture out and back. We asked of everyone who made it through if they knew whether or not the Roxas City airport was open and if there was transportation going there.

The culture of the land lends to unique challenges in communication. Not only do the people desire to give you the answers that you want to hear, but they also feel that it would be embarrassing to them to have to say I don't know.

I wandered over to a mini-bus driver who had made it through. "Hello, do you know if the road to Roxas City is open?"

"Yes."

"Are buses going to Roxas City?"

"Every day."

"Which bus line is going?"

"You try Peralta bus line."

"Is the road now open?"

"No more flood."

"Is the airport open in Roxas City?"

"Maybe."

"Are many people coming from Roxas City?"

"Sometimes."

"Do they ride on Peralta buses?"

"Maybe."

"Maybe I can ride a Peralta bus to Roxas City tomorrow?"

"The bridge is destroyed."

"When will it be repaired?"

"Repair crew cannot cross."

With that I wandered back to my room and the bus driver probably wondered why anyone would ask questions like that right after a flood.

The fifth day found us venturing out, suitcases in hand, having heard that someone had arrived from Iloilo City, the other side of the island. That news assured us that the road was good at least to where it intersected with the train track running between Roxas and Iloilo. If we made it that far, we could then decide whether to go on to Roxas or the longer trip to Iloilo.

Several agonizing hours later we stepped off the bus at the train station, the half way point if we went to Roxas, but only one-third if we needed to continue to Iloilo. The flood had not reached this far and the station was packed as usual. As we tried to decide whether to go West to Iloilo or East, the three-car passenger train pulled in from Roxas. We pushed toward the front of the mass of humanity waiting for the passengers getting off, still unsure if we should board for Iloilo or wait for the train going the other way.

At that moment Pauline spotted a man stepping off the train with a newspaper under his arm. She glanced at the date. Todays. She pulled us back. "The airport is open in Roxas," she exclaimed. I glanced at her, question in my eyes. "It's today's paper," she explained. "You can only buy them in Manila."

In Roxas, another day passed in a not so new hotel as we waited for the next available flight to Manila. The next day in the airport, we waited with tickets clamped in our sweaty hands. Suddenly Pahuline jumped up and headed for the gate out to the runway. Outside, four military officers were strolling in from two very military looking helicopters. An animated conversation took place. She then turned on her heels with head held high and an "I solved it," look on her face. The helicopters had

Chapter XXIII

returned several days prior from a circuitous flight around the island. They had been out to survey damage from a massive storm that had passed through. It was stalled over the mountains west of Kalibo at the headwaters of the Aklan River. Yes, their flight path would have taken them over Malay.

X-rays in a reputable hospital in Manila showed no damage to my back. Even the anterior fifth lumbar that had bothered me for so many years was no longer out of place. I questioned the doctor about that. He merely shrugged and explained that the trauma of lifting the house and the ensuing pull-twist to see the helicopters approach could have realigned everything.

And Mike? Definitely a case of severe salt shortage caused by the long hike the day before, then the adrenaline charged bicycle rides to town for medicine for his Dad. The fever? Paralysis? Yes, classic, the doctor assured.

As I lay on the bed in the S.I.L. guesthouse, mulling over the happenings of the past couple of weeks, Pauline entered, that same, "I solved it," look on her face. Slowly she eased herself down onto the bed.

"S.I.L. *did* get our telegram," she began, "and Joe French took off right away in the six passenger twin to come down." I took a breath as I waited through the dramatic pause. "Half way down he had to turn back because of the storm. They had no way of contacting us to let us know."

I nodded slowly. "I wonder if Paing made it back okay."

I was extremely grateful, but also wary. In the culture, if one person helps another to the extent that he helped me, I owed him my life. It was a debt that culturally could not be repaid but obligated the debtor to anything the other asked.

She stretched out on the bed beside me. "Let's go home," and she closed her eyes.

Chapter XXIV
INDEBTEDNESS

It wasn't too long after our return from Manila and a complete check-up that a runner came to us from Raphael saying that Raphael was critically ill and Dr. Prado was not able to help him. Without hesitation Pauline and I headed out the door toward the Jeep. Pauline had gripped in her hand her black bag and an assortment of possible helps. On our arrival at his place, two miles the other side of town, we found him unconscious with no detectable pulse. Dr. Prado paced the floor then left, not wanting to be present should the patient die, therefore releasing himself from any responsibility. Perhaps it was our prayers, perhaps Pauline's medicine and expertise, perhaps a combination, but Raphael pulled through. And now he owed us. The debt was not canceled. Now we owed each other. So here I was in a position to talk to this militant communist leader, at my pleasure, about the Lord, salvation, democracy, hopscotch, or any subject. And he was obligated to listen.

Chapter XXV
SNAKES

Snakes are as much a part of living in the tropics as mosquitoes. You quickly learn not to reach under anything, or open a box, without looking. In fact, a day passing without encountering at least one was rare.

One evening after the last of the patients had left and dinner was in the past, I leaned back on the bamboo bench built against the inside wall of the sala. Pauline sat beside me verbally unwinding from the day. I listened while letting my mind and eyes roam. We had left a gap of about a foot between the top of the wall and the roof for ventilation and the last light of dusk was finding its way through that gap. I had sat there many times under the same circumstances, but this time the long gap between the top of the wall and the roof was somehow interrupted. Unless the beam at the top of the wall had grown strangely, I was looking at something that shouldn't be there.

Pauline noticed my attention was focused and without taking her eyes off of my face said, "You see a snake, don't you?"

"Maybe." I stood slowly to get a better look. If it was a snake, it was big. "Mike, bring a flashlight," I said, not taking my eyes off the dark lump on top of the beam. It was at least a foot high and two or three feet long.

Pauline wasted no time scurrying up the stairs to the bedroom and in a moment Mike came down flashlight in hand. I pointed and he flashed. It was curled up on top of the beam, one coil sagging down the wall. It slowly turned its head toward the light, tongue flicking to pick up sound or scent. I took the flashlight from Mike as he headed back upstairs for the pellet rifle and pellet pistol. Firearms were not allowed in the Philippines, so the air guns and several machetes were all we had. "Hurry Mike!" I shouted as the snake, sensing movement, started moving across the beam toward the left. A few more feet and he would be where the young pine tree stood just outside. Mike was beside me in a flash. I took the air rifle and began pumping as Mike pumped the pistol. We both took hurried shots as it stretched toward the tree and safety. I pulled the front door open and hurried out under the pine tree in time to see it disappear into the darkness of the tree. Mike joined me with another flashlight. Next to the pine tree was a coconut tree, limbs and palm fronds mingling.

"I think it's in the coconut tree," Mike said as he circled to the other side.

"Be sure it doesn't come back," I said. I traded guns with Mike and shoved the pistol in my pants pocket, flashlight in the other. The lowest pine tree limb, the size of a baseball bat, grew just out of my reach. "I'm going up," I said. My plan was to leap for the limb and climb up to get a better view.

I leaped and wrapped my hand around the limb. Instead of the rough pine bark in my hand, what I was holding was smooth and soft. An instant shiver dropped my blood temperature at least ten degrees it seemed before my mind said that couldn't possibly be what my hand told me it was. I hung a moment before realizing the smoothness was the leaves of a vine growing out on the limb. I hoisted myself on up. From there I could get a better view of the coconut tree whose top was about eye level now. I still could not see the culprit.

Suddenly Mike yelled, "It's coming your way, Dad!" Flashlight in hand, I beat viciously on the palm frond, hoping the noise would stop his advance. I had no idea what I would have done if we had had a face-off. My gun was still in my pocket, other hand wrapped securely around the tree. "There he goes, Dad. He's crossing into the other coconut tree." I swung down, thankful it was dark enough to hide my shaking hands.

One coconut tree and a guava tree later we were able to terminate him with a few well-placed pellets. The Ati say they make good eating so we gave him to them . . . all eleven feet of him.

On another occasion pastor Terry and his wife came up for lunch and to discuss details before my business trip to Manila. As we sat in the *sala* chatting after lunch, a large rat ran from the kitchen, between us and out the front door. Pauline jumped up on the bench

Chapter XXV

where we sat and all eyes were on the front door where the rat disappeared . . . all except mine.

I wondered what would give the rat boldness to run out in the middle of the day with people present. I looked toward the kitchen and discovered it wasn't boldness that propelled the rat, but fear. Out from under the refrigerator swayed the head and about two feet of a cobra. It immediately slithered back under and disappeared. I went for my pellet rifle and Mike went for his *bolo*. We searched for some time but came up empty. There was a wide space between the split bamboo floor and the wall behind the fridge and it had escaped and was probably half way across the rice field by then.

We continued our business discussion in the *sala*, but everyone's attention seemed to have wandered and furtive eyes kept darting toward the kitchen, the walls and through the split bamboo floor. After Pastor Terry and his wife left, I turned to resume my packing for the trip.

"Oh no you don't!" Pauline said. "You're not leaving until you find it and kill it!" I knew she meant business and to ease her apprehension, Mike and I searched on. Neither one of us would admit it, but we had no desire to crawl under the house to search. The only place in the house we had not probed into was the hollow space between the two layers of fiberboard that formed the wall between the kitchen and bathroom, the only solid wall in the house.

So with Pauline's determined prompting, I pried the wallboard loose with a large screwdriver and shined the flashlight inside. The light reflected back at me from two brilliant eyes causing me to jump back and lose my grip on the screwdriver. By the time I recovered the flashlight, screwdriver, my pistol and myself it had disappeared. We continued our search, widening it to include the immediate area around the house. By then dusk was settling and Pauline's apprehension was rising.

Then Mike yelled from the back porch. "It's here, Dad!"

In a small mango tree beside the porch, it had climbed about eight feet up and was trying to act like a limb, but it didn't work and we quickly dispatched it with a few well-placed pellets.

Chapter XXVI
RABID DOG

While visiting with Pastor Terry one day, yells and hurt sounds came from children playing in back of the house.

"The kids got a new puppy," Terry anticipated our unasked question.

Oohs and aahs came from Carla and Mike. They glanced up at Pauline and me. We nodded and they quietly slipped out the back door to see the puppy. In a minute Carla returned looking not too happy. "It's biting everyone," she said.

We went out back to see a group of children surrounding the puppy taunting it. When one of the children would get too close it bit with the speed and sharp teeth puppies are known for.

"They shouldn't tease it," Pauline said with more than a little authority. The message was relayed in the local dialect by Terry and the kids backed away. I knelt down in front of the puppy and held my hand out, hoping to calm it. Mike and Terry joined me and before we knew it, all three of us were nipped. We gave up and suggested that Terry keep an eye on it for a couple days. Then after cleaning our puppy size wounds, we went on home. One purpose of our coming down the hill to the pastor's house was to see if they had any needs as I was planning to take the bus into Kalibo, the provincial capital, the next day.

The trip into Kalibo was always a major event as travel was either by the local bus, which came through town once a day, or by driving our four-wheel-drive Scout. In either case, it was from a four to twelve hour trip depending on the weather and tide. In rainy weather the rivers were often uncrossable and at high tide portions of the road which ran along the seashore were submerged. This time I chose to take the bus. I had been feeling fatigued and felt the bus trip would give me some time to rest. Not that it was comfortable. The wooden seats would not allow that, but it was usually so crowded, jammed tightly against each other that there was no need to hang on. I sometimes could even catch a few tidbits of sleep between jounces, until my head would bounce off the wooden window frame or I would need to shift my seat a bit to allow a different section to get the bruising.

The ride to the provincial capital was as I anticipated and my shopping successful. Next day I was back on the bus with my precious cargo of groceries and supplies that were available only in Kalibo: a few canned goods, sugar, coffee, fresh vegetables, fresh meat which I believed to be cow meat. Water buffalo meat could also be purchased but we found it to be too strong for our taste, a wild, pungent taste. Along with the usual, I had the essential case of Coke and a fifty-pound block of ice wrapped in a burlap sack surrounded with rice husks for insulation. A normal grocery trip.

Chapter XXVI

At the halfway point, the town of Pandan, the bus always made a rest stop. The bus heading the other way usually waited there also in case there were any needed repairs or news about road conditions to relay. It also gave the well-needed "pit stop" for the passengers. The men usually wandered off to the bushes, behind a nearby house, or by the riverbank. The women, the ones who desired privacy, were forced to wait in line for the "restroom" It consisted of a bamboo catwalk out over the river and a three-sided "room" just big enough for one person to squat. They had to carefully position their feet on the two bamboo poles spaced about six inches apart. That was all there was to the floor. Between the bamboo foot rests, several feet below, the river meandered slowly by. Timing was crucial as often children played in the shallow waters underneath.

As I headed back for the bus after my necessary stop, I tried appearing nonchalant as I hurried to get a window seat. To give an appearance of hurry, for any reason, was not culturally acceptable. As I sat, by the window, waiting for the bus to reload, a familiar vehicle lurched around the corner and heaved to a stop beside the bus. It was our Scout. Loaded with people. Mike was driving and Pauline seated next to him. She spotted me and waved almost frantically. She motioned me to get off and reluctantly I gave up my window seat.

She hurried to meet me as I stepped off. Then with the pause for emphasis that I knew well, "Hon, the puppy died yesterday and Terry buried it without telling anyone.

I found out this morning. I think it had rabies." Her eyes direct, unflinching, told me that she was serious and not to be questioned. I believed her and turned toward the vehicle and its human cargo. "I'm glad I saw you," she continued. "Everyone that was bitten needs to get rabies shots in Kalibo. That means you too."

"Everyone here was bitten?"

"That means you too," she added with emphasis.

I acknowledged the need, my mind trying to assimilate, sort and prioritize. "Why don't you go on into Kalibo on the bus, get the serum and bring it back and I'll drive everyone back and wait for you. Wouldn't that be easier than trying to find places for everyone to stay?" After a moment, she agreed, knowing as I did that it would be difficult to find places to stay.

The bus driver casually leaned against the bus waiting while I explained only what I needed to. He climbed deftly to the roof of the bus, searched out my cargo and began handing it down to me. I swung it to the top luggage carrier of the Scout and lashed everything down while Pauline searched out the driver of the inbound bus.

Within minutes I waved her off and I turned to my cargo of thirteen people, including myself, who were bitten by a small puppy that had since died of what appeared to be rabies. I knew that a person bitten by a rabid animal needed to have the anti-rabies injections within ten days or it was forever too late, and today was the third day.

Chapter XXVI

Early afternoon we arrived back in Malay. I advised everyone to remain close by because as soon as Pauline returned they would need the injections. The remainder of the ride home, Mike sat silently beside me his thoughts probably somewhere near mine: possibilities, probabilities, fears, and faith. As I topped the hill under the giant mango tree and descended the other side to our home, Carla was standing by the back door along with several of the Ati children. One of the Ati children stood alongside, Carla's arm draped over her shoulder. She was quiet, waiting.

"Where's Mom?" She glanced from Mike to me and back. We explained as we untied and unloaded supplies.

It was noon the following day when Pauline stepped off the bus. She was talking as she crossed the gravel road to where I waited. ". . . They only had one but it's enough to give skin tests to everyone. Manila. I'll have to go to Manila to get any more."

We drove in silence toward town and Pastor Terry's house. As we pulled to a stop alongside the house I could see the family at the kitchen table. Lunchtime. Terry saw us and met us at the door. "Gather everyone here in an hour, Terry," she started as the door opened. "Everyone has to have skin tests in case of allergies to the serum." Terry was backing into the living room nodding as he went. She turned toward the kitchen and greeted the family then breezed past me back toward the front door. "I'll be back in an hour," she tossed over her shoulder as she passed the door. Then for emphasis she stopped and turned. I braked hard to keep from running into her. "That's American time," she added with a smile, then we were off again toward home.

"That was a bit abrupt, Hon," I said.

She turned toward me as I drove, her eyes level, voice flat. "There are only six days left and I have to go to Manila and back."

I understood. More than once it had taken three days just to get to Manila. There was only one flight a day out of Kalibo and the bus from Malay could usually get to Kalibo in time for the flight. If the bus didn't break down. If the roads weren't flooded. If the tide wasn't high. If not, you wait till the next day. If the flight wasn't full. If it wasn't raining. If the flight wasn't canceled for no apparent reason, which it often was.

I gave the gas pedal an extra push.

One hour later we were back and so were a dozen nervous patients. Their fear of the horrible death from rabies had pushed them into American time. After swabbing a spot on the forearm, Pauline deftly injected minute amounts of the serum under the skin of each person bitten. "We should know within an hour," she said quietly as I sat opposite her to take my turn.

Within the hour we did know. Two were allergic. The skin around the injection sight flared up red. One was the pastor's son and one of the other children. "There's an alternate for those showing allergic reaction to the duck embryo serum," she said quietly as she sorted things

Chapter XXVI

back into her black bag. Her eyes were tired but I saw something else there too. She was thinking, unsure.

"I'll drive you to Kalibo in the morning." She turned toward me, an unspoken thank you in her eyes.

The twin turbo-prop engines screamed as the plane lifted off the gravel runway. It banked westward and would eventually swing north toward Manila. I was glad it was her on board that plane and not me, my mind said. I wouldn't know where to start looking for an alternate serum for those allergic to what 99% of people can take. I climbed back in the Scout and mentally calculated if the tide was low enough to cross the rivers on the road back to Malay. And it was day five.

Back home I immersed myself in the translation work and tried not to think of the possibilities if time ran out.

Day ten emerged no different than the past several, with the prayers and the anticipation that Pauline would return soon. But this day we could only pray that it would be this day. Tomorrow would be too late if that little puppy was truly rabid.

Mid-afternoon brought with it the sound of a vehicle topping the hill behind the house. It stopped before making the descent to the house. In a moment Pauline's tired strides carried her down the hill amidst several children. Two of them carried her overnight bag between them. In her hands she gripped a cardboard box tied with brown string. Carla and Mike were out the door and up the hill to meet her. Mike took the box from her. It was obvious she was fatigued but she seemed driven.

I strode across the yard from my office and helped her up the two steps into the *sala*. It served as more than a living room though. It was also our clinic where many had received healing and the bamboo bench had seen more than one patient breathe their last.

"I already talked to doctor Prado on my way in and he's coming up as soon as he can," she said as we crossed the sala to the kitchen. "I stopped at Terry's also and he's rounding everybody up to be here. It would hurry things along if you would drive down and give everyone a ride." As she opened the box with its precious contents, I pulled a Coke from the fridge along with two ice cubes.

"I'll go down in a minute," I said as I sat across from her at the kitchen table.

She pulled a smaller box from the one she had just opened. "Do you know where this came from?" she said setting it carefully on the table.

I shook my head slowly and waited. She looked up at me for emphasis, "It came from Thailand." She let that sink in while she took a sip of Coke, then continued, "It took me two days to go to every hospital in Manila, but no one had any of the special serum. So I had to go up to Clark and pray that they would have some on a U. S. Air Force base. And guess what . . . they didn't. I told the Major who was in charge what I needed and he said he thought they might have some at their base in Thailand, but had no authority in that area and would have to wake

Chapter XXVI

the commanding officer up. I apologized for having to wake him up on a Sunday morning.

"Don't worry about it. I'm always looking for a good reason to wake the old man up," the Major said with a sly grin.

"It didn't take long for the Colonel to come down, but he said he didn't have authority either unless it was a Filipino that needed the serum. Something to do with the laws, but it was two Filipinos and he got a message off to Thailand right away."

"So how did they get it so quick from Thailand to Clark?"

"One of our jet fighters was already scheduled to come to Clark so they put it on board then helicoptered it to Manila. As soon as I heard it was on the way, I grabbed the next flight back to Manila, explained to the authorities at the airport and they were obliging enough to hold the flight to Kalibo for me until the helicopter arrived."

"Yeah, obliging. Knowing you, you would have stood in front of the plane to keep it from leaving."

"This is the tenth day," she said with a finality that fit the situation.

I sat for a moment trying to absorb the improbability of the chain of events happening with such clockwork . . . especially in the Philippines and could only resign that God had a big hand in it.

As the sun set that evening, thirteen people gathered in our bedroom to receive what might have been a life-saving injection of anti-rabies serum. The dosage was determined by body weight and Doctor Prado had to turn away as Pauline filled the syringe twice in order to give enough for this one-hundred-eighty pound American.

Chapter XXVII
MOUNTAIN PEOPLE

"Mom." Carla, clipboard in hand, peered through the door of our house turned clinic. "There are some people here from Ta-oban with a sick boy."

Pauline didn't move, stethoscope in her ears, other end pressed to the chest of a man, his body looking much too old for his youthful face. She mouthed a word and he breathed deep, ending it with a spasm and a rattling cough.

"The baby's pretty sick, Mom. You better take a look."

"Just a minute Carla, there are several patients ahead of him. Get the vitals and I'll get to him as fast as I can," she said, but her mind was on the immediate problem. She moved the stethoscope, listening at various points on the man's back and chest.

"But Mom, they're from Ta-oban . . . the mountain people?"

There was a subdued urgency in her voice that prompted Pauline to look up. She shouldn't have had to hesitate, but at the moment she was in the midst of a rather complex T.B., emphysema, high blood pressure diagnosis, which with wrong medication could be fatal. She finished her thought and quietly stepped outside to meet her new patient.

Two dozen people, mostly tribal, stood or squatted in shady spots about the yard. Across the yard on the porch of my bamboo and nipa office another dozen rested, talked, nursed fussy babies and generally succeeded in inserting large cracks in my concentration.

Pauline had no trouble recognizing the new patients as she stepped out the door. Other than the fact that Carla was talking with them, they were the ones that stood alone, the ones that the others seemed to politely ignore. The man was the one that a trained eye would look for in a mob advancing toward you. Not the one leading with the loudest voice. The one off to the side who pulled the strings.

He was a rather handsome man, and quietly desperate. Pauline quickly became involved with his ill son and didn't realize until later what it was that set him apart. After her diagnosis, she turned to him and the woman who squatted on the ground slightly behind him. Apparently she was the mother so Pauline spoke to both of them.

"Your child has a sickness in his liver caused from dirty water. Now what you need to do is . . . ," She struggled to speak slowly and clearly as their dialect in the mountains was slightly different than the tribal language of the Ati, and she wanted no misunderstandings.

He listened attentively, eyebrows lifting in assent from time to time. His wife seemed to have trouble understanding and glanced furtively at him for

Chapter XXVII

affirmation each time he would assent. He accepted the medicine offered, but insisted on taking the child home instead of leaving him with his wife for a few days of observation.

"We will go home only to our place. My son will recover. Thank you." And with a wave of his arm indicating the direction, they turned with the child to go. Two men leaning against a nearby palm tree detached themselves and left with them.

"Mom, did you notice how alert and intelligent he seemed?"

"Yes Carla, and he carried his son instead of his wife carrying him. Not at all typical."

As she turned back to the other patients, the normal chatter picked up again. Not until a few well thought out remarks that she made to appear off-handed, and some alert listening did she discover that they were indeed some of the "mountain people."

The long tropical day had well ended before the last patient left and we were all able to unwind. I came in from my office and was seated at the window bench letting the deepening sunset iron out kinks in my brain. Too many hours leaning over my desk trying to make Biblical truths understandable in a tribal language that, until now had never been reduced to writing, did things to my brain. Learning an unwritten language is akin to skimming the surface of an unknown sea and stating that you know it. But to know it requires plumbing the depths of thought patterns and why a people think that way.

What stem of a thought, perhaps a century old, would cause association of two words that in another language stand poles apart? To ask would only prompt blank stares.

What, for instance, would cause women to fear washing their hair at evening and wait instead for morning? The answer to them is quite obvious; to wash hair in the evening causes blindness, and that answer would be given with the patience of a mother teaching a young child.

We search deeper: no towels to dry with, high humidity, wet hair, ideal breeding place for bacteria, eye infections, and blindness. But of course. And they know that just as surely as we know why black cats cause bad luck. But of course.

Two little kerosene lamps on the wood table struggled bravely against the darkness. Carla stood

Chapter XXVII

pensively in front of the wood stove poking at the fire under the pot of boiling bananas.

"Get much done on the translation today, Hon?" Pauline said as she slid onto the bench beside me.

"Oh, not as much as I'd like." I twisted my head, stretching a kink in my neck. "It's kinda hard to concentrate with so many right outside the door chatting, babies crying, you know—not that I don't want you to hold clinic every day, it's necessary, but I kind of wish it was away from the house a bit. You know, so you can walk away from it at the end of the day."

"Dream on, my love. We can't buy enough medicine to handle what we have here, let alone buy land and build something." She pondered a moment. "It does sound good though."

"Well, let's pray about it and see what comes up."

"What do you think I've been doing?" She said, sliding a hand up my back and squeezing tight neck muscles. "Honey, what happens if that boy doesn't recover?"

"Hmm? What boy?"

"I guess I haven't had time to tell you, but . . ." She went on to explain about the family and their companions from Ta-oban. ". . . And if the boy dies, do you think they'll blame us?"

I turned back toward the sunset that had now water-colored the universe in deep purple. I could feel my eyebrows growing heavy, as heavy as the silence. Taoban was known to be the home of hard-core communist guerrillas, the "mountain people", as they're called. Raphael's people. It was not unusual for someone who made them unhappy to quietly disappear, and to have a son die would certainly make anybody unhappy.

"I think I'll go talk with Raphael tomorrow," I said. Pauline's hand on my tight neck hesitated. I reached around, patted it reassuredly.

"Bananas are done!" came a call from the back porch.

"Let's eat."

Chapter XXVIII
SOMETIMES IT GETS TO ME

Not every missionary can sit across the table from a militant communist rebel leader with nothing between them but a cup of coffee and, with no fear of reprisal, illuminate the fallacies of communism as well as the realities of Christianity.

I could and I did. I had earned the right.

I had saved his life. Or more realistically, my wife, Pauline had. And by the culture to which he was bound, he had no choice but to listen, and if need be, to forfeit his own life to protect my family and I. That was his code, communist or not, and I believed him.

It was not the first time I had laid it all on the table before him, and I was praying it wouldn't be the last. Raphael Ong, or, Paing, as he allowed his friends to call him, was tough, but the knowledge of the ideologies for which he said he stood was quite limited. In fact we were quite sure at this point that he knew more about Christianity than about communism. His interest was not so much in ideologies as in allying himself with a cause strong enough to pose a serious threat to the country's dictatorial ruler. The New People's Army could certainly do this, so his allegiance was set. His highest goal was to give himself for the cause of his impoverished people.

That's all. But for the N.P.A., that was only a means to an end.

Pauline and I had gone to his home at Palhi for a different reason that particular evening. An evangelistic team made up of 32 young people from various Bible colleges across America and Canada had come over for a Summer of Service with our mission and was at that moment setting up their equipment in the town plaza for their crusade. We had already invited Paing, but thought it good to make this final appeal knowing that if he came it would greatly influence his followers.

Our visit was polite but to the point. I was playing with my second cup of coffee when a messenger came in. He appeared casual, stepping part way through the door then leaning easily against the doorframe. I had learned through the years that the casual attitude was a mark of the culture and not an indication of attitude or circumstance. His breathing was quite noticeably controlled, and I looked beyond to the glistening sweat on his face and chest. His eyes swept the room then he turned to Paing, speaking their dialect in rapid but quiet tones. I picked up enough to know there had been a stabbing somewhere and I knew he was here seeking Pauline for her medical knowledge. My wife could not refuse any emergency and she always carried her medical bag, so I knew we would be leaving immediately to help in any way we could.

Chapter XXVIII

Paing didn't move, then his face tightened. The young messenger's eyes shifted back and forth between us and he said in broken English, "I think he got dead."

Paing then turned to us. His eyes, normally suspicious and red anyway, had turned cold and I was reminded forcefully why no one ever challenged his leadership. "My cousin is stabbed . . . maybe you can help." It was a request, but not the kind to be denied.

"Where is he?" Pauline asked quickly as we stood to leave.

"At the plaza." His eyes bored past us toward the door. Pauline glanced at me and I knew that her thoughts, like mine, were on the team who were at this moment the center of attention there at the town plaza.

The messenger, turning back to Paing, then added a line to his message that tied a knot somewhere deep inside of me. *"Ho dian si Mike sa atubangan nana!"* Mike, our fourteen-year-old son, had been standing directly in front of the victim when he was stabbed.

Paing was out the door with us close behind. "Ride with us," I urged as Pauline clambered into the passenger side of the Scout. He didn't respond, already straddling his motorcycle. The motorcycle jumped into life and nosed down the trail before I got the Scout turned around.

As we sped down the narrowing beach toward town, I tossed up a quick thank you that the tide had not yet come in enough to block the way. Another half-hour, I estimated, and we'd have been stuck there for the night. Pauline was leaning forward in the seat gripping the grab bar, her face intent. "Do you think the team was involved?" I didn't answer right away. My mind shuffled over the possibilities, knowing the explosive nature of the people and the controversies that an evangelistic crusade can stir up in this Catholic nation, to say nothing of the assault on the cousin of a Communist leader. I forced my thoughts back on my driving.

"All we can do now is pray," I said as I slowed, waiting for a wave to recede before swinging around a fallen coconut tree.

As we braked to a halt at the plaza, the crowd was milling about and there was no sign of the team members. "They are there," someone said, pointing a lower lip toward the clinic across the plaza. A pathway opened as we picked our way through the crowd. The entrance to the clinic was packed. Necks were craning to see in and I picked up bits of furtive remarks in hushed tones.

"He's almost dead."

"His stomach is open from here to here." A finger traced a line from navel to backbone.

Excusing ourselves repeatedly, we pushed through the doorway. The victim lay writhing on the examination table. Doctor Prado was washing exposed intestines with a sterile solution and trying to remove bits of gravel and dirt. Pauline stepped alongside to help. Two men were holding the man's arms. He was conscious but delirious. I spotted the team at the far side of the room looking confused and helpless. Scared. As calmly as I could, I moved over to them. Carla and Mike stepped out as I approached. I don't know if it showed on my face or not, but relief eased the knot in my stomach as I saw my own children safe, and a quick inquiry verified that no one from the team was involved.

"How'd it happen?" I asked quietly.

"One of the old ladies had to leave the meeting early," Mike started, "and I carried her chair for her. Nonoy and a bunch of the guys were sitting on the fence and he said something to me as we passed."

"That's Nonoy?" I nodded toward the young man on the table.

"Yeah. We always played basketball together." Mike glanced toward the table then turned away quickly. "The guy behind him jumped up and I saw the blade. He had a rice knife, you know, the curved blade with a hook on the end. Nonoy tried to block with his arms, but he just couldn't so he turned to run. That's when he got him."

At that moment I saw my son as I had never before. He was growing up seeing the raw edge of life. Not the way a fourteen-year-old should. "What'd you do then?"

"He came and got me," Carla answered. She was never far away from her brother when he needed help. "And when I got there—"

"No," Mike said with a quick shake of his head. "First I tried to get a policeman." Then his eyes turned deep as he looked across the room toward his teammate on the table. "He just walked toward me with his arms across his stomach. His insides were hanging out. '*Mapatay ako, Mike,*' he said." Mike's eyes dropped to the floor. "He just told me he was dying." Mike shook his head. "I dropped the chair and ran for the police . . . I should have stayed with him."

"No Mike, you did the right thing."

"But Dad," he said, looking across the room in frustration, "the policeman wouldn't even come. I guess he thought I was just kidding or something." He glanced up at me in confusion, "Then when he finally did come, Nonoy wasn't there. I asked where he was but no one would even admit that anything happened. They just said, 'What fight?' and wouldn't help. Even when I pointed to the blood on the ground, no one said anything." Mike paused, reliving those few seconds. "Then someone across the street screamed. He was there. He had staggered over and fell in the gravel."

"That's when he came and got me," Carla added.

Mike looked up at me as if he wanted to shake someone. "Then I tried to get someone to go for the doctor, and no one would help me again, Dad." He looked around in frustration. "I don't get it."

Carla filled in, "I tried to put direct pressure on the wound, but . . ." She shrugged her shoulders.

Mike continued, "Then the chief got there on his motorcycle and he wouldn't even go for the doctor. Not enough gas, he said." Mike looked up anticipating my next question. "Paing's brother finally went for the doctor."

A commotion at the door caught my eye. Paing entered, his face twisted with hate. "He's going to be

Chapter XXVIII

okay?" he asked, stepping up behind Pauline to look over her shoulder. He took a long look then turned away, hate, hurt and fear for his cousin's life blazed across his face.

"We have to get him to Kalibo to the hospital," Pauline urged.

Paing's eyes flashed around the room then settled on mine. I shook my head slowly. "He can't take the jeep ride, Paing."

"I'll get a boat," he said and was gone out the door.

Pauline stepped away from where she was helping the doctor. "I think I should go with him to Kalibo."

I hesitated, weighing the risks. I knew nothing of medical care and could be of little help. One of us should stay and organize the team for safety sake. It was always dangerous to travel anywhere at night and it would probably be early morning before they arrived in Kalibo. But I knew Paing would be going and it would be unlikely that any troublemaker along the way would bother him. "Maybe you better go," I said, probing for a response.

"You're right," she answered after a tight hesitation. "But I'd like to take a couple of the guys. I'm sure I'll need help to hold him down. He's delirious."

I agreed, knowing they might also be a good deterrent if anyone thought about giving her trouble. I looked up, scanning the evangelistic team that had crowded around listening. My eyes stopped on Jim, tall, broad shouldered, the typical college jock, and a natural leader too. He nodded slightly before I asked and another young man also assented. The doctor was beginning to bandage Nonoy up and I knew we had no time to waste.

"Wait here," I indicated to everyone, "I'll get the Scout, we'll load him in and take him to the beach, then boat to Kalibo—come with me, Mike."

I wanted to shout, lean on the horn, race the engine, anything to get the milling, curious crowd to move, but that would only alienate me from the people and purpose of our being there. Slowly they parted and we backed the Scout to the clinic door. An army litter, procured somewhere in the past, was carried out and slid into the back of the Scout. Nonoy was unconscious.

"We'll meet you at the beach," Pauline said, her hand brushing my arm as she, the doctor, and the two team members hurried past to thread their way across the plaza toward the beach. Mike climbed over the seat to steady the litter and his friend.

At the beach, Paing pointed to the waiting boat and I backed the Scout, axle deep, into the shallow waters of the lagoon. Pauline and the crew were already on board and helping hands carried the litter to the boat where it was laid on the narrow deck. The boat was then poled back into deeper water and turned before the starter rope was wound around the flywheel and pulled. As the engine sputtered and hammered into life, Pauline looked back at me.

She was seated on the wood plank beside the litter on which Nonoy was strapped. On the planks in front and in back, Jim and his companion sat, positioned to restrain

Chapter XXVIII

the victim if need came. In front of them, seemingly detached, doctor Prado sat, leaning on his knees. Paing stood beside the boatman, in charge. In the gathering twilight I was aware of a tie of urgency and concern that bridged the widening distance. No one waved.

The boat receded and turned to parallel the coast toward Kalibo and a hospital. But for the sputtering of the exhaust pipe of the Scout, now submerged in the rising tide, quiet returned.

Mike stared silently to sea. I waited a moment, then turned, pushing through the clinging seawater to the door of the Scout. Mike followed and our purpose then focused on the more immediate need: getting the thirty-two team members and their equipment safely back to our house.

The collapsible screen, projection equipment, generator, and everything else had been taken down and packed for travel when we arrived back at the plaza. Team members were talking quietly with individuals in the milling crowd while keeping a wary eye on the pile of equipment. Mike jumped from the Scout to help load. Others pitched in and soon everything was on board.

"I'll take as many as can climb on and be back for more," I said as I slid behind the wheel.

"Papa," Carla gripped my arm to get my attention, "the group would rather stick together if it's all right."

I understood. "Okay. Have the guys walk in front and in back and stick close, okay? Mike and I will take the stuff to the house then be back to escort the parade."

I gave Carla's hand a squeeze and handed her the flashlight from the glove box.

The crowd thinned out as we edged through the rest of town heading home. Gravel crunched at the tires and swirled dust into the darkness. The three miles to the house was a dark road, an occasional flicker of a kerosene light from behind shuttered windows and silhouettes of coconut trees bent from the restless winds off the South China Sea. I estimated that I'd be back to escort the team before they had walked this far. To the right of the road, rice fields stretched off into the shadows of the hills where more coconut trees took their stand.

The air was still, thick, as it often was before a storm. In my mind a storm already raged and my attempts to piece together the damage seemed futile. The victim, cousin to a Communist firebrand—there was bound to be reprisal. Or was it aimed at disrupting the evangelistic meeting? Was the team in danger of reprisal? And above all, Pauline, strong, resourceful and in many ways vulnerable, who had inadvertently allied herself with Paing, the firebrand, was at that moment challenging the night, bandits, her own safety to save the life of a man she had never met.

Mike sat beside me, quiet, tense, gripping the edge of the windshield. Neither of us felt like talking. I sensed he wanted it that way. Then as I turned off the road to follow the riverbank up to our house, he drew it all together with one short sentence.

"Sometimes it gets to me, Dad."

Chapter XXVIII

"Sometimes," I echoed, not taking my eyes off the warn tracks that crowded between the brink of the riverbank and the rice fields. To wander one way was to plunge to the riverbed, the other, to be hopelessly mired in a rice paddy. No room for error.

After dinner, built as always around a large kettle of rice, talk touched lightly around the edges of the day's happenings. It was a day unusual even by our standards, how much more, I thought, for this conglomerate of Bible college students who had stepped out from the security of their known world.

"Will we be staying in local homes later?"

The original plan had been for the team members to be housed in homes of the various church members so they could get a feel for the very different family lives and perhaps draw some meaningful ties in the short time they were here. The pastor, however, could find no homes free from active tuberculosis.

"That was the plan," I answered, "but for now, we'll just have to put up with each other here." A few managed smiles, then eyes on me, they waited for blanks to be filled in.

"It's five hours to Kalibo at best," I said, not touching on the fact that night travel posed multiplied dangers and few dared travel after the sun set. "They should arrive at one or two in the morning, give another hour or so to raise a doctor willing to do anything at that hour . . ."

"Wouldn't they just take him straight to an emergency room?" a team member asked.
"What I'm talking about *is* the emergency room."

***

The next day late afternoon shadows were lengthening when voices drifted up the trail toward the house. The weary three had had no sleep except for the few nods while sitting on wooden planks stretched across the width of the open hulled outrigger. The hammering of the unmuffled single cylinder engine is enough to keep anyone awake. Then add to that the occasional wave lifting over the bow and sweeping everything with its salty brine and the constant need to brace against the toss and pitch of the boat. For some, the exhaust fumes offset the noise and splashes in the face and they actually do rest for the three hours. Then they stumble off the boat wet, red-eyed from salt spray, deaf, but for the continued ringing that usually subsides in an hour or so and partially numbed from the fumes. Pity the one who may have bladder problems.

While sipping an ice-cold coke, one of a case they had picked up before boarding the boat for the return trip, along with a fifty-pound block of ice, Pauline began to unwind. "If it wasn't for Paing, we never would have gotten anyone to drive us to Kalibo from Navas where the boat dropped us." She savored the cold luxury before continuing. "I don't know how much he paid them, but

Chapter XXVIII

they got us across the mountains in near record time despite a flat tire."

"You should have seen it," Jim interrupted, "it was like an Indy pit stop. Thirty seconds and we were off again. Funny," he brought himself up short, "we never passed another vehicle the whole trip."

"Remember the mountain?" Pauline pointed out. "The pine forest and the check-point with the bullet riddled walls?

"There was nobody there," Jim noted.

"Exactly. There was an ambush there awhile back. Some say it was the N.P.A., or maybe just bandits, but nobody travels that way after dark anymore. The army even abandons their check point at sundown"

"Comforting thought."

"Anyway, how was Nonoy when you left?" I asked.

"I don't know if he'll make it or not. I think it took close to two hours to get a doctor and team roused, and all that time he laid on a bed with a sliced intestine spilling poison into his abdominal cavity. We'll know in a couple of days. Paing stayed with him. "

Conversations began splintering that evening and Pauline and I both saw a need for the team to recuperate. They had not had time to themselves since their arrival from Manila almost two weeks ago. We had set them up for evangelistic meetings, which had included a movie based on the life of Christ, songs, and a few words by the pastors of the towns they were staying in, starting in

Kalibo, the provincial capital, then on to Banga, Navas, Pandan, Libertad, Buruanga, then ending in our town, Malay.

There was to be one meeting in each town, places to sleep, then on to the next town in the morning. Unfortunately some meetings were cancelled at the last minute, as were places to sleep. It seemed that some permission slips to have open meetings, obtained from local officials, could not be located and some who had agreed to house some of the students for the night could not be found. The Catholic Church had a strong hold in many towns and a few words in the right places was all it took.

With the unforeseen problems that arose with places to stay, transportation, food and ever-present hecklers, most of the team felt they had stepped off into another world.

Pauline turned to me quietly. "What's the plan for tomorrow?"

Then a reply from behind me before I could answer. "How about Taguatihan?" I turned as Carla laid her chin on my shoulder. She wore a smile on her face that no father could resist.

"I was about to say that, Pigeon."

"Yeah, right." Mike poked in

"I was . . . really."

***

Chapter XXVIII

The buzz of our 100 c.c. Honda startled me out of sleep. I rolled toward the window in time to see Mike straddling the red bike, engine screaming, front wheel barely touching the ground as it topped the hill and disappeared.

Outside the window, morning sun glistened off palm leaves. Miniature Dove orchids on the tree beside our window were beginning to bloom, and the fragrance, heavy with their first opening, was an all out attack on the senses. Sweet beyond description and with a slight tinge of acid, it stopped me in mid breath for its power. I rolled back, letting the fragrance riffle the pages of my imagination.

"Going to reserve a couple of boats for *Taguatihan*," Pauline mumbled from beside me.

I was drifting back toward sleep when the murmur of voices from the kitchen and living room tugged at my consciousness. A house full of young people. Hungry. What about breakfast? The smell of coffee slowly drifted through the walls and I knew all was well.

Dressed and trying to look more awake than I felt, I stepped out of our bedroom and was greeted by smiling faces, casual waves, and a few that looked like I felt. Carla, along with as many as could crowd into the kitchen were building a breakfast big enough to feed everyone. I was impressed.

Half an hour later young bodies guarding plates of scrambled eggs and fried rice sprawled across the floor, steps, benches, every available space. Mouths not chewing were talking or laughing. The recent tragedy was pushed aside for one soft morning.

The rattle of the Honda sliding to a stop followed by a cloud of dust drew attention. Mike stepped off, vainly brushing at the dust. "Boats will be ready in a couple hours."

Then as if responding to a cue, all heads turned toward Pauline and me. We hadn't told them.

"We're going on an outing." Pauline said with enthusiasm that brought cheers even from the most reserved.

"It's an island about a half hour out," I detailed. "Private, quiet, snorkeling, swimming. Or just doing nothing."

"I thought we could spend the night. How's that sound?" Pauline continued. Again cheers, wows, and a whole lot of smiles. "It's got a beach house and if everyone doesn't fit, a whole lot of soft, white sand to sleep on."

"When do we leave?"

"How fast can you finish eating?"

Except for chewing, rattling of silverware and some excited mumbling, the house became exceptionally quiet.

In near record time, loaded with all the necessities to sustain life for twenty-four hours on a deserted tropical island, I urged the Scout up over the hill and toward the road. A parade of young people, with high spirits,

Chapter XXVIII

followed. Mike had gone ahead on the Honda to try to round up transportation to the boats.

At the road, there were already three tricycles waiting. Built for two or three passengers in the sidecar and one on the back of the struggling Yamaha, Suzuki or Honda, these were the mainstay taxis in rural Philippines. Sometimes five or six people could be piled on, but with American size passengers and rough dirt roads, three was the limit. I knew there would be no problem shuffling everyone to the village four miles down the coast where the boats would be waiting. These tricycle drivers were all too eager for the few coins they could earn hauling passengers, especially American young people.

Surprisingly, the boats were waiting as scheduled and the half-hour boat ride across the channel was a first time experience for most of the team. With eager eyes, fingers pointing, cameras clicking and hands slicing the crystal waters, some were transported into that mystical, south-seas world: carefree, laid-back, where the only thing that goes wrong can be well handled by a straw hat. Others sat quietly, their minds still tortured by the night before.

Soon enough we were overwhelmed by quiet as the boatmen shut off their banging single cylinder engines to drift over the multicolored coral heads toward the white sand beach. They slid to a stop, bow slicing the white sand, and in a matter of minutes we were unloaded. Then with another reminder to the boatmen to not come back until the next afternoon, they were waved off and everything was packed up to the beach house.

Sitting thirty yards from the water at the far edge of the white sand and shaded by obliging coconut palms, the beach house snuggled up against a cliff. Built only of bamboo with a palm thatched roof, it was already showing signs of its battle with the elements although only two years old. It was constructed on three levels. The front level, just four bamboo steps above the sand, had no walls to obstruct the dazzling view.

In front of the house, the wide flat beach was dotted with driftwood and patches of seaweed. Whitecaps flashed out on the channel, and beyond, on the main island where we had come from, the green mountains rose quietly into the brilliant blue of a tropical sky. At the rear of the house the underbrush crept down the cliff from the mini-jungle that topped the island above the twenty-foot cliff.

From the front level, five steps led up to the upper level, the sleeping area. Open too, except for a three-foot high wall, it afforded privacy without suffocating a breeze or the view. Underneath this room was an enclosed area for storage, and over an elevated walkway, a discreet distance away, a combination dressing room and toilet.

Brief instructions were given, then like ants out of a jar, eager young people scattered each to fill their own personal curiosity. Those who had not worn their swimsuits under their clothes waited their turn to use the

Chapter XXVIII

dressing room. While waiting, shards of conversation spilled out, to be continued by the next in line.

"Wow, what a place."

"Just the boat ride over makes it worthwhile."

"Not the same as the boat trip down from Manila, huh?"

"Oh please, that was a bad dream. Twenty-two hours, we were told."

"Sure, if the engine had kept running."

"For all we know, we'd still be out there."

"A ship load of skeletons, adrift forever."

"Not to worry, it wouldn't have stayed afloat that long."

"But we always had the lifeboats."

"Oh right! Did you see them? Rusted clear through. I mean, holes you could stick your fist through."

"Sure strengthens your prayer life, doesn't it?"

"I think some of us needed it."

Nervous laughter, unnecessary throat clearing and averted eyes confirmed what Carla had already confided to us.

Before leaving Manila we had prepared the team as best we could for the adventure of the boat trip down. "Take enough food and water for a twenty-two hour trip. Everyone who values their health does. Sometimes you can buy soft drinks, but don't count on it."

Glances of disbelief had followed my statement until Carla and Pauline confirmed with simultaneous nods.

Many heads were turned as the thirty-three white-skinned, blue-eyed young people strolled two by two up the gangplank of the inter-island ship. Light talk and laughter was in order as they swung Styrofoam coolers between them filled with junky foods that many of the locals would have considered gourmet.

No one knew that twenty-four hours later they would still be floating in the South China Sea, helpless, the ships engine dead and food and water severely rationed. And some, while their companions slept, would reach quietly for an extra ration of food or water. "*I'm bigger and need more food*," some thoughts tried to justify. And others, '*I'm smaller and don't have the reserve*." All manner of claims float on the winds, but only when tests blow in are the authentic revealed. Fortunately, engine repairs were successful and the next day the ship limped into the harbor where we anxiously waited.

On the beach that evening, flames from the campfire climbed to melt into the sunset. The gold of the sky reflected off the white sand, danced on the curl of each wave and illuminated young faces pleasantly tired by the activities of the day. The sunset tinted their laughter with gold and pushed plans and schedules far into the background.

It softened the numerous veneers that we burden ourselves with: veneers expected by leadership, peers, commitments, life-styles or other perceptions, real or imagined. And they began peeling away one by one. And beneath those veneers lay fears, questions, doubts that we hope to never have to face, or have come to understand that they should not even be there. Or have been told that if we are who we say we are, they don't exist. But they do and to deny it only gives more time form them to ferment, build pressure and blow that veneer at the most inopportune time. You hope that when it does blow you'll be alone in a safe place, or at best a trusted, understanding friend is present who can help you through the mess.

Better yet to have that trusted friend there before pressure builds. Someone who has been there, knows the process and can guide you to the right answers and still remains an understanding friend, an arm around the shoulder, a soft word, a prayer. Or just a silence that says, I care.

That evening we all became a little more real. Authentic. Stronger.

Chapter XXIX
KILLER BEES

All too often life was disrupted by the unwanted, so when pleasant disruptions occurred they were most welcomed. A young man, American, about twenty-five showed up on our doorstep wanting to see how "tribal missionaries" lived. We welcomed the excuse to take a day off and planned a weekend on Taguatihan, but plans are like the wind or one misstep. Wind can bring rain, and one misstep can bring worse.

***

"There!" Carla pointed through a break in the foliage. As abruptly as it had started, the half-acre jungle ended. In front of them, beautiful in its starkness, pushed up from the guts of a young world millennia ago and sculpted by sea and wind, fingers of lava pointed grotesquely at the brilliance of a tropical sky. Thirty feet beyond, the display ended at a cliff above a rock strewn beach where crystal waters pulled white sand between coral heads.

"Wait." Robb touched Carla's arm and stepped back, "Don't move." He pulled the camera strap off his shoulder and unsnapped the leather case. "No, no, don't move. I want you in it too. This I want to remember and you're certainly a part of this." A smile lit up her face as the shutter snapped. To get a better perspective, Robb stepped back two steps and one sidestep off the trail. The sound of the shutter snap was drowned by the angry drone of a thousand bees disturbed by one foot in a rubber thong as they rested from the heat of the day in the underbrush.

Carla turned at the sound of Robb's cry to see him as if frozen in time looking down at the swarm that covered his bare legs and quickly rose to engulf him.

"Run! This way!" she called, reaching a hand toward him, her other arm stretching toward the lava field and the sea beyond. It flashed through Carla's mind that her mother was deathly allergic to insect stings and the thought of inherited allergies made her turn and run as Robb moved toward her, slapping at his legs. But before she had taken two steps the bees caught up to her and angry pricks of fire stabbed at her arms and back.

They stumbled and ran, sharp fingers of lava cutting their feet. Robb, not accustomed to walking in thongs, lost his, and his feet were quickly torn and sliced on the lava. He stumbled, his shoulder catching the edge of a jagged formation. Blood splashed on the rocks from his feet and the deep gash on his shoulder but neither of them noticed.

They swung wildly, slapping at the bees that relentlessly pursued. Their bodies were quickly covered with stabs of fire as they raced toward the cliff. They hesitated at the edge.

Fifteen feet below, the sea lay calm, clearly revealing soft white sand framing massive coral heads just below the surface. Carla pointed to a sandy spot and hand in hand they jumped. They hit the water together and went down, their feet sinking into the sand six feet below the surface. The shock of the water-cooled and numbed their bodies for a moment. Surfacing, they gasped for air, the pain returning. Each sting a pit of fire.

Carla looked at Robb, already red welts forming on his face. She knew she looked the same. "What was that?" he managed to say, bewilderment mingling with the pain.

"*Potiokan*!" was the only word Carla could gasp. It was the native name for the wild bees of the jungles and wilds of the Philippines. Not unlike the so-called killer bees coming up from Central America, now found in the southern U.S. their sting was little more than that of the common honeybee. When aroused however, every bee became inflamed, stinging anything that moved.

The fire in Carla's veins was magnified by her thoughts of possible allergic reaction. Robb pulled at a bee struggling in his hair. Then another and suddenly their reprieve ended as the bees once again swarmed around their heads. They dove under water scraping at their faces with their hands to dislodge the stubborn bees, then turned toward the open sea, their lungs burning. Surfacing, they gulped for air only to find the bees had followed. They swam on, splashing water in each other's faces to drive away the bees.

Chapter XXIX

Carla felt herself weakening, her muscles trembled and knotted. They couldn't be more than two hundred feet off shore but it seemed like a mile. Struggling to keep her face above water, she turned toward Robb. He wasn't doing much better. A bee crawled across his head having already planted its stinger in his scalp. Blood stained the water from Robb's torn shoulder and the thought of sharks surfaced in Carla's mind. They locked eyes for an instant—or an eternity, it didn't matter. Then Robb's eyes shifted and widened, focusing on a point beyond Carla's shoulder. What was to have been a Saturday of relaxation and fun had ended.

It began Friday afternoon late, the end of an unusually hectic week. The last of the patients had made their way to the edge of the yard, turned and with a wave of the hand toward the mountains indicated their departure. A welcome quiet settled.

Pauline leaned against the bamboo doorpost of our house, the weariness in her face failing to dampen the satisfaction in her eyes. She unconsciously fingered the stethoscope that hung from her neck.

Carla and Robb sat on a bench in the living room. Carla was diligently transforming scribblings on odd bits of paper into personal health records on three by five cards and handing them to Robb. With much coaxing Robb then filed them alphabetically—not that Robb could not spell, but many of the tribal people had no last names and he was not familiar with the family groupings. They were involved in quiet conversation.

I stepped out of the one room bamboo hut across the yard that I called office and rolled my shoulders trying to loosen tight muscles. Translating portions of the Bible into an unwritten language was a slow, grinding process. Words are only vehicles to carry meanings, and correct meaning was my goal, not a literal word for word translation.

I ambled across the yard and stepped up beside Pauline. "Hard day?" It was more a statement than a question. "Anything planned for tomorrow?"

"No." Her eyes were still on the empty trail toward the mountains.

"How about Taguatihan?"

"Can we, Papa?" Carla's ears had perked up and her eyes sparkled more than usual as she fumbled with the last card. Then hurrying on before an answer could be given, "Tomorrow is Saturday you know, and we always do something on Saturday." She stood, hands on hips and leaned forward trying to emphasize her mock sternness.

I returned her scowl, but knew she was right and the corners of my mouth must have twitched a tad because she quickly turned to her brother, whose head suddenly appeared from his bedroom door.

"Mike, go rent a boat! We're going to Taguatihan!" Before the words were completely out of her mouth, Mike was down the steps, out the door and straddling the Honda.

"All right!" Could be heard over the buzz of the motorcycle as he kicked the starter.

Chapter XXIX

"And don't forget to ask permission from Mr. Talosa." But her shout was lost in the dust of a 100 c.c. motorcycle and a fifteen year old boy as they weaved up the hill between the old Mango trees.

Then as quickly as the sound and dust faded, so did the excited little girl, and it was a mature young lady of nineteen who turned back to face us, poised as if she had just escorted the last of the guests from an afternoon tea. But she didn't really turn to face us as much as to Robb.

Robb had endured the arduous trip down from Manila two days ago to see how "tribal missionaries" lived. He was completely taken aback by the contrasting civilizations that lived virtually side-by-side in the Philippines. The modern city life of Manila was a world away from the illiterate tribesmen who walked the trails here, their machete swinging by their side just as important a part of their identity as was their loincloth or bare feet.

Robb was one of the many young summer missionaries who made their way to various countries to help the old timers for a few weeks each summer, and left with their view point of the other world drastically altered if not changed completely. He was young, inquisitive and with an adventurous side that brought him here where few others dared. And he was most likely the only Caucasian that Carla had met since her teens had changed her outlook on boys.

"Taguatihan is a private island just a few minutes boat ride away." Her words had a matter-of-fact sound to them, but her voice seemed to be floating over toward Robb, as was she. "Mike's going to get permission from the owner and nobody else goes there and it's beautiful and . . . ." She caught herself starting to bubble and turned to the family with a set in her eyes that started me nodding in approval before she finished her explanation. "And it's going to be fun, right?"

We all knew it would be. In spite of the work of preparation, it always was. Mike and I would spend most of our time spear fishing or just enjoying the freedom of weightlessness gliding among the coral heads and numberless variety of fish, some flashing brilliance as they dash for safety. Others would eye us indifferently while still others, quite possessive of their territory, would attack with a mock furiosity which at times provoked bursts of laughter quickly sending us to the surface for much needed air.

At quieter times Pauline and I would drift on the surface of the shallow lagoon enjoying the same beauty without the need to fight the current of the deeper area or of keeping a wary eye on the murky depths beyond the drop-off where sharks were said to prowl. Or we would walk hand in hand among the grotesque beauty of tortured lava outcroppings on the heights of this five-acre bubble of solitude. Often we would simply sit on the lip of the cliff on the seaward side feeling the cool spray of the waves storming the cliffs. There we would imagine the waves bringing greetings from across the Pacific,

Chapter XXIX

greetings of hope, an assurance that we were not alone, that home had not forgotten us.

But mostly Pauline's enjoyment came from the shade of the cliff overhanging the other end of the beach. Stretched out on the soft sand she would search for miniature seashells or pour over one of her ever-present medical journals. Her desire for knowledge in order to help others, whether physically or spiritually, never took a day off.

***

Saturday dawned with a hum of activity. Accompanying the four of us was Emma, a tribal girl abandoned by her mother. Emma had severed an achiles tendon from a broken bottle carelessly tossed into a muddy rice field. She lived with us many weeks while the tendon healed and her mother "gave" her to us as payment for our medical care. Ruthie, a young Filipina lady who helped us in the church work and around the house was also a welcome companion.

The ice chest was packed with what little ice our kerosene refrigerator could produce and a few precious cokes. Sandwiches with bread baked the night before were checked off one by one and packed in a box. Matches, a machete, and of course a first aid kit with everything needed from suntan oil to suturing supplies and anesthetic were accounted for. If it could happen, Pauline was prepared. She rolled up two magazines and pushed them down into the box. No one needed ask what they were.

"Come on, Papa, everything's loaded and waiting."

"Coming, Carla. Just one last check." I went through a mental checklist; back porch locked, toolbox, back door, all windows. Did they get all the boxes, the cooler, all the paraphernalia? Blankets? "Mike, got your spear gun, masks, and fins? Did anyone cut any bamboo sticks to roast fish on?"

"What fish?" A voice taunted.

"The fish we're going to catch, of course."

"You catch some, and we'll have no problem praying up some sticks."

A smile tugged at the corners of my mouth as I slid the door shut firmly and dropped the lock through the hasp.

"Are you doubting Mike and my ability to catch fish?" I challenged as I slid behind the wheel of our much-depended on four-wheel-drive Scout. In constant need of repair, the Scout was nevertheless roomier than the old World War Two Jeep which decided on its own to retire.

"Are you doubting the power of our prayers?" Came the reply from the back seat.

Some guffaws came from the back seat as well as a good-natured slap at the back of my head as I slipped the Scout into gear, transfer case in low and four-wheel drive.

Chapter XXIX

Lurching off up the hill and past the Mango trees, we made a brief stop at the neighbor's to tell them where we were going. It was customary, although it was doubtful if there was anyone who didn't already know. Few things ever slipped by the jungle grapevine. The path, which with a little widening accommodated our vehicle, wound through the village of Cogon, then skirted the riverbank down to the dirt road that followed the beach. Five kilometers and four fishing villages later we wheeled onto the beach where the boat waited.

Mike had told the boat owner nine AM, and it was already almost ten. No one was expected to be on time in the Philippines. The boatman sauntered up as we started pulling cargo from the back of the Scout. By his look at the pile of gear, he was most likely wondering if this was going to be a picnic, or a permanent move.

"We'll be returning by three, okay?" Pauline emphasized the hour knowing he would be late anyway.

"Yes, three okay," he replied in the local dialect as he hoisted a box to one shoulder and grabbed another in the other hand. Robb and Carla swung the cooler between them and Mike and the girls scooped the rest of the gear up while I locked up the Scout.

As usual there was little conversation on the way over to the island. For some reason, the boatmen equate power with noise and the mufflers are the first things to be removed on their little one-cylinder power plants. The hammering of the engine coupled to an off balance propeller shaft left everyone to retreat into their own thoughts. Except for Robb. Everything was new to him and when he wasn't pointing his camera, he was asking questions, which made it necessary for him to slide very close to Carla on the wooden plank seat in order to be heard. She didn't seem to be complaining.

The fifteen minute boat ride was beautiful, and the quiet as the engine was shut off was overwhelming. The boat seemed to float on air over the emerald hued crystal waters and multicolored coral heads. It then slid to a stop, bow slicing into the white sand. In a matter of minutes we unloaded and with another reminder to the boatmen, we waved him off and everything was packed up to the beach house. After we checked out the bathroom to be sure it wasn't occupied by any surprises, we filled the rest of the short morning with swimming and bursts of laughter and of races across white sands and of softly floating on the bay. Drifting but a few feet above a silent world of color and undulations indifferent to the tensions of the week, we felt them dissolve one by one into the crystal waters.

But all too soon it was time to start thinking about lunch, so Mike and I headed for deep water for some serious spear fishing.

Time seemed to disappear and we reluctantly turned back toward shore and lunch. As we climbed the beach-house steps, Pauline was stretched out in the shade with a medical journal.

"Whatcha reading?" I asked, dropping down beside her.

Chapter XXIX

"Emergency treatment for massive insect bites." Her eyes never left the page, but a slight change in her voice began to deflate me as she added, "How many fish did you get?"

"Well," I hesitated searching for a reply. "I don't see any bamboo sticks. Did you pray?" I countered.

"No-o-o." There was a definite lilt in her voice now. Then she looked up with a sparkle. "Did I need to?"

I feigned an embarrassed grin and searched the horizon for a new subject to change to, but all I saw were Carla and Robb approaching up the stairs, and from the look on Carla's face, I knew she had overheard.

"What's for lunch, Papa?" She asked choking back a laugh.

"Come on, Dad," Mike ran interference while retreating down the stairs, "We better help with lunch".

"Right." I rolled to my feet. "I better find some firewood."

"For what, the potato salad?"

It was a perfect day and a cold lunch only added fuel for laughter.

Lunch over, we submitted to the warm breeze stirring the palm leaves and the gentle murmur of the water. Choosing a likely spot on the bamboo floor, I stretched out, letting the softness of the day massage away the kinks of the mind as well as the body. Pauline went back into her book. Mike was already in dreamland, and Carla and Robb with their backs propped against the railing, were quietly discussing things young people discuss.

After what seemed only a few moments, I opened my eyes to quiet footsteps as Carla and Robb tiptoed past and down the steps. Seeing my eyes open, Carla pointed to her mother fast asleep, put a finger to her lips and motioned toward the far side of the island with its miniature jungle and cliffs facing east. Robb raised his camera for me to notice and I waved them on. Propping myself up on one elbow, I spotted Mike half way down the beach with his diving gear. I decided to join him.

The afternoon went quickly as Mike and I glided and probed the coral forests on the north end of the island. We were constantly aware that the beauty and quiet of the water world had its own dangers also. A Moray eel let us know which territory was his and we honored it, keeping an arm's length between us. Drifting over a sandy stretch, we kept a wary eye on a black and white striped sea snake winding its way along the bottom. Most sea snakes are poisonous and we didn't care to debate which species this was.

Experience had also made us aware of a type of silvery seaweed that did its slow dance swaying to the rhythm of the ebbing tide. To touch it was like an electric shock. My first experience sent a jolt up my leg as I brushed against it and left a red streak that burned for several days. Beauty is seldom without risk.

As I drifted along the surface I sensed a shadow angling in at me from the side. Turning, I saw Mike

Chapter XXIX

approaching. He motioned toward the beach and I looked up to see a boat approaching. Pulling my mask off for a better view, I recognized it as the boat we had hired. Could it be three o'clock already? We turned reluctantly toward the beach, and swam slowly not wanting to miss any part of this peaceful oasis. We knew we'd most likely be back in a couple of weeks, but so much happened in a week that we had learned not to postpone one moment of life. It was so fragile.

Waving to the boatman as we pulled ourselves out of the water, we told him we weren't yet ready and he smiled and leaned back against the engine housing as if to say, no problem.

At the beach house, Emma and Ruthie, seeing the boat, were busying themselves packing and tying boxes for the return. Pauline waved her magazine at me as I climbed the steps. "Finished." she said triumphantly.

"Great. Did you get in the water at all this afternoon?"

"No, but it was relaxing for me, really. Next time I'll get in . . . honest." I smiled knowing that she truly did enjoy herself.

"By the way, has anyone seen Carla and Robb?"

"Not since they left after lunch . . . do you think someone should go look for them?"

"Well, maybe if—"

"Mom, look!" It was Ruthie pointing excitedly towards the beach. "It's Carla and Robb, but how did they get there?"

A small outrigger boat was slicing into the calm of the lagoon. Two men paddled briskly and between them sat Carla and Robb. Robb was waving and Carla appeared to be slumped over. As the boat slid to a stop on the sand, Robb scrambled over the side and reached back to help Carla out.

"There's something wrong." Pauline was on her feet and down the steps in a flash, but Mike reached them first and took Carla's arm to support her. Her head was down and her steps uncertain. Robb wasn't too steady either. Even before the rest of us reached them we could clearly see that their faces, arms, and every exposed part of their bodies was swollen and red. Carla was shaking uncontrollably.

"*Potiokan*!" Called out Mike as we met and turned back toward the beach house. Carla and Robb in their swimsuits had little protection.

"Robb's feet . . . ," Carla managed to get out between chattering teeth. His feet and ankles were covered with blood still flowing from deep lacerations on his ankles.

"I lost my thongs." His voice was calm but weak. "We stepped on some vines and they came up from the ground, they were everywhere . . . we ran . . . I dropped my camera!" He looked up questioningly.

"Don't worry about it. I'll get it later." I heard myself say calmly, but inside everything was racing. I knew Pauline always carried an insect sting kit for her allergy, but I was wondering of the probability of it being

Chapter XXIX

hereditary, and how long it would take to get to the doctor. The only one within many miles was in town and even with the boat already here I knew it would take us close to an hour. I glanced at my watch. Not yet three. Why was the boat so early? I didn't remember consciously praying, but I most certainly was. I knew if the allergy was hereditary there was little chance of reaching the doctor in time.

In the few precious moments it took to reach the beach house, Pauline had run ahead and was frantically tearing open one neatly packed box after the other searching for her sting kit. Finding it, she called out instructions and Emma and Ruthie were both fumbling for a cup and the little bit of water that was left.

"Here, take these. Benedryl!" Then to no one in particular, "We're going to have to get them to the doctor . . . fast." Her hands were sure and steady in spite of the near panic that must have been in her mind.

"Epinephrine," she said quietly as she wiped a spot on Carla's arm and injected half the liquid from a small syringe. Then the remaining half for Robb.

I was vaguely aware of movement behind me and turned as Mike, the boatman and both girls, started off toward the boat with the gear.

"Shall we go?" I tried again sounding calm but was carefully watching Carla and Robb's reactions and reflexes. They were getting slower. Dull.

"My ear, Mom." Carla raised a hand to her head. Pauline moved her hand away and with her own fingernail pulled a dying bee out of her ear and flipped it away, and when she turned to me, I could see her efficient, compassionate eyes begin to cloud with tears. The next hour was going to be an eternity.

Mike put his shoulder to the bow of the boat. Pushing and lifting, he freed it from the sand and jumped aboard as the boatman poled it back into deeper water before starting the engine. Everything seemed to be in slow motion as he labored to turn the boat, leaning into the bending bamboo pole. As the bow slowly swung around, the boatman took a long look over the side assuring himself that he was out far enough for the propeller to clear any coral. Then placing the pole carefully alongside the outrigger, he secured it before turning to the engine. Taking the starting rope, he wound it carefully around the flywheel, set the throttle then pulled. The engine rolled over several times without response. Again.

Pauline looked up at me with eyes pleading—demanding—that I do something to help.

A third time the rope was wound carefully and pulled. The engine coughed, and with a fourth pull it came to life filling the air with its unmuffled hammering and exhaust fumes. Never was that sound so comforting. He set the throttle and from the sound it was set higher than usual. I had to remind myself that it was not the custom of these people to show signs of anxiety or hurry. I was sure that if my knotted stomach muscles could have propelled that boat it would have gotten us across much

Chapter XXIX

faster. I tried not to look at my daughter shaking and leaning heavily on her mother. To do so I was sure would cause me to scream at the boatman for more speed though I was sure he knew the limits of his own engine. I only prayed that the tired little engine wouldn't be overstrained and quit, as they often did.

It seemed hours before the boatman shut the engine down and we silently glided onto the rocky beach where our Scout was parked. Mike leaped from the bow before the boat stopped and was off and racing up the beach toward the Scout. By the time we were unloaded, he was backing down toward us. In no time we were loaded and down the dusty road to town and the doctor who we prayed would be there.

Speed was always tempered with caution and as we approached one of the narrow wooden bridges that crossed the numerous streams. I remembered that only last week this very bridge had been closed for repairs for several hours and I sent up a little thank you to God.

***

"Yes, the doctor is here. Come in please." The house-girl greeted. As we stepped through the large doorway we could hear laughter and many voices. It was a party. I once again felt the tightening in my stomach. In this country parties were seldom disrupted . . . for anything. It just wasn't done. The house-girl offered the wooden bench, stood a moment, then started asking what had happened. Pauline touched her on the shoulder with a cold calmness.

"Would you please get the doctor . . . NOW!" The house-girl left quickly, her fear of disturbing the party overcome.

"So, how did you get in the fishing boat?" I asked trying to ease the tension of waiting.

"We tried to beat the bees off with our towels," Rob answered. "Then we ran to the cliff . . . ."

"Robb lost his slippers and camera," Carla added in a weak voice.

Robb continued. "We jumped off the cliff. Carla pointed to a sandy spot between the rocks and we jumped. If the sand hadn't been soft I'm sure we would have broken something. I don't think the water was four feet deep."

"And at low tide it would have been zero," I put in.

"Jumping off a fifteen foot cliff onto even soft sand isn't too healthy." I added, trying again to down play the seriousness of the moment.

"The bees followed," Robb took up his story rocking his head slowly from side to side. "We swam away from shore splashing each other to keep the bees away. I didn't see the boat till we were almost to it. Carla shouted something to them and . . . ."

"I just told them it was Potiokan." Carla's head rolled back against the wall, eyes swollen closed.

"They helped us into the boat and brought us around."

"I was going into shock, Papa. If Robb hadn't pushed me into the boat I wouldn't have made it." She reached a hand out to Robb, but he didn't see. His head was hanging low, eyes closed. A lump grew in my throat.

Doctor Prado and Pauline had worked together on numerous medical cases and he had never departed from the measured indifference so predominant of the Philippine culture. Now, however, he was visibly troubled. These were American lives in his hands. And one was the daughter of a friend; a friend who was respected by the commander of the Provincial Security Forces. By a twist of fate that the doctor could not understand, he was also respected and protected by the local commander of the rebel forces: the highly militant New People's Army, as the communist underground was called.

Doctor Prado gave an additional injection of epinephrine to each, then he paced. He glanced at the rapidly growing crowd of curious outside his home and office. Then he prescribed rest and close observation . . . in their own home. Besides, he assured Pauline, her expertise and treatment were very capable. His parting advice was to not let the bee stings get wet lest the patients skin fall off. Pauline agreed that home treatment would most likely be best.

At the house, two cots were set up side by side in the living room and Carla and Robb were made as comfortable as possible. Throughout the remaining afternoon and evening their blood pressure dropped to a dangerous 60 and pulse rates also slowed to well below the comfort level before they began to stabilize, and it was a full week before Pauline dared call them recovered.

The next day Mike and I returned to the island to search for Robb's camera.

"You wait here and I'll go up and look for it," I said as the boat slid onto the shore. I buttoned the sleeves of the long sleeved shirt I donned in case the bees were still there, and double-checked the rubber bands around my pant cuffs. I had nothing to cover my face and head, but felt I could swat away enough of them to be effective.

"If I'm not back in fifteen minutes, come looking for me." I grinned at Mike in a feeble attempt at humor. It didn't work.

Thankfully the bees were nowhere to be found and I recovered Robb's camera, along with its leather case imbedded with twenty-one bee stingers.

Through this, we were brought to a more severe realization that faith is not necessarily synonymous with safety, nor with courage, but is more closely related to strength; a strength coming from a very concerned God.

Chapter XXX
MALAY MISSION HOSPITAL

It wasn't a large ceremony: a small group of friends, a prayer, a rusty shovel turning over a clod of dirt, and the Malay Mission Hospital had a start.

But where did it really start? The first promise of funding? The first realization of the need? The first prayer? First unnecessary death witnessed by first time missionaries in a remote tribal region in a province of the Philippines that some countrymen didn't even know existed?

Where do you start a story that seems to be just one link in a chain that you call life?

Maybe we could start the story when my wife, Pauline, and Carla our sixteen-year-old daughter, became inundated with patients at the house; thirty, forty, or more every day. Sometimes patients would walk miles for medical treatment they could get nowhere else. With few exceptions patients came from daybreak to sundown. The tribal people usually didn't like being on the trail after dark, so that gave a little breather until the middle of the night when we would all too often hear a small whisper outside the bamboo grating of our bedroom window, or a polite clearing of the throat. It was quite impolite in the culture of the tribe to wake someone, so it had to seem as if it was not intentional. "Oh, Sir, as long as you're awake, my daughter is almost to die, can you come?" Then away we would go on an emergency for perhaps a couple of hours, or many times all night, only to begin again at sunup.

So many times we would all be completely drained physically, emotionally as well as spiritually. Physically because of the shear hours put in; emotionally from seeing sick and dying people depending on us, their last hope, and not having the time, medicine, or knowledge to help. Have you ever watched someone laying on a bench in your own house and they look at you with that last ray of hope and you have to tell them, perhaps not even with words, that you can do nothing and they are going to die? Then they look away and within minutes they're gone because hope had died.

It drains you. Your chest squeezes and you try to swallow a hot, growing lump in your throat. And last, but by no means least; there's that spiritual drain. You haven't yet learned the language well enough to explain the love of Christ that motivated you to be here in the first place. And now they will never know.

***

Like any living organism, and this hospital is indeed a living organism, there is first the implanting of the seed, then a period of gestation where the seed of life grows, develops and is for the most part unseen. Then that never to be repeated time when it springs forth to perhaps totter a bit then step out on its own to fulfill whatever destiny it may have.

    The seed perhaps was planted on one of our necessary jaunts to Manila for mission business. We were telling our mission director of the medical overload we were under when he calmly gave us the answer. "Why don't you build a hospital down there?"

    Wonderful thought. Why didn't we think of it? Our personal financial support level was below what the mission required to start with. Where were we to get the money to build a hospital? Our visionary director then deflated us by quickly adding that the mission did not have the personnel, equipment or money to undertake such a project. But the seed had been planted. And it grew.

    We went back to the tribe with a new prayer. We had no idea how, but we just kind of slipped it in front of God for Him to evaluate and sort of perform a miracle. Well, miracles do happen. Sometimes one just drops in on you, sometimes you have to look around a lot to see where He put it. And sometimes He zaps somebody else with a thought, and in your wanderings you pick up on it and, low and behold, a miracle. That's how this happened. At least the beginning of it. Miracles are sometimes like the living organism I mentioned that takes time to grow and develop.

It was somewhere in the midst of the gestation period when a young businessman from England named Peter Daws dropped in just for a visit. Our mission director had suggested he drop down to see how "tribal missionaries" lived. He was very cordial and we took an instant liking to him. "Why don't you build a hospital here?" He asked after seeing our situation. Where had I heard that before? He stayed for a couple of weeks and during that time concreted in our hearts that somehow, it was possible.

About two miles from us on a flat peninsula jutting out into the South China Sea was a fairly well maintained grass airstrip. I could find no one who really knew who built it, but it was used by the Japanese during the war and then subsequently by the American liberation forces. It was still maintained because an occasional tourist would fly in from Manila to scoot across the bay in one of the many outrigger boats and play on the white sand beaches of a then insignificant little island called Boracay.

It occurred to me that a hospital adjacent to the strip would be ideal in the event of a needed medical emergency where a patient needed additional care we couldn't give, or where a doctor might fly in. I knew that land there would be at a premium and no one in their right mind would sell knowing the prospect of the tourist trade increasing was a real possibility. But there it was, a piece of land adjacent to the strip, big enough for a hospital. And for sale at half the going price. Why did he want to sell? I never knew, but I said yes. Money? I didn't know that either. I had enough to put a small earnest deposit on it and that was it.

As a businessman and business consultant, Peter Daws suggested that one of us would have to return to the States and raise money. It didn't take a lot of time, or a great business head to realize that the someone should be Pauline. She had the charisma and the sincere interest in people to appeal to the ones who needed to be appealed to. Of course God is in the miracle business, Peter frankly pointed out, but He also gave us minds to work out the details.

"I've never raised money in my life," Pauline argued. And truth to tell, most of the public speaking in churches to raise our needed support had fallen on my shoulders. There were still a few churches that were not clear about a woman's authority to fill their pulpits. With all of her charisma, Pauline was terrified to speak in public. One on one and small groups were her forte.

"That's exactly why it should be you," Peter said. "People are fed up with professional money raisers." With that he drew up a check for four thousand dollars, calling it seed money. He was a little bit off with that statement. The seed had already been planted. This was watering time.

We purchased the land and it lay silent while the necessities of life went on and we waited for the next step. The expense of flying back Stateside to raise money was one of those certain necessities that loomed large, but there were other steps in the plan that had to be climbed first. We wrote letters, we asked advice of Christians and non-Christians alike, we strategized, attacked it from the supply and demand angle, the logistics, God's view, and even common sense—not that God doesn't use common-sense, but I mean our own version of it. The only positive feedback came from the people themselves. They wanted it, they needed it. But not the government, not the town mayor, nor our mission could help and we were beginning to wonder about God's viewpoint.

Then one day Dr. Prado came for a visit. Even considering the non-confrontive, oblique approach prevalent to the Philippines, it was obvious this wasn't a social visit. He was visibly upset, embarrassed, almost at a loss for words.

He had received word that an official protest had been filed at the national level. Pauline, my wife, the missionary dedicated to all that is right, the well-being of the people and God, was being accused of practicing medicine without a license. Someone local filed it. "Was it true?" The doctor finally asked.

"True," She had said, not knowing that such a thing as a license was necessary in a remote tribe.

Well, all she had to do was say she wasn't practicing medicine. That was the doctor's advice. Just testify that everything she did was under his supervision. She couldn't. We discussed it, prayed about it, and wondered if God would be honored by just this one little lie. After all, lives were at stake. And for her to stop treating them, would their deaths then be on her hands?

Dr. Prado then suggested the name of an attorney we could see in the provincial capital. We did.

"Just deny it," The attorney said. Same suggestion.

"What can be done to me?" She asked.

"You can be imprisoned, fined, deported, or all three."

Chapter XXXI
INTERROGATION

Pauline went to Manila alone. They didn't want to see me. I wasn't important to them. After all, I was just translating God's Word into an unknown language. That's all, and that wasn't illegal. And besides, someone had to watch the camp.

    The taxi took her as straight as any taxi could to the main gate of Malacanyang Palace, the White House of the Philippines. After identifying herself, one guard stepped into the guardhouse and picked up the phone while not taking an eye off of her. The other guard stood behind her, automatic weapon at the ready. A military car soon appeared and she was driven to a side door of the palace. The door opened and another well-armed escort took her in where she eventually sat in an overpowering room looking across a massive desk at an imposing military figure. Two men in civilian clothes flanked him. They stood. She felt as if she too should stand, but remained seated as she had been asked to do. The military introduced himself.

    "I'm General Ver," he said, his voice not unpleasant, but sending waves deep into Pauline that may well have been identified as terror. He was President Marcos' right hand man; General of the Armies, might be a title that would fit him. Other titles flashed briefly through Pauline's mind: killer, military genius, cold tyrant. He was said to put people to death for the smallest suspicion of inconsistency. He was feared by friend and foe alike. Many had been imprisoned by him never to be seen again. Those flanking him were both doctors of high national standing.

After the necessary exchange of pleasantries, the doctors sat down and began questioning her at will on her medical knowledge. " If a patient came to you with . . . what would you do . . . And suppose you didn't have that medicine what would you substitute . . . but if it's a woman and she's pregnant, would that apply? . . and if in case . . . . "

The questioning went on for hours, and as it slowed, Pauline realized that they had not asked one question she could not answer. Silently she thanked God that He had guided their thoughts and questions because there were volumes they could have asked that would have caught her short.

Seemingly satisfied with her answers, the General leaned forward raising his frame taller than she thought any man could without standing. He laced his fingers together and smiled. "Your medical knowledge is impressive," he said. Then without a pause, "Are you practicing medicine down there without a license?"

All I have to do is say, no, she thought, then I'm home free. But have I come this far for nothing? "Well sir," she heard herself say, her mind searching for words

Chapter XXXI

as she spoke, "If you mean am I seeing patients, diagnosing, dispensing medicine and receiving pay for my work, the answer is no. But if you mean am I looking after the needs of the minorities who would otherwise die without my help; if I am sacrificing my time and myself to physically, mentally and spiritually help the people of your country without taking any pay, then the answer is yes."

His expression did not change. Nothing in the room moved. As if she had never spoken. Then without breaking stride he continued. "Tell me this then, are you giving the Gospel down there?"

Her mind spun wildly. Quite unusual, she thought later because her heart had seemed to stop completely. Again the question and the choice. As boldly as she could from her position below his overpowering presence she answered. "Yes sir!"

His fingers unfurled and a palm came down flat on his desk that ruffled papers and would have brought tears to her eyes had her brain not been temporarily short-circuited. "Good!" his voice rang. "That's what we need in this country, now what can I do for you?"

When her mouth could open and close properly, "We're wanting to build a small hospital in our area and we're going to need to bring equipment in and can you let us bring it in duty free . . . sir?"

"Done!" His voice rang again. "What else?"

Why stop now? "We need to bring in American doctors, can you get them licensed for me?"

"Done! What else?"

"Can your government supply us with some medicine?"

He nodded. "Anything else?"

"Can I go now?" She hoped she was still ahead with that last request.

***

What with other business that Pauline had to do in Manila and a chance for her heart to slow down, it was two weeks before she returned to Malay and the little family and lots of friends that were earnestly praying for her.

In the meantime one man living in town disappeared. He was one of the few and the most vocal who opposed our being there, and some had secretly said was a government spy. Government transfer we were told. It wouldn't have been polite to ask, but we thought we had it figured out who it was that reported us. News travels fast.

As she was replaying her story to me on her return, she reminded me of the story in the Bible of Joseph. How his jealous brothers threw him in a pit then sold him to some slave traders passing through and told their father that some wild beast had gotten him. Later, as you remember, God did a few miracles and Joseph eventually became the number two man in Egypt. Then about that time there was a great famine and these same brothers went to Egypt looking for food. They of course had no

Chapter XXXI

idea Joseph was still alive, let alone be in some power role. Too many years had gone by and they didn't even recognize him. Now there they were negotiating for food with the very man they had sold off. After he let them sweat it out for a while, he told them who he was, then they really sweat.

But he, being who he was, was gracious and explained all that God had done up till then. Then the punch line. "You meant it unto me for evil, but God meant it for good."

The man, who had since disappeared, meant it to her for evil. But God turned it all around and used that very thing to get us permission to build the hospital, and permits, and government medicine, and even equipment in with no duty charge. One big step for mankind. From a very big God.

Plans then seemed to go into high gear as we watched things fall into place. An American builder who wanted to be simply called Wally who was in Manila to help out the mission for a while, came on down to take a look. At the same time, a missionary doctor who we knew from our home church in Kansas City, on his way home from a four year tour in Saudi Arabia, visited and we all sat around drawing plans. My architectural background helped with the actual pencil and paper part while the doctor's input had to do with efficiency; the fewer steps the doctor actually has to take, the more efficient he is. Then the builder added construction feasibilities, footing sizes, how much steel reinforcing, etc. All the time I scribbled out more plans, erased, reached for more paper until we all nodded and leaned back.

Another step, then another problem. That's what going forward does. If it wasn't for problems then everyone would be doing it and there would be no needs left in this world and we'd all be perfect. But guess what?

Now who's going to run this hospital that we have already built in our heads? Our mission wasn't prepared to take on such a project, and we fully understood.

With the exception of ourselves, Action International Ministries, our mission, held its concentration on the overwhelming task of reaching the homeless, the starving and the physically as well as spiritually lost in the easy to get lost in city of Manila. There are in that city thousands of children who simply wander away from home and can't find their way back. And there are those who found home so unbearable that they didn't want to find their way back.

We needed someone with a tried and true track record in the medical side of missions and who was also unflinching in their stand for Christ.

Only one name came to mind that filled both slots; the Association of Baptists for World Evangelism, or ABWE as they are called. With Pauline's medical expertise it was decided that she would go to Manila to try to find Dr. Nelson, the ABWE doctor who headed up its medical arm. It was often a toss-up which of us would go to Manila when it was warranted for one of us to go. The trip out was fatiguing at best but a well needed break

Chapter XXXI

in routine for Pauline who often felt imprisoned by the needs of the people. When she would leave we would pray that no emergency showed itself. Perhaps my prayers had a little different slant to them. I didn't want to be the one responsible for someone's death. The usual list of chronic patients was written down, the ones needing their scheduled medicine or injections. I never did get used to giving injections; not that I didn't know how, but many patients were so thin and their skin was like leather which meant the resharpened needles we had needed to be really pushed to get through.

I escorted Pauline as far as Kalibo to catch the plane for Manila. We spent the night in the Glowmoon Hotel, as the first flight out was not till the following day. We checked in, sprayed the beds with bug spray then went to dinner while the spray did its work. On returning I shushed a mouse back into his hole in the wall and tried to rest. The following morning found us at the airstrip waiting for the plane. Thankfully it hadn't rained that night and the plane arrived reasonably on schedule. Many times we had stood right there and watched the plane circle the field and return to Manila because of a rain softened gravel runway.

Chapter XXXII
CEZAR

On another one of her times away an emergency struck. The kind that strips the missionary to the bare bones and puts his faith to the test that many don't pass; when the life of his own child is laid on the line and there is absolutely nothing he can do.

    I had been absorbed in my language study and translating. Carla and Mike, having finished their morning home-study courses, went about doing what nine and twelve year olds do. Carla quietly curled up with a book and Mike went out to play with one of the eagerly waiting tribal boys his age. Stripped to their shorts, they ran, tagged, wrestled and whatever little boys that age do. They mingled laughter, sweat and more than their share of grass stains and mud as they wrestled.

    Lunchtime came and Carla roused herself to set the table and throw on a pot of rice. As the wood stove took so long to get going and seemed a waste for just the three of us, she fired up the butane stove. Mike came in to clean up and Cesar, his wrestling mate, crawled up on the bamboo bench in the living room to rest for a while. He soon fell off to sleep until his older sister appeared at the door scolding him for not coming home to eat. He roused himself groggily and followed her to their hut a hundred-fifty yards distant.

After lunch we fell back into our routine; the children back to their schoolwork and I to the intricacies of deciphering an unwritten language. Learning to speak a language that has never been written is one thing, discovering, analyzing and describing the many rules of grammar, syntax, etc. is something else. Even if they have never been written, there are many hard and fast rules. And there is no one to tell you why they say it that way and not another.

Afternoons were usually quiet as it was too hot to do otherwise, so when the wail came from the direction of the village it rang clear, mournful, a sound that cannot be mistaken. Someone had died. It seemed only seconds later the sound of bare feet pounded down the trail. A young girl's face appeared in the open doorway. Cesar was dead.

I rushed to the village, praying that any medical knowledge that I had picked up from my wife would come to the front of my memory.

Cesar was indeed dead. He was still covered with grass stains and mud from the morning fun. But no laughter. His brown, naked body lay still, lifeless. I searched him thoroughly for insect bites, stings, bruises; anything at all. I asked questions of the grieving mother: What did he eat? Did he vomit? Diarrhea? Fever? Nothing unusual, no, no, no.

The answers did nothing to throw light on the sudden death. I turned toward home baffled, my mind trying to dig up any reason why a young boy, seemingly as healthy as my own son, would suddenly die . . . My own son with whom he had mingled sweat, laughed and wrestled with a mere two hours earlier. I took a deep breath trying to loosen something that was tightening in my chest.

Carla and Mike both met me in the doorway and tears welled up when I verified their fears. I tried to downplay the possibility of any type of fast moving contagious disease but knew at the same time that uncountable still were the types that plagued tropical areas of the world such as this.

When the very real possibility existed of one of my own children being stricken down and killed suddenly by an unknown, the mere intensity of prayer could certainly work miracles. There is no way to build a wall around them not knowing which way the attack will come or when. You pray. You watch closely. And you try to convey an all-assuring confidence.

A week had passed before Pauline returned from Manila. That time she had gone to Manila for her own medical needs. She had been plagued by fatigue and her red blood count had dropped alarmingly low. The doctor in Manila had given her massive iron shots that filled her with new life, but no sure answers for the reason behind the anemia. With sadness she had listened as we explained about Cesar. She searched through her medical

Chapter XXXII

knowledge and joined the vigil. Nothing ever came of our fear, nor did anything come to light concerning Cesar's death. Some things just cannot be explained.

Chapter XXXIII
DOCTOR NELSON

This time in Manila, in search of Dr. Nelson, Pauline had settled in at our mission guesthouse exhausted. The trials of the trip had overtaken her and her hemoglobin had again dropped to a dangerous level. On the edge of anemia, she tired quickly and had planned the very next day to get another iron shot to bolster her. More often than not the condition of the body and that of the mind are closely related and this was not to be an exception. She was discouraged.

She had no luck locating Dr. Nelson. One of the ABWE personnel thought he was in the city. No, he had gone to their hospital on the island of Leyte another said, and didn't know when he was expected back. He was a busy man, very busy. At the moment she was too tired to care.

She lay back on her bed, her mind unable and not wanting to concentrate on anything. She mentally pushed aside the fact that she needed to go to mission headquarters to order supplies before returning to the tribe. Getting some type of transportation was always a problem, and even though the office was only a short walk away she knew she wasn't up to it that day.

Chapter XXXIII

A pounding at the compound gate only blended with the ever present and irritating noises of the city. Oh for the quiet of the tribe. The pounding continued until she realized that the girl in charge of the home had left to do some shopping. Her body didn't approve, but she struggled to the door, then out to the gate where she could see an American man standing.

"Could you tell me where your mission headquarters is?" he asked. He stood tall and carried himself well for someone she guessed to be in his sixties. His eyes revealed an open, light hearted out-look on life. The kind that makes you glad just to be around him. And he had a car.

"If you can wait a moment while I change clothes, I'll take you there," and opening the gate she ushered him in, glad for the ride to the office.

"By the way," he held out a steady hand, "I'm Doctor Nelson, but most people just call me Linc".

Pauline's first opinion of the doctor had turned out to be right on the money, but underneath the light hearted face she found a man earnest and dedicated to his work and the Lord. After laying her cards on the table concerning the proposed hospital and ABWE's possible involvement, Dr. Nelson suggested we visit him at their hospital on the island of Leyte so we could get to know each other and also get a first-hand opinion of the work.

It was a month before we could make time to schedule a flight to Leyte. Nothing went anywhere without starting in Manila, so back to Manila we went.

Without much trouble we looked up Yvon, an old friend who had flown us to our location a couple of times past when the commercial flights were either full or delayed for some one of a hundred reasons. Yvon was a Frenchman we had gotten to know someplace in the past. He owned a single engine Cessna that he used when he felt like escaping the city for a while. Once in awhile he hired out to tourists who wanted to get to some exotic out of the way island, that is, if he wanted to see the place too. For us, we liked to think he flew us in and out just because he liked us. His primary income came from a small French restaurant that was well worth visiting. It strained our budget but we managed it from time to time.

Single engine planes were not new to me. I didn't think anything could beat skimming mountaintops and stomach lurching drops into hidden valleys. I knew the man at the controls would not endanger himself or his plane. I enjoyed every minute. On one such flight on the way to a mission conference high in the mountains of northern Philippines we plunged over a mountaintop and leveled off with nothing beneath but miles of forests. I knew we were nearing our destination and I eagerly scanned the treetops for what may resemble a landing strip. Any clearing barely one hundred feet long and wider than the planes wingspread would do. "Where's the strip?" I shouted over the roar of the engine.

"There." He was pointing up rather than down. I looked up and there directly in front on a ridgeline was a clearing. Barely twenty feet wide, it ran up the ridge,

Chapter XXXIII

ending at a small hut where several people stood. Trees had been topped on both sides of the runway for the wings to clear. The pilot aimed the nose of the plane at a hump a third of the way up the strip, touched the top of the hump and rolled on up the strip to a nonchalant stop in front of the hut. I was impressed.

While there a plane from New Tribes Mission came in but with a slight miscalculation. He hit the hump too hard, breaking his tail wheel.

That conference was my introduction to Jo Shetler, by far the most remarkable woman missionary I had the pleasure to meet. In her early days, it took three weeks to hike in, but now with the airstrip it was a matter of hours. She had hiked in and planted herself in the midst of several warring tribes who now sat side by side listening to a white-woman tell of the God who created them all equal.

After the conference, we stood beside the little hut and watched the New Tribes pilot calmly climb in with his not so calm passengers. As they climbed in, he instructed the three passengers to lean forward as far as they could on take-off. Then with his little engine revved high and dust engulfing everything, he lowered the flap on the tail elevator until the windblast from the prop lifted the tail with its broken wheel off the ground. Slowly he released the brakes and picked up speed, keeping the tail wheel in the air as he hurtled down the ridgeline. He hit the hump, catapulted into the air, raised the flap and he was on the way back to their home base north of Manila. Once again I was impressed.

This trip would not entail mountains, but miles of open sea. After checking his schedule, Yvon agreed to take us to Leyte and pick us up in a week. He was sure he could find a tourist or two who would be wanting to fly back and therefore make the trip worthwhile for him.

The sky wasn't promising as we walked out to the Cessna that morning. A few clouds hung loose and weather reports indicated a front moving in toward the South where we were headed. It was a six hour trip, about twice the distance as it was to our place; in fact we would almost fly over our place on the way. As we taxied down the strip I wondered idly if any of those little rattles and strains coming from various parts of the little plane meant anything. At times like that I liked to be in a position so I could watch the pilot's face for any signs of strain. There never were any so all was okay. Or Yvon had been in the Philippines long enough to perfect their nonchalant, everything-is-okay-in-spite-of-the-flames, outlook on life. At any rate he took a very serious approach to his airplane, and that we liked.

As he pulled the throttle back and the plane picked up speed down the bumpy runway, I knew we had essentially put all conversation on hold for six hours. Our ears quickly closed off to the drumming of the engine and we settled back to enjoy the scenery. We picked up altitude and circled south crossing over the Pasig River that cut through the heart of the city. It ran black with raw sewage of every description and I shrank inside knowing that even now there were children down there swimming in that. Mothers who hadn't a clue what a germ was or where diseases started were also there washing clothes, beating them against the slime covered rocks. And if they knew, what choice had they? It was the only water they had and one of those row upon row of four by ten tin sheds was all the home they had, perhaps from generations past with little if any hope for the future. I looked away.

We climbed, passing over a corner of Laguna, the four hundred some square mile lake that fed the Pasig River. It was shallow, always brown and crisscrossed with geometric lines, fish traps, some a hundred yards across. Round, square, each one marking the boundaries of one fisherman's claim. Past the lake, houses thinned out. The road wandered away to the south-east with clumps of thatched roofs showing at intervals, or rusted galvanized roofs glaring back the sun, marking small businesses or rich men's homes. To our right the mountains rose and on the horizon, Lake Taal, the deep blue waters of the sunken volcano; a magnificent contrast to the torpid waters of Laguna. In the center of the lake stood the still smoldering volcanic cone, its black ash sides sliding into the blue waters, beautiful but foreboding, a constant reminder that there was still unfathomable energy just below the surface that could blow any time. It was called, "the island on the lake on the island."

Directly below us now, steam rose from a geothermal plant tapping into the heat of that liquid rock, barely touching the virtually unending source for electric power. I wondered how many generations would pass before the full extent of the power could be harnessed. And over there to the north of Manila millions were being spent to develop a nuclear power plant. We reached for altitude as we approached the coastline.

The promised weather front was sliding in and I caught just a glimpse of the graying ocean before it was covered. The little plane could not climb above the gathering, rolling cloud front, so through them we went. At times buffeted by strong winds we flew on blindly, the clouds effectively closing off everything beyond wingtip. I watched as Yvon kept his eye on the compass, and twisting dials, triangulated in on known radio signals. I wondered off-handedly how many other planes just like ours were in the area, their pilots eyeing their compasses and seeing nothing past wingtips.

I remembered another time he had flown us to our location through a rainstorm. As we approached, he dove down through the clouds, his eye on the altimeter, and finally breaking under the clouds when the altimeter was reading below one hundred feet. I had felt like ducking my head as the clouds seemed to push us down toward the rolling seas. We had skimmed the ocean, having to actually climb as we approached the shore to clear the coconut trees. There were seldom times when we had to remind each other to pray. It was as natural and necessary

Chapter XXXIII

as breathing, which we hoped we could continue engaging in for a while yet.

The little Cessna droned on. Shadows flashed past as we dove from one cloudbank to another. My eyes darted to each shadow, half expecting another plane banking toward us on a collision course. This flying blind was not for me. Yvon began checking his watch regularly now. "Getting close?" I shouted over the drone. He nodded while adjusting the radio frequency.

Soon I felt us dropping. "We should be here," he said. "We better be here," he added more to himself then not. He pointed us down, pushing through the clouds. I again watched the altimeter unwind heading for zero. I began wondering how low he would dare before lifting. I could feel my feet pushing against the floor, as if that would help. Then suddenly we left the clouds above and leveled off at four hundred feet. Over our heads, the clouds boiled downward, and below, the coastline. Staggered rows of houses crowded a road and off to the left the unmistakable and only straight line in view; an airstrip. Over five hours flying blind with only a compass and radio signals and here we were, dead on course.

We rolled to a stop in front of the building called a terminal. The sign read, Hilongos, Leyte. This was the right place. The trusty engine shuddered into silence as a jeepney wheeled onto the runway heading in our direction. Brightly painted with every conceivable geometric shape painted in rainbows of color, streamers flying from wires sticking out from the hood, fenders, windshield, strings of glittering tinsel like shapes hung in front of the driver. I wondered how he could even see. It was no different than the thousands of others that vie to be different. Behind him two tricycles kicked up their share of dust. The same paint jobs, same streamers, the little 100 cc noisemakers sporting Yamaha and Honda names had been patched, repaired, wired and modified so much I doubted if any manufacturer would take credit. They sported side cars built for two, but could hold six or eight, that is if at least one would run alongside pushing then jump on as momentum grew.

We unloaded our bags and chose the jeepney, invited Yvon to join us and he did. He wanted to see the hospital, he said, and besides, there might be someone wanting a ride to Manila.

Our week as houseguests of Linc and Lenore Nelson at the Leyte Baptist Hospital was a most informative and encouraging time. But above all it was refreshing and restful. Dr. Nelson was an accomplished and well-known physician and surgeon who chose to give his life and career for the spiritual and physical well-being of those who could not help themselves. In other words he cared. He and Lenore, his life long wife and medical partner, had to date spent nearly thirty years on the mission field. To them every day was a challenge, a reward; a day they could add to with their skill, their compassion and their humor. They were loved, respected and admired by all and I for one could find no reason to think otherwise.

At the designated time, the little Cessna buzzed the hospital and headed for the gravel airstrip, the signal that our week of reprieve was over. But we left with hearts lifted and an outlook that we prayed would not fade.

Back in Manila, we managed to snag a room at the SIL guesthouse. It was always our first choice of places to stay. We felt at home there as we had taken our linguistic training with them. We also felt free to pick the brains of the linguists there on particular trouble spots we had run into in our struggle with the local language. They were a dedicated and hospitable people who never hesitated to share from their storehouses of linguistic knowledge.

Chapter XXXIV
AUNT SADIE

It's always restful to mingle with others of like mind. It strengthens, encourages, boosts spirits often times flagging, and sometimes, just sometimes, brings someone across your path who throws a sizzling beam of light on one of those nebulous pieces of puzzle floating around in a dark corner of your mind. It's a piece of the puzzle of life with the big "WHY?" written across it.

That's what happened to me in that very same guesthouse three years prior. It was summer of 1977 and Pauline and I had just completed the three day ordeal that it usually took to leave our allocation in Malay to make it by foot, out-rigger boat, truck, finally island hopping by plane to a business meeting in Manila. In those days it was only then that we saw another American face, and we treasured the times we could converse in English without the strain of a foreign language, to say nothing of the somewhat convoluted and indirect approach that was the Filipino conversation style. Dinner had ended and the couple we shared the table with had excused themselves. We were settling back with that last cup of coffee when she approached.

"I feel God would have me talk to you," were her first words as she stepped up to the table. And how could

Chapter XXXIV

I deny such a conversation opener? We exchanged introductions and we felt genuinely honored to meet this sparkling eyed legend. Her name was almost a byword in missionary circles in the Philippines. She was known simply as Aunt Sadie. Since before anyone could remember, and most likely before many of them were born, she was a helping hand, an encouraging word, and most of all was known for the strength of her prayers. And she wanted to talk to me.

She didn't waste any time, but immediately launched into her life story. I cradled my coffee cup in my hands and leaned back. I was eager and interested to learn this page, and I was sure an important one, of missionary history in the Philippines, but more than that, I was curious. Curious because I felt her first statement to me more than just an introductory opening. My years of struggle to learn indirect, between-the-lines type of communication that was the mainstay in this country led me astray at first. I was looking for a hidden meaning, a crack in the facade of conversation to get a peek into the true communication. But there was no facade. Her eyes were as direct as her words, and I almost missed something important.

"I first came to the Philippines in 1937," she was saying. "And on the long voyage over I met a young American family. They were on the way to the Philippines too—well, at least it was the first time for her and the children," she interrupted herself. "They had two children, a girl, and a boy about one-and-a-half," she went on. "You see, the husband was a Filipino, and I think that's what first drew me to them . . . or maybe it was her. She seemed lonely already, and I guess I . . ."

By then I was leaning forward, my mind recapturing the story my mother had told so often of our arrival in that year of 1937. And how after a stormy crossing I had to learn how to walk all over again. Of another first-term missionary who had invited Mother to her cabin, and there they had prayed every day. And how that young lady named Sadie had held me and carried me often on her walks across the rolling decks. She had been a strength to Mother, and Mother had somehow relayed that strength to me through the telling of the story. Now I was beginning to see that there might have been something more than just a bond between two friends.

In telling the story Mother would often wonder aloud what ever happened to Sadie. Had she been captured during the war? Had she met the same fate as fourteen of our close friends in a hidden valley ironically called Hopevale?

Each time my mind brought up the scene of the massacre at Hopevale, with it would come the question of *why*? Why was I not included with them? Was there a purpose in my survival? Or was it just an incident without reason? A random choice?

There are times when by faith we must accept that God has His reasons and get on with life; but my heart was not so easily satisfied. I had been taught that to question God was lack of faith, and I relented to that, but

Chapter XXXIV

again, it did nothing to quench the burning that often accompanied the thought.

Aunt Sadie's searching eyes never wavered as she continued her story. "In 1941 I went home on my scheduled furlough not knowing what happened to that family. Shortly after I landed in California the war started, and I agonized in prayer for them, but no word came."

My mind was rushing along a parallel circuit, filling in answers to her questions. It was December 19, of that year, 1942, my sixth birthday when the Japanese planes bombed Iloilo City. It was expected by then and the city had been pretty well evacuated. We had since moved out of the town of Calinog into the countryside and that day began the two and a half years of animal-like existence in the jungles and mountains of the central Philippines.

" . . . And I have not ceased to pray for that family every day for the past forty years," Aunt Sadie was continuing, "especially for their little boy because he's the only one who's name I remember." She paused, lowering her eyes to the coffee cup that I was slowly turning. Reaching out, she laid her hands on mine. Looking up, our eyes locked and she went on. "They called him, Carling, but his name was Carlos. Would you happen to know?"

My eyes blurred. I could not speak. Yes, I knew. I knew of forty years of questions, and now of forty years of prayer. It took a few moments before I could say, "I'm that little boy." And the rest of the evening was filled with the wonder of a faithful warrior of prayer seeing the fruit of her faith.

And I? I was filled with the wonder of the faithfulness of a God. Even when at times we turn our backs on Him in indifference, He's still there with the quiet, yet persistent voice, urging, reminding and at times provoking us on until we see below the sometimes troubled surface into the depths of an eternal plan.

Chapter XXXV
A.B.W.E.

Our next step was to talk with the business end of ABWE. At ABWE headquarters we were extremely fortunate, they said. The two top men we needed to talk to just happened to be in Manila.

Without much delay we were ushered into an office and there began unfolding our plan to the two men authorized to make the type of decision we were hoping for.

ABWE operated two hospitals and one clinic in the Philippines. One hospital stood on the far southern island of Mindanao. Another was on Leyte, about two-third the distance from Manila to Mindanao. The clinic held its own on Palawan, a three hour plane flight southwest of Manila. Our location was nearly three hours East of Palawan and between Leyte and Manila, an ideal spot. Even more alluring with the makeshift airstrip on our property line.

After much discussion and nodding of heads, the man who seemed to be more in charge of the logistics side agreed with our assessment of the need and our ideal location.

"ABWE would certainly welcome the opportunity to expand in this way," he said by way of prelude. "But there is just so much involved in the construction of another hospital, what with licenses, the growing rebellion problem and, as you know, the graft and corruption involved with trying to line up a good work crew, material and the red tape of the local government." He didn't need to say any more but he did anyway. "We just can't take on the project at this time."

As his rambling and profusely apologetic refusal wound down, I found that my mind had been running a parallel course, negating each item as it surfaced. The license issue was already clearly taken care of through Pauline's unwelcome invitation to Malacanyang. A rebel leader owed me greatly and was under obligation to all in his power to protect the hospital, and we had grown quite close to a Chinese merchant in the provincial capital our first year there. Among other things he owned a lumberyard and hardware store, and to put a sort of binder on our relationship, they had named Pauline as godmother of their newborn daughter. As for a labor force, there were twenty or thirty willing Ati men who could be trained quite readily and a few trained carpenters in town that were regular attendees at our clinic. Isn't God good?

I was undaunted and before he could catch his breath, I challenged, "If we built it and equipped it, would ABWE run it?"

He didn't come back quite as quickly, but it was legitimate. "It would take two to three years to get an adequate staff assembled. And as you know, any one

Chapter XXXV

feeling the call must still undergo the sometimes long process of raising their own support after their acceptance and then their training before coming out."

He meant it as an argument but I took it as an acceptance. A few more items were presented which I thought to be insignificant, then he capped off his argument.

"Of course nothing can go any further until our scheduled board meeting in May."

It was only November then. Pauline and I left the meeting still assured in our hearts that the hospital was God's plan, but foggy about the schedule that God wanted. We caught the first possible commercial flight back to Kalibo and then to our home. We were a bit anxious about having left the children for that long in the tribe. Not that we were anxious about their safety—we knew there were a number of the Ati men who would be willing to protect them with their lives if need be. It was the constant threat of disease that was the concern. For our children as well as the tribal folks. More than once we had returned from business in Manila to be greeted with the news that during our absence someone had died. Could we have helped had we been there? Each time we agonized with the question before reluctantly turning it over to God. It's just not that easy when you're the one in the driver's seat—unless you're God, then it's no problem. He sees the road all the way to the end of course, He built it.

***

A month passed before we received word back from the several people we had written to concerning our hospital construction plans. They were all positive. Some offered places for Pauline to stay while she was Stateside. Another offered a car. Several would be contacting their church pastors for opportunities for Pauline to speak explaining the needs. We did the dreaming, others filled in the blanks.

***

Hospital plans were formalized and after several trips to Kalibo for plan revues, the needed officials all nodded heads and we had our permits and construction started with what little seed money we had and our good credit at the lumber yard in Kalibo.

The floor plan was all staked out and digging of the footings was well under way when I recognized one of the building inspectors as he stepped off the bus from Kalibo. After informal greetings he informed me that we could not build there. He saw my obvious confusion and went on to explain that the federal aviation department had informed him that the structure if built there would be too close to the airstrip.

I listened politely knowing that to argue would certainly be detrimental, but my mind was not at peace. How could it be too close? Coconut trees surrounding the proposed building would tower over the two-story structure and there were other buildings much closer anyway. To clear regulations, he said we would have to move everything back thirty feet. Oh great, just great. We didn't have enough property to move back.

With trepidation, prayer and a supreme effort to appear casual and nonchalant, I approached the owner of the land behind us. Fortunately he was in full favor of a hospital being built next door to him and was willing to sell us enough land to make the thirty foot step back from the airstrip.

As we began measuring for the setback, I realized a large tree toward the back of the property had to be cut down. Not only cut down, but had to be dug up, roots and all. It stood where a corner of the hospital would be and to leave the roots would mean as the root system deteriorated, it would leave a hole that the corner of the footing would gradually sink into.

This particular tree was special to some of the older folks. The species of tree wasn't special, but they still used it as a place to sacrifice to their gods for healing. Whether it was a chicken, a goat, bowl of rice or whatever, it was an appeasement to their gods. It was no secret that we served a different God, the living God, but neither did we feel that cutting down a tree held sacred to them would further our cause. It wasn't our purpose to chop down their gods, but to introduce them to ours.

We also knew it would be counter-productive to call a tribal or community meeting to discuss the issue.

That would only lead to cultural pride and opposition, so we just let the news seep out on the tropical grapevine, which grows very fast, and waited.

Not many days passed before the verdict came down. We would be allowed to cut down the tree only because our purpose was worthwhile. Of course the fact that they had already witnessed the power of our medicine at our home clinic may have had something to do with it. Their gods had presumably agreed to it and that was fine with us. The process saved face and kept the momentum going.

The tree came down and the root system was chopped out leaving a hole a decent size truck could get lost in. The stump was rolled off to the side, the hole filled with sand from the beach and progress picked up again.

Chapter XXXV

***

Whenever one or both of us needed to go to Manila, we checked first at the grass runway adjacent to the land and the now-in-construction hospital at Caticlan. If per chance a tourist had flown in and could give us a lift to Manila, it would cut off a two or three day trip to Kalibo and a wait for a seat on the commercial plane to Manila.

The day prior to Pauline's planned departure for Stateside, we heard that there was indeed an airplane at Caticlan and they were going back to Manila that day. We hurried through the remainder of her packing and rushed off with a prayer and fingers crossed. As we drove up to the grass strip we could see a group of people gathered around a two-engine plane. We parked alongside the strip and walked out to them.

Yes, they were leaving for Manila shortly. And yes, they would be glad to give Pauline a lift. I walked back to our vehicle to get her bag with a twinge of doubt in my heart. The two men spoke with heavy German accents, but appeared amiable and friendly. When I returned with Pauline's bag, she was more at ease than I and we agreed that she would go with them.

I watched the plane climb into the sky knowing that before we met again she would have been half way around the world and back, spoken in several churches raising financial as well as prayer support and met many with the same vision and drive as she. Or so we hoped.

With that vision and drive I had little doubt she would meet with success even though her health was still a growing concern for all of us. Only with massive injections of iron was she able to function anywhere near normal. Something was still depleting her blood of the needed iron causing anemia that debilitated her if not for those ongoing iron supplements. I prayed she'd be able to contact the right doctors while Stateside to give her the answers she needed.

As the drone of the twin-engine plane faded, my ears tuned into the labored hammering of the single-cylinder engine on the cement mixer at the hospital site. I drove the hundred yards to the construction site where half a dozen tribal men worked tirelessly shoveling sifted sand, one bag of cement and the proper amount of water into the little mixer. They were mixing a very dry mixture for the cement block maker. After the proper mixing time, the load was dumped into a wooden trough. Then it was shoveled into the waiting block maker, tamped lightly and the form carefully lifted off and the blocks left to cure. The form made two blocks at a time.

Before the completion of the hospital, over ten thousand blocks would have been carefully made by tribal men who, before our arrival, knew nothing about mechanical equipment beyond a machete and an occasional shovel.

Chapter XXXV

The scheduled time for Pauline's return was quickly approaching. And a few days after that, her birthday. To her, special days were always special days and I had nothing or nowhere to go to buy anything for her. I tried pushing the thought to the back of my mind and concentrate on what needed to be done, but to no avail. Then a vine-covered lump at the edge of the clearing caught my eye. The sacred tree-trunk we had dug up. I pulled the encroaching vines away and examined the tangle of its root system still intact. Yes, it would work and soon I had two men with their long two-man bucksaw puzzling at this crazy white-man's instructions. Soon they were busy cutting the trunk off at its widest point, which was where it had emerged from the sandy soil. Then turning it over, they cut the roots off about twenty inches down. From there I had much help loading it into the back of our vehicle and took it to the house. A few more precise cuts, many hours of sanding, several coats of varnish and I had a presentable present. That coffee table with a story would grace our home for many years to come.

Chapter XXXV 354

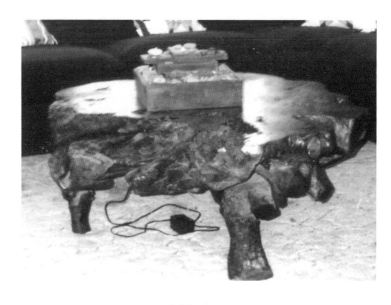

***

I stood on the skywalk at Manila International Airport as the massive 747 rolled to a stop below me. It was August 1st, over two months since Pauline climbed aboard the twin-engine plane on the grass runway and disappeared into the northern sky on her way to this airport and on to the States. This was her scheduled flight back and I strained my eyes as passengers began stepping out the door, down the rollaway steps and into the oppressive heat of a Manila summer, a drastic change from the air-conditioned flight.

    The passengers stood in a slow moving single line in the smog filtered sun as a customs official casually examined passports. Then I spotted her bypassing the lumbering line, her long hair streamed behind. The confidence in her stride alone told me she had met with success. She went directly to the customs desk. A brief conversation and she was waved toward the terminal doors.

I turned for the stairs to meet her knowing she had successfully convinced them of her need to immediately get out of the sun, or some other plausible reason for jumping the line. She would not stretch anything into a lie, but she could give truth an immediacy that would cause heads to nod and action to start. She was good.

The next several days, while waiting for a flight back to our island, we stocked up on needed supplies and I listened to her bubbling over with news of everyone at home, her renewed strength, and the success of the money-raising endeavors.

One Christian organization had vowed a large sum of money for the hospital. Along with a longtime friend and advice from well-connected doctors, she had gained access to medical warehouses where obsolete medical equipment stood awaiting for just this moment. Obsolete by American standards, it still served well in most parts of the world. There, by simply pointing to what she wanted, she was handed equipment to furnish a complete operating room, laboratory, delivery room, as well as an x-ray machine. Churches she visited volunteered the shipping costs and friends even volunteered to come help in the construction.

She saved the best news to the last. "And remember the German tourists who flew me to Manila?

When I told them what we were doing they handed me a check for forty thousand dollars when we arrived in Manila. Isn't God good?" She was radiant.

While in a shopping mall gathering what we knew could not be found down in the province, by chance we ran into the same two ABWE personnel who we had talked to ten months earlier. They had advised us not to get too excited because it would take time to get approval, gather funding, staff and begin the organizational wheels turning toward the construction of the hospital. "Well, good news," they began enthusiastically. "The board met in May and approved the plans to run the hospital if you build it."

Pauline had no problem outshining their enthusiasm. "That's wonderful. It's already half built and the equipment is on the way over even now."

It took several minutes for their organizational thinking to fall into line, but before we left Manila, formalities were taken care of and a partnership formed that benefited many.

Finishing the Hospital

Chapter XXXVI
FISH POISONING

The afternoon sun was already tinting the dusty air yellow when they first started arriving. By ones and twos they came, announced by the rattle of tired little motorcycles pulling overloaded sidecars and dust. Then they came by Jeep loads. Some were helped through the doors by friends and relatives with pleading eyes. Others were carried in, a woven mat slung under a bamboo pole, or piggy-back fashion. A young man, his wife alongside, stumbled through the door. He hugged a small limp form to his breast. A still, small arm protruded from the bundle.

Those who knew Pauline sought her out. Those who didn't followed. She wasn't troubled by the first few cases. After all, a day wasn't complete without at least one emergency.

For almost ten years, before the Malay Mission Hospital became a reality, Pauline, had attended to almost every kind of medical emergency in our home. Her genuine love and concern for the well-being of the individual, both body and spirit, had made her what she was: loved, sought after, and in control.

In some ways, this day was no different. She quickly and efficiently diagnosed, prescribed, reassured, gave orders to staff and turned to meet the next victim through the door or check on dwindling supplies. But that was where the similarity ended. As the number grew, sleeping mats were rolled out on unfinished corridor floors and I.V. bottles hung from four inch nails hammered into freshly varnished walls. Nurses hurried from one patient to another distributing medicine and checking dropping blood pressures.

The only doctor was already occupied in the emergency room quietly attempting to suture back together the victim of a drunken machete attack. Friends and relatives of the victims mingled about confused and frightened. A woman slumped in one corner, eyes sunken, clenched fists pressed against her cheekbones. Somewhere a child cried. A mother sobbed quietly over a small, still form. No one noticed as a skinny dog slinked down the corridor searching for its master.

Neither did I notice the unusual number of vehicles in front of the hospital as I coasted to a stop and stepped off the Honda. My mind was still occupied with the conversation I just had with my friend Raphael out at Palhi. It always took me some time to sort out fact from fiction when I returned from Palhi.

Palhi, the enchanted land. So named because the rugged yet beautiful peninsula jutting defiantly at the South China Sea was honeycombed with caves out of which swarmed clouds of bats at dusk. Caves through which the wind moaned, and during the stormy season moans turned to howls and screams. Just in case there were those of the local superstitious townsfolk who had

Chapter XXXVI

not heard the mournful sounds drifting over from Palhi, Raphael made mention of them often. It was a successful deterrent to even the most curious. The labyrinth of caves also created a quite safe place to store a cache of considerable size safe from prying eyes. A fact Raphael did not make mention of.

Raphael was so openly vehement about his hatred for the government and his verbal sympathy for the underground communist movement that most people thought him to be only that, verbal. But from the tribal people who lived in the foothills and the mountains, a different story emerged.

They knew what was happening high in their mountains where few lowlanders went, and they trusted and confided in Pauline and me. It was troubling that Raphael's outbursts against the government and warnings of rebellion were verified by sightings in the mountains of armed men moving at night.

Pauline called one of the staff to cover for her as she spotted me stepping through the door. She hurried over and quietly explained the situation. In keeping with the culture, she refrained from embracing me and satisfied herself with a gentle touch on my arm as we talked. "You've got to get to Kalibo for more medicine right away," she finished. Her voice, low and urgent, was neither a request nor a command, but simply a statement of fact.

"Easy, honey." I said, trying to assure myself as well as her, "I really don't see anything that can't be handled with what you have here. Besides, it's after six and I don't relish five or six hours out there after dark."

"Honey, someone has to go! I have a strong feeling many more will be coming." Her voice strained, "And one has already died."

She was right, of course. There was really no decision to be made, no one else to go. I just needed a few moments to let the adrenaline pump me up. My mind went ahead down the road trying to see where the darkness would swallow me. Ten minutes to prepare, I thought, then twenty or thirty minutes would put me past the village where these people came from, past the mining company and into the mountains. But no! I first had to go home and gas up the bike. Rats! That would mean another half hour lost.

***

Darkness was already settling in and the bouncing headlight erased shadows that should have outlined ruts and humps in the road. I was jarred into remembering that things look different at night as the Honda staggered over rocks I should have missed. I was barely ten minutes down the road when the mining company dump truck and a Jeep rumbled past scattering gravel and blinding dust. It barely registered in my mind that it wasn't normal for a dump truck to be out at night loaded full. Full of people. I had things more urgent on my mind.

Chapter XXXVI

The people here say that night belongs to the Aswang, the witch that drifts through the black skies and lurks in shadows. It also belongs to the communist guerrillas and the bandits. No one leaves the safety of town after night has conquered. Not the police. Not the army. No one.

I knew that. I knew it well. Ten years had earned me a well-rounded education in the ways of the Philippines. This proud little country had been embattled, beaten and ruled over by more aggressive nations for four hundred years. Her brown shoulders had been often bowed, but now hope was once again glimpsed, if only briefly, in the lightning bolts of rebellion which were flashing unpredictable and fierce. A new generation was now rising. One that was climbing unsteadily to its feet supported by the strength of darkness and saying, "That's enough!"

The tropical night, like a black shroud, quickly engulfed me and only the lonely headlight pushed blackness from the gravel interlude that passed for a road. It dodged between tangles of tropical growth and fought its way through barely perceptible interruptions in the cliffs and mountains. Shadows seemed to duck and hide as the lone headlight sliced and parried its beam with every twist and bounce of the bike. So many times I had covered this three hours between Kalibo and our tribal home, and my little Honda was tired, but I urged it—pleaded with it—just this one more time.

Much as I had become familiar with the road, the country, and the people, it was always different . . . especially now. Anger pumped more adrenaline into my over-loaded system as my thoughts swept across the restless sea of frustrations Pauline and I had gone through during the building of the tribal hospital; tangles of red tape, especially if "bonuses" were not paid in order to "expedite" paperwork. Officials couldn't understand why I wouldn't pay their usual "bonuses," after all; anyone building a million peso hospital just for tribal people must be skimming a good share off the top. They always did, it was a way of life. If construction had only gone smoothly it would have been finished by now, and this trip would not have been necessary.

Kalibo, the provincial capital, was the closest place where food and medicine could be purchased, or legal matters accomplished. This time however, lives were at stake—and it was night. My mind could not turn away from the rumors of armed men moving at night in the mountains, these mountains, and I remembered again my recent visit with Paingl. The cultural demand for extended greetings, oblique approaches, and calculated nonchalance was usually skipped with Paing, but years of practice had made it second nature with me.

"Chuck, my friend", Paing had greeted, "Come inside, let's drink coffee."

"Of course, my friend. Why else would I come to Palhi but to drink coffee and to ride down the smoothest road in the province?" I gestured down the long stretch of shining beach as I eased my leg from the Honda.

"But only at low tide, my friend, or the beach is gone and your Honda becomes a submarine."

A chuckle passed between us, an arm on the shoulder and we went into the house.

"I saw Princie in town," I probed as I slid into one of the well-worn chairs at the heavy wooden table.

Raphael's eyes snapped. "She and the kids moved to town with her sister. She says it's too far to walk to school from here and besides the kids need companions, you know."

His voice softened and his eyes broke away to steal a glance at the fire-blackened coffee pot. " Anyway, it's too lonely out here for her."

"Yes it is," I ventured, "and so many strangers coming and going. Maybe she doesn't like . . . . "

"These are my amigos." His voice lowered, coarse. "And she's supposed to be my wife, but if she doesn't like them . . ."

He stood, cleared his throat, crossed to the window and spit between the wood slats. He faced the window a moment, his eyes following the steps that wound up the cliff to the old house, its wide portico and arched windows a weathered reminder of an age past.

"My father believed in Palhi," he said, his eyes distant. "When everyone in town said he was crazy, he still worked. But this place made him rich. Now with the price of coconut so low . . . I can't even afford to pay my men." He turned toward the boiling coffee pot.

"Raphael, maybe something else can grow up above besides coconut. Maybe coffee?"

"Sure, my friend. Something else is growing up above."

His eyes never changed, but something did. Something insignificant to one not sensitive to the culture.

"Oh? What are you planting?"

A chuckle. Coffee pot in hand he turned. Our eyes met and at that instant I knew that what was being planted could not be harvested, but would before long reap a whirlwind. It did not have green leaves but red sickles.

Raphael's face darkened as he approached. "What did Princie tell you?"

"Oh nothing," I answered a little too quickly, "only there are too many strangers."

"That's not her business." he motioned angrily toward town, sending steaming drops of black coffee exploding across the table. "Anyway, she's not here now." He reached apologetically for a rag and swiped at the dark stain spreading on the table. "Stupid woman." he muttered, "anyway I'm not gonna let them take Palhi." A change of subject defused the moment.

"Take Palhi? Who wants to?"
"Land Reform."
"Oh?"

Chapter XXXVI

"Yeah. They say everything over seven hectares you must sell to the tenant."

"Only if they want to buy, is it not?" I raised a finger for emphasis, "and only if they have the money, and your tenants do not have the money, right? But anyway, what can you do about it?" I added trying to draw out the darkness that stirred in him.

There was that change again. "My people are strong, Chuck. Soon comes the end!"

"Maybe, my friend" I leaned forward reaching for my coffee for support, "But how many will die?"

"Much blood will spill!" His voice was low. He shook out a match, his face hidden behind cigarette smoke. "As much as needed."

"Maybe even your own kids?" I ventured.

His eyes blazed. "They'll be safe. I'll get them out."

Slowly I leaned back in my chair, lifted my cup to my lips trying unobtrusively to steady it with my left hand.

"And my kids, Raphael, do you care?" I felt my pulse in my throat and swallowed it with some coffee.

His eyes bored passed me and seemed to lock onto something bigger than life itself. Then they swung, bringing that something directly between us as a monument, a pledge, and he uttered a phrase slowly, deliberately, as an oath followed by an explanation. Not that I needed one, but that there would be no doubt that Raphael Ong was not one to forget. "You saved my life before, my friend Chuck. I will not allow your children to be harmed."

I lowered my cup and took a breath to say something then stopped. I remembered clearly. Raphael had at one time supplied us with food, medicine and eventually transportation when I had been bedridden for days with a back injury. I echoed back the phrase that was to these people almost sacred. *"Utang na lo-ob."* I owed him my life. There was nothing else to say.

Pauline, in her completely non-partisan concern for people, had once saved his life, and he in turn had saved mine. A bond of uncancellable life indebtedness going both ways had been forged.

Slowly I pushed my cup away and turned toward the open door.

Raphael followed my gaze. "The tide is coming in."

"Taob na." I echoed. "Maybe I should go." Outside, I straddled the Honda and looked up at my friend. Raphael shifted his eyes and became suddenly interested in a sun-bleached seashell at his feet.

"Paing," I said quietly. It was a name Raphael allowed only his close friends to use, "I must complete this hospital . . . for the people."

He squinted into the afternoon sun and the waves rolling in, narrowing the long strip of sand between the sea and jutting cliff. His pause was not so much in deliberation, but to solidify something in his own mind.

"Yes, it must be so." His words were solid.

Chapter XXXVI

"But it'll be *kanogon* if the revolution destroys it."

"No, it will not be a waste." His words were measured. "When the revolution comes, we need the hospital as much as you. You finish it. It will not be harmed. I guarantee."

I searched his eyes and believed, then turned toward the incoming tide and narrowing beach. I had to leave or be stranded. Time seemed always to be an enemy.

***

Time. I tapped the shift lever for another gear as I began the climb toward Campo Verde. Yes, time was indeed an enemy. An unfinished hospital, dwindling supplies, a strange deadly epidemic, armed men moving in the mountains and now Raphael, the young communist leader pledging that the guerrilla action would not hinder the construction. Could he be trusted?

I remembered his oath and gambled on it. Culturally we were indebted to each other for life, and cultural demands were strong. Raphael wouldn't break his word. He was bound by it, and his oriental pride. Suddenly my own safety came back to my mind. Through clenched jaws I smiled to myself at the irony of the thought. Sure, Raphael's men wouldn't ambush me, but in the darkness, bullets don't choose. On the other hand, who else but the *"Cano"*, the American, was foolish enough to challenge the night?

In the oppressive heat of day, everyone knew me. My 6'2" frame gave my dark eyes a clear view over most everyone's heads, and my hair, mostly gray now and usually windblown, was as good as a flag floating above the undulating neatly groomed sea of black heads. Eyebrows long ago pulled into a perpetual scowl by the tropical glare were at times a point of offense, which I struggled to correct whenever I saw the effect reflected in their eyes. To the Philippine people expressions and attitudes of fear or anger were unacceptable, and to be accepted was important to me.

I eased off the throttle as I topped the last rise at Campo Verde and slowed for the police check point. They knew me and usually waved me on through. That is, unless the Colonel himself was there. Then they would proceed with the formality of a search, but now only silence and the darkness challenged me. My headlight swept over the guard house with its bullet punctured walls, and I was sharply reminded that after that shooting incident the army, too, had retreated with the sun.

Twisting the throttle with a snap, I groaned at having forgotten, ducked low under the barricade as the Honda gasped and clawed at the gravel. Quickly picking up speed down the hill, I felt vulnerable. Shadows seemed to come to life and jump behind each bush as I passed. I poised my thumb on the light switch to flick it off at the least sign of trouble. Raising my eyes to the far reach of the dodging headlight beam, I wondered how far I could drive without a light if I needed. The rear wheel slid as I braked hard coming into the first turn much too fast. A reflex twist on the handlebars and I was safely around the turn and out of sight. For more than one reason, I was glad to be alone.

I thought of the Colonel who had ordered the check-point abandoned in the face of danger and knew it was not fear, but rather the patient oriental game of give and take that prompted his move. I had known the Colonel when he was still a Lieutenant. That was ten years ago when martial law and gun control were first implemented. I had turned in my .22 caliber rifle that I had brought with me from the States and had met with the Colonel on several occasions since then for various necessary permits, occasional gifts of government medicine, and just to keep updated on the political situation. No meeting can ever take place without lengthy social amenities so it didn't take long for us to become acquainted.

I knew the Colonel to be a just and fair man—even Raphael referred to the Colonel as honest and brave, but added it was too bad he was a "government lover".

The Colonel was a Christian, and pro-military. A rare combination, I had noted, and a good man to be on the right side of. And that's the side I wanted to remain on, but that could change if the Colonel decided to press me for information about Raphael. Up until now he had not, but if the situation deteriorated more, his military position might demand it.

Many times I had mentally shuffled the Colonel's oriental heritage, military training, and his Christian awakening, trying to decipher his possible actions, but had not as yet seen a clear answer. I theorized that if the Colonel did press me, culture would allow me to discreetly skirt the answer without offending. But the Colonel was indeed oriental and would know I had more answers than I was telling, no matter how skillfully I tiptoed around the subject. Then he would smile, and before long I could expect a very discreet deportation of myself as well as family . . . at the least.

It was like a giant chess game, and I knew the rules. However there was another set of rules in my heart that shouted louder—rules that said the individual was noble, and his dignity, well being, and soul were not pawns to be sacrificed for the sake of the game. And souls were at stake.

***

The flash of headlights caught Pauline's eye as the large dump truck swung into the circle driveway and hissed to a stop. The dust cloud that chased it caught up and settled.

One man being helped out over the side of the truck slipped and fell, landing on the gravel in a disheveled heap. He didn't even try to catch himself. He moved slowly trying to get up, seemingly stunned. Pauline rushed over calling for help as she knelt beside him. His right arm protruded from under his body at an odd angle,

Chapter XXXVI

but something else caught her attention. This man was gravely ill. She gave quick instructions and helping hands carried him in to the hospital. Her mind grappled a moment at what confronted her: a truck load of ill and desperate men, women, and children helping or carrying others like themselves, only worse, down out of the truck and into the door. The driver half climbed and half fell to the running board and there sat, head in hands, dark vomit spilling down one leg. He didn't notice.

"Can anyone drive this truck?" He choked out as he was being helped to his feet.

Pauline quickly stepped over to help. "I don't think so," she replied. "Come, you've got to get inside."

"No!" He shook his head loosely and coughed, trying to revive himself. His eyes were sunken, glazed. "I have to return." Taking a deep breath, he straightened up, still trembling. "There are more." He turned, groping for the truck door.

"Oh Lord," Pauline prayed out loud, as she helped one through the door, "I hope Chuck saw this truck and orders five times more medicine."

She heard her name and hurried over to a young boy laying on a gurney. The nurse straightened, letting the stethoscope dangle from her neck.

"He's fibrillating." There was no hope in her voice. "It's too late."

Pauline grabbed a syringe as her eyes scanned the tray for a long needle.

"Epinephrine, STAT!" Her voice pierced the confusion of sounds. Valuable seconds passed before the nurse returned ripping the protective cap off the vial. A quick swipe of alcohol across a spot on the chest and the long needle sank deep, reaching for the heart.

A few moments later, Pauline stepped back and turned to once again check their supply of drugs as his breathing steadied and his heart regained a more normal rhythm.

As she glanced at the meager inventory, she wished she could just project her thoughts to Chuck and let him know what additional items were needed and how desperate it was. "Hurry, hurry honey, but be careful." Then arrowing her thoughts higher, "Lord, take care of him. We need him."

Someone called to her and she stepped over to where an elderly man lay on the floor. The nurse beside him was removing the blood pressure cuff. "What's his history?" Pauline asked, reaching over and turning up his eyelid.

"He's one of our regulars—advanced T.B. He doesn't look good."

"That's not what he's here for though, is it?"

"No. It's the same as the others."

"What's his B.P.?"

"70 over 20."

"We don't have enough medicine," Pauline said quietly to the nurse. "Save it for those with hope." She met the eyes of the woman squatting next to him and said

Chapter XXXVI

nothing, but they communicated. The woman sank down beside the still form, one hand combed through his hair while the other, tight in a fist, beat rhythmically against her own chest. She cried quietly.

Pauline reached for the nurse's shoulder for support as she stood and turned away, tears welling up. "Not now! Not now!" she commanded her tears, "I don't have time."

***

"Around the curve, across the bridge and we're in Kalibo," I spoke out loud to my Honda—it helped my concentration. "Then to find someone that will open their doors to us at midnight." I released the throttle as I felt the smoothness of the concrete bridge under me. My whole body relaxed and only then was I aware that my right arm was numb. Letting my hand drop in my lap, I rolled my shoulders back trying to release the pinched nerve. I reached for the handlebars again as I came off the bridge and leaned into a right turn that would take me to Tamayo's drug store.

It was a one-way street, the other way, but it didn't matter at midnight. The only witness was a tired street lamp that seemed to nod approval as I passed. I wheeled to a stop in front of the store, avoiding the open sewer, and welcomed the quiet as I shut off the ignition. I knocked on the boarded up door, the sound echoing down the sleeping street. Again, I knocked, trying to make it sound casual but loud enough to be heard upstairs. I waited, then calculating they would probably be awake by then, I listened for a familiar voice. Stepping back a couple of feet from the door, I turned, looking up at the second floor window. The shutter opened slightly. I stepped farther out into the light so they could identify me and came back.

"Good evening, little sister." I gave the proper greeting in their language. "Please excuse me very much, it's quite late, but there is an emergency in Malay. I need medicine."

"They are not here," the window replied apologetically. "They went to the city to buy supplies. You try Alba's."

After a pause, the shutter opened enough for a small brown hand to show itself and wave up the street towards the government hospital. "They are open all night."

"Thank you very much." The hand disappeared and the shutter closed slowly.

Kicking the Honda into life, I apologized to the street as sleeping stores mumbled back at the noise of 125 tired c.c's.

Alba's drug store was open. As was custom, the government hospital across the street provided no medicine, and if it was needed, the friends or relatives watching the patient had to find it, no matter what the hour. The flickering yellow light of a kerosene kinki revealed a hole in the boarded up door large enough for a

Chapter XXXVI

small package to be passed through. After several knocks, I leaned down and peered through the hole. I could make out the outline of a form curled up on the wooden bench. A louder knock and the young lady stirred, almost rolled off, then sat up eyes still closed. I called to her. Her eyes opened and turned in my direction. A greeting, a few words of explanation then she finally woke up. I started over again then handed my order through the hole.

She shuffled down the aisle, searching the shelves and setting bottles on the counter. "You came from Malay?" she said without turning. "Just now?" She stopped at the hole in the door again to check my list. "You're not afraid?"

"Yes, but God is with me."

She looked up at me. Her eyes seemed perplexed at the concept. Then wrapping each bottle carefully in old newspaper, she placed them in a box and tied it securely. Checking off the items on the list which were not in stock, she suggested where I might find them.

"You wait," she said, a new thought occurring to her. "I'll telephone first." She pushed my change to me and shuffled to the back of the store.

I turned to my bike while waiting and idly loosened the nylon rope holding my ever-present tire pump and removed it. I'd need to rearrange things to fit the box of medicine. A sudden thought came to me and I turned back to the hole. The girl was off the phone and back with an affirmation.

"Marianing store has what you need. I ordered for you," she said, the pride of her accomplishment showing through. I knew where it was. I heard the bar sliding from the door and she opened it enough to hand the box out. "You're returning to Malay now?"

"*Ho-o*, many are waiting for the medicine."

"*Áy na ako!* Maybe it's best you wait until it becomes light."

"Maybe, but I must return tonight. Excuse me, but do you have enough medicine to double this order?" I said, hefting the box.

"Yes, but not the other, Marianing has that."

"Good! I'll buy two times this amount if you can box it carefully and put it on the bus, the first trip out to Malay." She looked blank. I set the box down and taking out my list, doubled everything and handed it to her with more than enough money. "First trip to Malay Mission Hospital. Okay?"

"You're going now?" There was concern in her voice. I reached for the box and set it carefully on the carrier. The bike settled under the load.

"You have a flat tire."

I paused, then slowly lowered the box to the ground. Sinking down beside the rear tire, I let my breath hiss out between my teeth. "Well, it's sure better than having one in the mountains," I said. The door slowly closed to save me from embarrassment. Reaching for the tire pump, I hoped it was only a small leak. As briskly as my tired arms would allow, I pumped until the tire

Chapter XXXVI

rounded out and hardened. I listened. Nothing. Then quickly tying the box and pump on, I headed for Marianings. It was only three blocks, but as I pulled up in front of the drug store, I felt the tire sag—along with my spirits.

The door opened and I attempted to wipe away the heaviness. "Your order is ready." she said trying to look alert.

"Thank you." I sat astraddle my Honda as the tire hissed out its last complaint.

"Oh, you have a flat tire."

"Thank you." I fought hard to not let sarcasm leak out. "Where can I find someone to repair it?" I looked up, wiping fatigue from my eyes. "I must return to Malay tonight"

"Tonight?"

"Tonight." I stood, dragging a weary leg across the seat.

"My cousin can repair it."

"Thank you. Where is he?"

"Sleeping. He gets up at maybe six. You just wait, it's not long now."

"But I must return to Malay tonight. The medicine is needed badly." Pulling a crumpled bill from my pocket, I slowly straightened it and turning it over, studied it thoughtfully. "Maybe he would fix it for ten pesos?"

She studied it too. "Maybe," she said turning to a back room and a cousin who would not get all the sleep he wanted that night.

***

The night didn't let up. Nearly one hundred had now been treated for the strange poisoning, for that's what it was decided had attacked the village. Some were released after medication, with instructions to come back if symptoms returned, some lay paralyzed, muscles numb and unmoving. It affected the breathing, the heart: three had died.

The father of the young boy who had fibrillated, although himself quite ill, had pulled the I.V. needle out of his own arm and gone home, leaving his wife to watch the boy and their youngest daughter, who was also ill. He had to find their other daughter. The doctor, having finished his long work on the machete victim, helped for a while then retired to the labor room and gave in to a sleep of the exhausted.

Raphael came with some of his men and helped, taking control as he always did. When his people needed help, he was always there. When he spoke, men obeyed, out of respect as well as fear. He was Pauline's first Sergeant, seeing to it that requests and needs were met, even anticipating needs. She appreciated his help but hoped it wouldn't be misunderstood by any as an alignment with his ideologies. But sometimes, she thought, it just doesn't matter.

***

Chapter XXXVI

The sight of the familiar building, now ablaze with lights, signaled the end of reserve energy for me. The stress from the heavy load and tension of night travel had been offset only by the urgency of the hour. My tired mind now told me my job was finished.

Silhouettes of various vehicles were scattered about in front. As my headlight swept across I could see two Jeeps, several motorcycles, and a dump truck. My weariness suddenly forgotten, I pulled up at the side door by the pharmacy. Helping hands quickly untied the heavy box and carried it in. I stepped through the door and stopped, trying to comprehend what I saw.

"Salamat sa Dios!" came a voice from behind me. Recognizing the voice, I turned to grip an eager hand.

"Yes, thank God." I agreed, but no one was smiling. I walked on in past thankful hands that reached out to me and looked for Pauline. Someone pointed down the corridor.

She was kneeling beside a mat on the floor. On the mat lay a young boy. He was very still. I hesitated a moment, glancing around at the situation. An empty packing crate, the one the x-ray machine had come in, still lay on its side in the unfinished waiting room. Two forms were sleeping inside and one on top. There were hundreds of people, some lying in groups, some leaning against the walls. There was scarcely enough room to walk.

I picked my way between them down the corridor and dropped to one knee behind Pauline. Her eyes were closed. She turned at the touch on her shoulder, and seeing me, gasped out, her eyes coming alive. "Oh, thank God you're safe! Did you get the medicine?"

"Some of it . . . all I could carry. The rest is coming by bus. First trip."

She sighed deeply, closed her eyes and leaned back, resting her weight on me. I held her and watched the tears spill over and run freely. "We were able to revive him three times," Her voice faded, "but just couldn't make it again."

I looked down at the small form. He looked so healthy.

"Others we revived successfully, but this little one. . . ." She raised her arms in futility and let them drop. "There was too much poison. Everything just stopped. First his uncle, now . . . ."

"His uncle?"

"Yes, and the man with him said they didn't even eat any of the poisoned fish."

"Poisonous fish! So that's it, but how could so many make a mistake like that? They know the difference . . ."

"But that's just it. It was *Bangus* and everyone eats *Bangus*. It was freshly caught and, anyway, his uncle and the other man didn't even eat any. A dog had died and they had barbecue instead."

I felt my eyebrows pull down, "What killed the dog?" She straightened up. It made sense.

Chapter XXXVI

"Oh, dear God! What kind of a poison are we dealing with that can kill a man at that distance—the dog must have eaten some fish, and they ate the dog. We eat *Bangus* all the time."

"Not any more!"

***

It was mid-morning when a nurse took Pauline aside to talk with her. As she listened, Pauline's face registered disbelief, deep sadness, then finally dissolved into concession. She leaned back heavily against the wall. Her eyes searched the room, then rested on a woman sleeping on the floor beside a small child. I walked over to her and followed her gaze.

"He died." I put my hands on her shoulders and pulled her to me. She leaned her head on my chest and I waited. "The man who pulled his I.V. out and went home to look for his daughter."

She turned her face up to me. "The boy we worked so hard on who died, that was his son. His wife and daughter are there sleeping," she indicated with her eyes. "And I'm not certain the daughter will make it. And they don't think she should be told now, she's had enough sorrow," Pauline continued. I must have tightened because she looked up at me. My mind was sifting through pages of culturally correct etiquette I had stored and was coming up blank.

"When is the right time to tell her?"

"They say wait till she goes home. She'll be better able to bear it then."

"There really is no better time, is there?" She leaned back on my chest and I smelled the scent of medicine and of fatigue and had no answers.

***

I roused myself and looked at my watch. One p.m. I had chosen a secluded spot behind some shelves in the pharmacy and rolled out on the floor just for a few minutes. I shook my head and took several deep breaths. Coffee would sure taste good. So would something to eat. Stepping out of the pharmacy, I spotted Pauline and headed her way. She was moving slowly.

"Are you feeling any better?" Her eyes were deep and red.

"I don't know, I'll tell you when I wake up. Looks like my few minutes turned into about three hours. You should have kicked me about two hours ago—have you rested?"

"Not yet, but I think I'm going to have to soon."

"Take a few minutes and let's get a bite to eat over at Esting's."

"I can't right now, but you go ahead . . . Oh Hon', their daughter died too."

"No. You mean the father that went home and . . .?"

Chapter XXXVI

"Yes, about an hour ago. And the mother will be going home soon. She still doesn't know her husband is dead. It's better that way, they say. I want so bad to reach out to her, but I suppose I shouldn't right now."

I shook my head slowly. "I hope she survives."

"Me too. We'll visit her next week." She paused, took a deep breath. "One hundred seventy-three."

"What?"

"Poisonings. And five didn't make it." Another pause. "You go ahead now. I'll get a bite later."

The atmosphere was subdued as I walked down the corridor towards the door. I passed a nurse and two other staff on duty. In spite of their obvious fatigue they were pleasant, understanding and comforting as they circulated among the ill. I slipped through the door and squinted into the glare of the afternoon sun. The laundress greeted me as I passed. Two little boys ran naked down the trail laughing in their innocence, dragging sticks behind them. Some things were winding back to normal. Some things never would. I knew one village that wouldn't.

What good could come of it? We needed to visit in a couple of days. How many more lives could have been saved if we had been prepared. I thought of a woman going home to an empty house, and she didn't even know it was empty. I slapped at a banana leaf as I passed. No answers.

Esting's greeting reached out to me with sadness as I climbed the steps and seated myself on the bamboo bench. She set the thermos and instant coffee in front of me and eased down across the table. It was after lunch and the little Bamboo and Nipa leaf cafeteria was empty. I welcomed the quiet. She slid the sugar bowl toward me.

"The people are saying that your hospital is different, Chuck." Esting never wasted time when she had something important to say. She knew I usually had little time to talk.

"Oh? What are they saying?" I was deep in thought but tried to be polite.

"They say it's as if everyone here really loves them. Not like it's just a job. No one speaks loud or gets angry when directions are not followed. It's good. You tell your Mrs.!"

"I will Esting, I will." I had needed that. From the beginning Pauline and I had wanted this hospital to be a place of healing for the spirit as well as the body. A place where the desires of a Holy and caring God could be lived out. I felt my eyes blur and looked away out the window framed in red and white bougainvillea. "I guess we were prepared."

***

The sun slipped quietly below the horizon but not without mirroring its panorama of colors against the waiting clouds. I slowed the Jeep and wheeled to the right, winding between coconut palms to stop short of the receding tide. Hushed waves rattled seashells against the rocky beach and muted iridescence reflected back colors of the sky.

Two weeks had passed and we were returning from a visit to a somber yet thankful village. The people smiled and talked of tomorrows but their eyes still spoke of a yesterday.

It was a small but highly poisonous crab that inhabited the river tributaries more than a mile from the sea. Even the youngest of the villagers readily recognized it and kept clear. This was its egg-laying season and a rare out of season storm had washed the crab eggs into the sea. A large school of *Bangus,* attracted by the heavy run-off, stuffed themselves on their last meal. And a last meal it was also for five of the villagers and one hapless dog.

The sky shimmered from its yellows, orange, down to streaks of blood red before giving way to the deep royal purple that signaled the end of the day. But the tomorrows that were talked of would come, and new hopes with the sunrise.

NOT THE END

***

Epilogue

For some time, I had been questioning as to what God had for me next. Was I destined to just lean back in my recliner and watch the rest of my life stumble by, or was that really part of His plan? I decided to get out of my recliner and find out. If God said no, then He would stop me.

There were definitely times in my life when I had hoped that God would hit the delete button, but He had not.

There was a tragic car accident that took my daughter Carla's life along with her unborn baby. Her husband had miraculously survived and went on with his life. Many years after that, as often happens when parents lose a child, Pauline, my wife of nearly 40 years handed me divorce papers. Her life had taken a different path and so did mine; however, my relationship with my son was solid and I cannot imagine anything that could break our bond.

After a year of living alone, I met Alice and we have now been married seventeen wonderful years.

It's now been thirty years since we left the Philippines. My son Mike approached me with a question that was meant to dig beneath the surface of my, leaning-back-in-my-recliner-gazing-at-the-peaceful-desert, lifestyle. It did.

Epilogue

"Dad, why don't you go with me this year?" Mike had been returning to the Philippines almost every year to be with the people he grew up with, to help them and encourage them in their many struggles—and he wanted me to go with him.

I shook my head slowly. "Mike, I can hardly walk and you want me to trudge the muddy trails again?"

"Dad, it's not the same now. We can get off the plane, rent an air-conditioned car and drive most of the way to where the Ati live."

"Really? Well, let me think about it. Right now the pain in my back makes it hard to make a logical decision."

Alice, my faithful wife of seventeen years, sided with Mike. Really? "Honey, you're going to hurt whether here or there, so why not?"

"I really don't want to . . ."

"It's for them, Dad. They want to see you."

Mike threw in some details that punched holes in my logic. Many of the Ati that I had known were now passed away. Life expectancy for them is quite low, but they had told their children and they wanted to see this man who had first introduced them to Christ and a better life—the one who was instrumental in constructing for them a hospital and two churches. They knew the stories, but they wanted to see the man.

After I agreed, we consulted with friends and without exception they agreed that if this was God's plan, He would provide a way. How much was this venture going to cost? Mike figured about $2700. That was about how much I did not have. We sent out inquiring letters to friends. Prayers and financial support came in quickly from the loving supportive community we now call family. That settled it.

Mike decided on December 6 as a take-off date. That coincided with an Ati Christmas celebration. The ball was rolling and I now had to prepare myself. There was a passport to be renewed and shots to be had. I started on a heavy daily dose of vitamin B1. For some reason that vitamin helps to keep mosquitoes away. Sure, a good repellant works too, but one can't be too safe. No one wants to bring home a case of malaria or dengue fever and the mosquitoes over there are loaded with it. I also started a more vigorous exercising of my legs. I had been quite lax in that area since my knee surgery. I hate pain.

Mike worked on the flight scheduling. He finally landed us an inexpensive plan. It meant four plane changes, but it would work. First flight was from Phoenix to San Francisco, then from San Francisco to Taipei, Taipei to Manila then down to Malay. That was a total travel time of around 22 hours. Alice bought me a pair of knee-high constricting socks that would push the blood back up my legs. The pooling of blood in the lower legs is the biggest problem associated with long periods of sitting.

December 6th came soon enough. Alice drove me to Phoenix where I met up with Mike and we were off. The first three legs of the trip were long but uneventful.

We landed in Manila close to midnight, then grabbed a cab to the Wycliffe center to spend the night. It was a four mile drive which took two hours—at midnight. That defines Manila traffic. The next morning was a short plane hop to Malay.

The Malay airport of 30 years ago that I remembered consisted of a flat grassy strip long enough for a twin-engine Cessna to land and take off—that's it. Now it's a concrete runway where nine or ten commercial jets fly in every day. To make the strip long enough they had to remove a small mountain. So they did. The terminal is now adequate for a dozen or more busses to come and go shuttling passengers to and from the beach where most of them boarded boats for their destination: the white sands of Boracay island. Boracay was an almost deserted island 30 years ago. Now it is crowded with resorts, opulent houses and marketplaces where almost anything can be bought at inflated prices.

That wasn't our goal. Ours was a small, now outdated hospital built 32 years ago on the edge of a grass airstrip. It is now destined to be torn down to make way for a larger air terminal. From there we would go five miles down the road and up a back trail to where the Ati live.

After a short visit to the hospital which we started 32 years ago, and an enthusiastic request that we return the following day, we were off to visit the Ati. A friend had loaned Mike a minivan and we drove to the rental house we were to call home for the next two weeks. We dropped off our luggage, acquired a change of clothes, and we were off. The stretch of pot-holes that passed for a road led us to within a half mile of the Ati village and it was a muddy trail the rest of the way. Thankfully, I had brought along my cane as I really needed it.

On the trail I passed a tribal man and was reminded of the clashing cultural aspects that the tribal folks faced. He was barefooted, wore a ragged pair of shorts, a machete hung on his side and in one hand he carried his cell phone.

The jungle grape-vine is an unexplainable phenomenon. Somehow, they knew we were coming and we were welcomed with open arms. A banquet was already in progress and the tribal folks were dressed in their Sunday best. Some even wore rubber flip-flops but most were barefooted, and some were equipped with the traditional machete hanging on their side. I didn't count, but estimated around 300 men, women and children mingling and laughing. Long tables of sorts were laden with an array of foods from chicken, shrimp, pork, various vegetables, a couple of unknowns and of course heaps of fresh, steaming sticky-rice. That variety of rice is a delicacy not to be readily found in America. The chicken was cooked whole. Pieces had to be ripped off with a fork. Shrimp also was whole. That's where the fingers came into play. Messy but good. Folks that were children when we left now had families of their own and we were the guests of honor. It was quite humbling. For many this meal might be their only one for the day or maybe for more than one day. One lady, about sixty years of age, approached me with a twinkle in her eye, ran a hand across my balding pate and said, "You must be very rich, you own your own landing strip." Peals of laughter followed and I was introduced to a different type of humor.

Then conversations followed which I understood only enough to make basic replies and raised eyebrow assents to. Thirty years can erase mounds of language knowledge. They were very courteous and understanding. Mike, being younger and returning mostly every year was still quite fluent in their unwritten language. At one point he made a quite lengthy appeal to them for unity and peaceful living. It made an impact. A division had recently formed in the tribe. On the one side was the tribal leader and his quite large family and followers, and on the other side was the ousted leader with his equally large family. He had recently been removed from power for supposed cruelties and unwise tribal decisions.

That afternoon as we prepared to leave, the rain started in earnest. We slipped and slid our way down the trail, arriving at the minivan completely soaked, but satisfied that relationships were strong and that we enhanced our connection with a tribe of people who had for the most part been left behind in the somewhat thin façade of civilization.

Back at the house we took cold showers—that's the only kind available—and stretched out in the only room with an air conditioner in a window. It struggled valiantly but held its own in the 100% humidity. In the rest of the house the humidity condensed on the concrete walls and ran down making slippery puddles on the floor. The second floor was unfinished with bamboo lattice work not doing much of a job holding the rain out of the doorways and windows.

The following day Mike drove to the provincial capital to negotiate paperwork pertaining to the relocation of the hospital. The powers that be were only willing to give us what we paid for the land thirty years ago before bulldozing the hospital down. That price was approximately four hundred dollars, as opposed to the greatly inflated current land price of over a quarter of a million.

I hailed a passing tricycle to take me to the hospital for a visit. A tricycle is the name given to the local means of transportation. It consists of a 100 or 125 CC motorcycle with an attached sidecar. The sidecar can hold 6 to 8 passengers plus two or three behind the driver. With such a load, usually the last person on would jump off and push the tricycle to get its momentum started. How much is the fare? The equivalent of one U.S. penny.

As we pulled up to the hospital I noted an unusual number of vehicles parked in front. We were ushered directly toward the rear of the building where people were mingling. Many turned my way as I approached. Both my hands were grasped and I was ushered to a table heaped with food. To those I did not know, I was introduced as the founder of this hospital that still functioned, giving spiritual as well as physical healing. I was the guest of honor and greatly humbled.

The next day we ventured into town and met with the widow of Paing, the man who made the construction of the hospital possible. In his position as leader of the communistic rebel group he had assured us that the hospital construction would proceed without fear of bandit attacks or well needed equipment disappearing in the night. Paing had since passed away, the victim of something that even his influence and strength could not overpower. There is still no known cure for Alzheimer's Disease.

As the door swung shut on our short visit, we were reminded that God was still in control, but in my heart, I also questioned why more people did not step up and answer His call. We had, and it was the most gratifying experience of our lives.